Ton

PLAYS FOUR

Tony Harrison was born in Leeds in 1937. His volumes
of poetry include *The Loiners* (winner of the Geoffrey
Faber Memorial Prize), *Continuous, v.* (broadcast on
Channel 4 in 1987, winning the Royal Television Society
Award), *The Gaze of the Gorgon* (winner of the
Whitbread Prize for Poetry) and Laureate's Block.
Recognised as Britain's leading theatre and film poet,
Tony Harrison has written extensively for the National
Theatre, the New York Metropolitan Opera, the BBC,
Channel 4, and for unique ancient spaces in Greece and
Austria. His film *Black Daisies for the Bride* won the
Prix Italia in 1994; this and his volume of film/poems
The Shadow of Hiroshima and Other Film/Poems and
his feature film *Prometheus* are published by Faber and
Faber. His most recent film/poem was *Crossings,* 2002.
In 2007 his *Collected Film Poetry* was published by Faber
and his *Collected Poems* by Penguin. His play, *Fram,*
premiered at the National Theatre in 2008. Tony Harrison
was awarded the first PEN/Pinter Prize in 2009.

TONY HARRISON

Plays Four

The Oresteia

The Common Chorus
Parts One & Two

**Introduced by
the author**

faber and faber

This collection first published in 2002
by Faber and Faber Limited
Bloomsbury House, 74–77 Great Russell Street,
London, WC1B 3DA
Published in the United States by Faber and Faber Inc.
an affiliate of Farrar, Straus and Giroux LLC, New York

Typeset by Country Setting, Kingsdown, Kent CT14 8ES
Printed and bound by CPI Group (UK) Ltd, Croydon, CR0 4YY

The Oresteia first published in Great Britain in 1981 by Rex Collings Ltd,
published in 1985 in Dramatic Verse 1973–1985 by Bloodaxe Books,
published in 1986 in Theatre Works 1973–1985 by Penguin Books
© Tony Harrison, 1985

The Common Chorus first published in the U.S.A.
in The Agni Review, 27, 1988, and in Great Britain in 1992
by Faber and Faber Limited © Tony Harrison, 1992

The Common Chorus Part II (The Trojan Women)
first published in this collection in 2002, © Tony Harrison, 2002

Introduction to The Oresteia © Tony Harrison, 2002
Introduction to The Common Chorus © Tony Harrison, 1992

A CIP record for this book is available from the British Library

ISBN 978-0-571-21046-6

Contents

THE ORESTEIA

The Oresteia
of Aeschylus
in an English version
by Tony Harrison

Introduction

EGIL AND EAGLE-BARK

Aischulos' bronze-throat eagle-bark at blood
Has somehow spoiled my taste for twitterings!
Robert Browning, *Aristophanes' Apology* (1875)

The date on page one of the first of what became over a
dozen thick notebooks devoted to my workings and
reworkings of the *Oresteia* is 8 March 1973, about two
weeks after the opening of my *Misanthrope* at the Old
Vic, which was the home of the National Theatre before
the new building on the Thames was completed. The trilogy of Aeschylus finally opened in the Olivier Theatre on
28 November 1981 after a false start aborted owing to
industrial disputes at the NT in 1979. So the style of it had
a long gestation, owing partly to a protracted grappling
with the Greek and partly to the Gargantuan birth pang
of a newly opened 'theatre industry' complex on the South
Bank. I have written pieces for all three auditoria of this
complex but most have appeared in my favourite of the
three, the Olivier – inspired, said the architect Denys
Lasdun, by the ancient Greek theatre of Epidaurus, where
to my great gratification the National Theatre's *Oresteia*
became in 1982 the first foreign production ever to be
presented in its two-thousand-year-old space. One of the
things that attracted me to the Olivier space was that it
was inhospitable to the clichés of naturalistic drama that
have become the norm on TV and in most theatrically
anaemic modern drama. It seemed a space ready for poetry,
a verse drama that was public and presentational and
owed nothing to that of T. S. Eliot, who, perhaps apart
from *Murder in the Cathedral*, forced verse theatre into

anorexia in order to squeeze it into the proscenium draw-ing room, and made it so discreet and well bred in its metrical gentility you wondered why it bothered to go public at all. The kind of theatre I was most exposed to as a child, the last days of music hall and pantomime, introduced me to verse in the theatre in both the comic monologue and the panto in rhymed couplets which, though often crude, clumsy and gauche had a vernacular energy to crackle across the footlights and engage an audience. The language and the style of playing, the butch male 'dame', the glamorous leggy girl 'principal boy' have always been in my mind as something which could, given a serious context, suggest clues for a kind of theatricality I was looking for as a poet, and which made me use the languages I'd learned and the earlier poet/dramatists to clear a space for a new verse drama.

Once I had agreed to work with Peter Hall on the *Oresteia* I had a vivid dream – unusual because I dream very rarely. I've always supposed it's because I spend most of the waking hours of my days dreaming. But on this occasion I dreamed that there was in my hallway in New-castle a large, rather ornately bound visitors' book, but its engraved cover read *Oresteia*, or, to be precise, ΟΡΕΣΤΕΙΑ, as it was embossed in Greek script. I think it was meant as a kind of audition roster for the chorus of Aeschylus' trilogy. In my garden at dawn, or even before dawn, there was assembled a long queue of men, all old men. They all wrote their names in the book and left without a word. Each of them seemed to have no trouble with the Greek script on the cover and they each ran a finger over the gilded Greek, and then opened the book, ran the same fin-ger down the list of previous signatories and then signed themselves, then closed it again for the man behind to read and trail his finger on the ancient Greek. Strangely, though it was a repeated action, each signatory brought to the occasion his own definite individual style. When the last one had left, I picked up the book and read the names. They were all the names of the comedians I had seen in panto as the dame, or as a solo act, at the Leeds Empire, or Grand Theatre: Norman Evans, Frank Randall, Nat Jackley, Robb Wilton, Arthur Lucan ('Old Mother Riley' but for some reason without Kitty), Jewell and Warriss etc . . . the list went on for pages. The kind of theatricality that they had, though still defiantly alive in the last days of vaudeville, had more or less disappeared from so-called 'serious' theatre, and I carried their presences with me as a sometimes grinning and girning, but always supportive, chorus, paradoxically, into the quest for an Aeschylean *gravitas*. One of the essential secrets of that theatricality, still preserved in the popular forms, is that the audience is there to be addressed, entertained, moved, accosted, not to be eavesdroppers on some private happening. This simple fact is behind almost all the pieces I created for the Olivier, but perhaps most obviously in *The Trackers of Oxyrhynchus* (1990) and *Square Rounds* (1992), both of which I also directed, in order to allow the old men who signed my *Oresteia* visitors' book to be there at every stage of the productions. In the unashamed coupling of 'high' and 'low' the theatrical poet finds his most persuasive voice.

Leading into our collaboration on the *Oresteia*, I also felt that Peter Hall was looking in his own way for an equivalent theatricality to fill the Olivier, and very early in the history of that auditorium he made discoveries in it that, though they have to go on being rediscovered, made him ripe for our *Oresteia*. His production of Marlowe's *Tamburlaine* in 1976 was the first in the Olivier space to show its exciting potential. Harley Granville Barker had likened the relation of actor to character in *Tamburlaine* to that of the black-clad handler to his puppet in Japanese Bunraku. 'Marlowe,' he wrote in one of his marvellous *Prefaces to Shakespeare*, here to *Hamlet*, 'had made the character something rather to be *exhibited* than acted.'

Peter Hall was evidently of a similar opinion, and one of the ways he found of reaching this was by playing on the NT terraces to anyone who happened to be passing. He notes in his *Diaries*:

> An actor cannot speak thirty lines of blank verse to another actor's eyeballs. It must be shared with the audience – told like a story-teller.

Full daylight, the conditions in which most of the great verse dramas were played and where actor can see the audience as clearly as they see him, is a great way to discover the nature of this kind of theatre, and clearly the cast of *Tamburlaine* learned to fill the Olivier by being in the openair makeshift spaces of the NT terraces. On the Easter Saturday the following year we also played *The Passion*, which I had adapted from the Northern Mystery Cycles, outside on the NT terraces, and the experience similarly helped to unlock the public style of the drama which was then fed into the Cottesloe performances indoors. In another note in his *Diaries*, Peter Hall observes of Albert Finney, who was to be a wonderful Tamburlaine, that he was 'in terrific form: one feels all those years of his youth in Manchester studying stand-up comics' (9 July 1976). In a similar way I felt that chorus of old comics cheering me on to the serious business of Greek tragedy. I believe that when we started the sadly aborted first rehearsals in 1979 both Peter Hall and I agreed on the points he records in his *Diaries* for that day, 27 Febuary:

> I started the *Oresteia* . . . Three main factors – the use of masks, the use of percussion, and the whole text being spoken by the actors to the audience was understood from the start.

We never got to play or rehearse on the terraces a drama that was created for the light of day. Granville Barker also wrote of Greek drama, and indeed of open-air full daylight theatre in general, that it suffered in the transition 'from sunlight to limelight. The mere transference from outdoors in will prove deadening.' All through our workshops and rehearsals we kept the original conditions in mind – large, open-air theatre, masks, all-male company, not in the spirit of pedantic archaeology but in order to discover a theatricality the Olivier space cried out for and, sadly, even now, rarely gets. We weren't to know then that we would eventually take the *Oresteia* to Epidaurus, though, alas, perhaps tragically ironic after what I have said about the theatre of daylight, the Greeks hold their festival performances at night in lighting conditions more suitable for the football pitch than to the dark tragedy, originally flooded with spring sunshine illuminating equally actors and some 15,000 in the audience.

Looking at the theatre of Epidaurus we were to play in seven years later, Peter Hall wrote in his diary for 19 May 1975:

> I long to do a play here: with nothing, and with daylight, with the hillside pouring into the auditorium. But, say the Greeks, it is too hot. Well too hot in July and August, when they have the festival, but orginally Greek theatres were built to operate in the spring, in March and April.

II

I brooded over my much annotated Greek text, with its alliterative clusters underlined in red, for years, though in the period I also worked on other theatrical projects for the National Theatre, like *Phaedra Britannica* 'after Racine' in 1976; and *Bow Down*, a music-theatre piece with Harrison Birtwistle, who was to contribute the music to our *Oresteia*; and *The Passion*. from the alliterative medieval

Northern cycle of mystery plays, both in 1977 – all of which fed into what became the obsessive quest for the right form of English for Aeschylus.

The style I eventually came up with for the National Theatre's *Oresteia* (1981), after a great deal of experimentation in workshops with masks and music, was characterised by alliterative metrics and compound words which I invented for reasons I will explain below. Two of my Anglo-Saxon-style neologising inventions – or what I'd thought of as my own inventions – namely 'yokestrap' and 'hackblock', I recalled suddenly, at a later stage, I had lifted from Robert Browning's much maligned *Agamemnon* of 1877, though I never felt tempted to lift the more archaising chivalric 'troth-plight', which, unlike the former examples, sounded too 'poetic' for me to want to plagiarise. I think it might be true to say that the seeds of my principal choices were lurking there in Browning from the beginning without my fully realising it.

John Keats, to whom the melody of vowels was the principal essence of verse music, spoke of the ancient Greek tongue as 'vowelled Greek'; but Robert Browning, in his probably unplayable, unperformable and even, to many, unreadable but, to me, constantly fascinating version of the *Agamemnon,* corrects Keats in his preface and uses the phrase '*consonanted* Greek'. Though clearly both modes of articulation are necessary to speech, immoderate affiliation to or affection for one or the other can polarise poetics. Dr Johnson called English a language 'overstocked with consonants'. Henry Lawes, the composer who collaborated with Milton, envying the vowels of Italian for sung text, said in 1651 that 'our English seems a little over-clogg'd with consonants'. It is only 'overstocked' or 'over-clogg'd' if you have a distaste for them or want to use vowels and their capacity for sustained drone as a sort of operatic helium. The repeated consonants of medieval Northern drama helped the words to carry directly over the unstructured hubbub and bustle of a Corpus Christi crowd in the York streets.

Aristotle thought vowels were of the spirit and consonants of the body. The poetic seeks first to inhabit flesh. 'Consonants are secular,' wrote Mandelstam, 'vowels are monastic.' My poetics are grounded in the flesh and the secular. Since I was a child I have loved the consonantal play at the heart of Yorkshire idiom and was delighted when I worked in Prague and began to learn Czech to come across a tongue-twister, '*strč prst skrz krk*', which has not one vowel in it. So my affiliation, no doubt conditioned by my Yorkshire accent, was heavily consonantal, and my instinct was to go with the clogging but to search for a metrical current that had enough force to carry the consonantal crag-splinters with it. It is certainly Browning's feel for the consonantal, potentially clogging, energy of Aeschylus' verse, his awareness of the oral physicality and what George Steiner calls the 'aural density' of the original language, that distinguishes Browning's *Agamemnon* translation. It may clog but it never cloys like so much inferior Victorian poetry. Somewhere though, almost more than in any other English-speaking poet who has tackled Aeschylus, I have always felt, even before I began to think of translating him myself, there were clues to the way Aeschylus might sound in English in the Browning version. Already using a kind of poetic compounding, and happily combining 'grind' or 'grate' and 'strident' in the Miltonic 'griding' (*Paradise Lost*, VI, 329), both resources he would use liberally to match Aeschylus almost forty years later, Browning talks of the Greek tragedian in *Sordello* (1840) thus:

> The thunder-phrase of the Athenian, grown
> Up out of memories of Marathon,
> Would echo like his own sword's griding screech
> Braying a Persian shield –

I also took to the word 'braying', as I'd used 'bray' even as a toddler in Leeds to mean 'give somebody a beating', and to the subdued alliteration that enacts the striker and the struck in the voiced and voiceless counterparts of 'b' and 'p' in 'Braying a Persian shield'. There is also a similar pairing of voiced and voiceless consonantal counterparts in the previous line's 'sword's griding screech'. The following are examples of Browning listening to that 'griding screech', that 'bronze-throat eagle-bark':

And – so upsoaring as to stride seas over,
The strong lamp-voyager, and all for joyance –
Did the gold-glorious splendour, any sun like,
Pass on – the pine tree – to Makistos' watchplace.

or:

The old men, from a throat that's free no longer,
Shriekingly wail the death-doom of their dearest.

or:

And when a messenger with gloomy visage
To a city bears a fall'n host's woes – God ward off! –
One popular wound that happens to the city,
And many sacrificed from many households –
Men, scourged by that two-thonged whip Ares loves so,
Double spear-headed curse, bloody yoke couple –
Of woes like these, doubtless, who'er comes weighted,
Him does it suit to sing the Erinues' paian.

or:

But blood of man to earth once falling – deadly, black
In times ere these –
Who may, by singing spells, call back?

or:

And blowing forth a brisk blood-spatter, strikes me
With a dark drop of slaughterous dew – rejoicing

> No less than, at the god-given dewy-comfort,
> The sown-stuff in its birth-throes from the calyx.

Or in Clytemnestra's dominating response to the chorus
after she has killed Agamemnon and Cassandra:

> Now, indeed, thou adjudgest exile to me,
> And citizens' hate, and to have popular curses:
> Nothing of this against the man here bringing,
> Who, no more awe-checked than as 'twere a beast's
>   fate –
> With sheep abundant in the well-fleeced graze-flocks –
> Sacrificed *his* child – dearest fruit of travail
> To me – as song-spell against Threkian blowings.
> Not *him* did it behove thee hence to banish
> – Pollution's penalty?

Browning's devices, his dragging parentheses weighted between hyphens (no poet uses more hyphens than Browning!)
that he uses in his own poetry but on a more colloquial
base than in his Aeschylus, his crabbed word order, his
compounds, all seeking to give weight to the line, once
familiarity and fluency have mastered them, have an
indisputable force and a power uncharacteristic of English
outside its earliest forms, Milton, or Browning's contemporary, Gerard Manley Hopkins. Mostly, however, sequen-
tial meaning struggles with word order and coinage.

Browning called his version a 'transcription' rather than
a translation. This is not only aptly applicable to the deliberately non-Latinate transliteration of Greek names like
Klutaimnestra, Kalchas, Skamandros, Kokutos, or Threkian
etc. – a habit Browning bequeathed to Ezra Pound along
with much else – but also to the way he tries to reproduce
word order and grammar. 'He picks you out the English for
the Greek word by word, and now and again sticks two
or three words together with hyphens . . .' wrote Carlyle,
who came to regret that he had personally encouraged
Browning to translate Greek tragedy, once he was faced

with the virtually unintelligible text of the *Agamemnon*. The kindest contemporary judgement was that of Sir Frederick Kenyon, who called the work a 'perverse *tour de force*'. But somewhere, I think, those very perversities point the way to a means of making the text massive and megalithic, doing honour to the daunting *Dunkelheit* of Aeschylus but without renouncing the intelligibility at the heart of all theatrical communication. The sense of the weighted net of Aeschylean verse is in the Browning version sporadically, but the movement of the metric and the narrative clarity become clogged, not so much by the compounds (which are a characteristic of his original) but because of Browning's commitment to a Greek, or at least a highly Hellenised and un-English grammatical word order. In his preface he says he is translating 'in as Greek a fashion as the English will bear'. John Aldington Symonds, in his diary for 1 November 1888, noted:

> Browning's theory of translation. Ought to be absolutely literal, with exact rendering of words, and words placed in the order of the original.

He comes up, he concludes, with something 'neither English nor Greek'. 'Browning's translation is the nightmarish product of the nineteenth-century dream of reproducing the past "as it actually was",' agreed the more contemporary translation theorist, Reuben A. Brower.

Browning's *Sordello* (1840), another of his notoriously 'obscure' productions, and long regarded as the least comprehensible poem in English, was understood by so few readers that the poet offered to publish a more reader-friendly edition in which, though he would change nothing, he would write in 'the unwritten *every-other-line* which I stupidly left as an amusement for the reader to do'. In Browning's *Agamemnon* there is a written '*every-other-line*' which can only be the original Greek of Aeschylus. You feel you are reading one of those interlinear texts of the Bible I used to use in school chapel services so that the act of worship I always thought ridiculous would not go to waste, and I would use the occasion to learn some Greek or Latin, or sometimes Lutheran German. A contemporary reviewer of Browning's *Agamemnon* claimed that the poet, who had always 'tortured' the English language 'now tortures it even more fiercely'. Browning's rare apologists, like his contemporary Dr Edward Berdoe, thought that it was the very ruggedness of Browning's verse that was required 'to interpret correctly the ruggedness of Aeschylus'. Browning certainly constructs a hurdle course, daunting at first sight, but once the reader learns to clear these apparent obstacles to smooth forward progress, the motion is by no means sporadic, lamed, hobbled, hamstrung or encumbered, but each leap increases the forward, even at times stylish, momentum. Browning's 'semantic stutter' can reach a weighty eloquence. What G. K. Chesterton called Browning's 'staccato music', except when it is laboured and deliberately self-retarding or struggling vainly to ignite its dragging 'lumberingness', can rise to Aeschylean marmoreal grandeur. The 'lumberingness' of Browning undermines the dramatic need for momentum. Metrical verse serves as the guarantor of momentum. 'Metre', said Coleridge, is 'a stimulant to the attention.'

The momentum should appear unstoppable and keep the spectator spellbound and therefore never able to interrupt or intervene to relieve the sufferer or prevent an enacted consequence. In this respect the audience shares something of the condition of the Greek chorus which is drawn into performance but never intervention through action. This sets up a kind of half-way house that ensures the basic decorum of theatricality. The speech of Clytemnestra as Agamemnon walks up the blood-coloured carpet strewn for him prevents the audience, by its spell-binding rhetoric, from behaving like kids at the panto and yelling *'Don't go inside!'*

Actors need to be encouraged not to provide chinks in the momentum when the play runs down and the dramatic propellant leaks through the overlong 'psychological' pause, or the naturalistic prosifying of rhythmical verse used, in most cases, for its very quality of unstoppability and relentless, inexorable, though not boring, momentum. Yeats was probably feeling the same when he wrote:

> But actors lacking music
> Do most excite my spleen,
> They say it is more human
> To shuffle, grunt and groan . . .
> 'The Old Stone Cross'

In the aborted *Oresteia* workshops of 1979 I listened to actors reading Browning's version aloud with some difficulty. We also read a dozen others. As Peter Hall wrote in his *Diaries* for 5 March 1979: 'All were totally unspeakable and undramatic.' I have always thought that one of the ways to make it both speakable and dramatic was to find an English verse which would have maximum *weight*, of the kind that Browning recognised in the Greek of Aeschylus and was aiming for in his English, *but* with a maximum *momentum*.

The weight, the ruggedness of Aeschylus consists partly of craggy alliteration and compounding. A few random samples suffice:

τὸ μὴ βεβαίως βλέφαρα συμβαλεῖν ὕπνῳ (*Ag.*, 15)

πῶς φής; πεφευγε τοὖπος ἀπιστίας (*Ag.*, 268)

And Agamemnon's contemptuous reference to the ashes of Troy with his contempt for the effeminate sighing smoke carried by repeated πs:

σποδὸς προπέμπει πίονας πλούτου πνοάς (*Ag.*, 820)

This appears in my version as:

the ashes of surfeited Asia still sighing
the sickly cachou breath of soft living and riches.

στείχει γυναικῶν φάρεσιν μελαγχίμοις
πρέπουσα; ποιᾳ ξυμφρᾳ προσεικάσω (*Ch.*, 11–12)

πρὸς ἔρυμα τόδε κἀκων κεδνῶν τ᾽
    ἀπότροπο ἄγος ἀπεύχετον (*Ch.*, 154–5)

θεῶν τις οὐδ᾽ ἄνθρωπος οὐδὲ θήρ ποτε (*Eu.*, 70)

Or over several lines binding the grief of Electra in
strangled knots:

δμωὰι γυνᾶικες, δωμάτων εὐθήμονες,
ἐπὲι πάρεοτε τῆσδε προοτροπῆς ἐμοὶ
πομποί, γένεσθε τῶνδε σύμβουλοι πέρι·
τί φῶ χέουσα τάσδε κηδείους χοάς;
πῶς εὔφρον᾽ εἴπω πῶς κατεύξομαι πατρί;
πότερα λέγουσα παρὰ φίλης φιλῳ φέρειν. (*Ch.*, 84–9)

That ruggedness, that weight, that craggy mass of the verse
which Dionysius of Halicarnassus likened to those vast
piles of Cyclopean masonry we associate with the citadel of Mycenae, and which John Cowper Powys called
'megalithic', was certainly given, intermittently, an English
counterpart in Browning who, in a letter written in 1876,
a year before his *Agamemnon*, proposes publishing it along
with photographs of Schliemann's recent excavations at
Mycenae in 1874, where the notorious fantasist gazed on
the face of a wizened anonymous mummy, and called it
Agamemnon.

His mistake, I always felt, even long before I undertook
the *Oresteia* trilogy myself, was to dam the natural flow
and current of English syntax and word order, that would
have the necessary strength and clarity to move the boul-
ders of massed meaning and craggy lexical invention, so that
the dramatic momentum was remorselessly maintained,

for in the unstoppable ongoing momentum, the forward drive, the inevitability of rhythmical progression lies as much in the meaning, especially of the *Oresteia*, as in any local crux deemed to deserve infinite glossing in any *apparatus criticus*. No one had programmes or copies of the libretto to consult at the performance of the *Oresteia* in 458 BC. There was no 'rewind' mode in the inexorable one-off of Athenian performance. Meaning was delivered moment by moment. 'No Attic dramatist', writes Bernard Knox in the *New York Review of Books,* 'could afford to leave his audience puzzled.'

A style that deliberately compels *re-reading* is not one that will communicate on one *hearing*. Weightiness in verse was a Victorian preoccupation, except, perhaps in Swinburne, who recklessly jettisons poetic cargo to swing along with untrammelled momentum. But in Browning, though the vessel groans, it carries valuable cargo, not ballast.

On my way back from Prague in May 1976, after researching the geographical and economic background for Karel Sabina's scenario for Smetana's *The Bartered Bride* in Bohemia, I took the train to Vienna and saw the Ronconi production of the *Oresteia* at the Burgtheater, a building presided over by an Apollo with his lyre, and directly opposite the Parliament building presided over by a giant statue of Athena. I would use a projected slide of the Burgtheater Apollo in a sequence of the dictator deity on almost all the Opera Houses and National Theatres in Europe. I filed away all this for future use in *Trackers* and, though I took notes on my reactions to Ronconi's production, I remember sitting after the show in the Café Landtmann looking at my Greek text covered with notes in different colours, but primarily I recall still hearing in my head what was a Germanic echo of my text in its stocky compounds like *Blut-Klumpfen* and *Mutterblut.* Hearing such as these, which are natural to modern German as they were in the Old English of my models, I went back to

Britain confirmed in my choices. And I delivered the first draft of *Agamemnon* on 27 July 1976, almost exactly a century after Robert Browning's.

III

Some, including the Greek scholar W. B. Stanford, see in another Victorian poet Francis Thompson's poem *The Hound of Heaven* 'one of the most Aeschylean in English'. Thompson's favourite poets were Aeschylus and Blake, and he carried the Athenian tragedian in one pocket and the English visionary in the other when he left Preston, Lancs., for London and lived as a destitute match-seller round Charing Cross. Certainly some of his lines could be said to be inspired either by Aeschylus or, for hostile critics, by the addict poet's 'morphomania', which finally helped to kill him. Professor Stanford's citation is from *The Hound of Heaven*:

> To all swift things for swiftness did I sue;
> Clung to the whistling mane of every wind.
> But whether they swept, smoothly fleet,
> The long savannahs of the blue;
> Or whether Thunder-driven,
> They clanged his chariot 'thwart a heaven
> Plashy with flying lightnings round the spurn
>   o' their feet . . .

And characteristic of Aeschylus is this synaesthetic image:

> The long laburnum drips
> Its honey of wild flame, its jocund spilth of fire.

'Its jocund spilth of fire' is on the way to being authentically 'Aeschylean', though I find his poem *A Corymbus for Autumn* more like Aeschylus, even if it is only because

its surface paganism throws off Thompson's encrustations
of Catholic guilt:

> Hearken my chant, 'tis
>   As a Bacchante's,
> A grape-spurt, a vine-splash, a tossed tree, flown vaunt 'tis!
>
>   Suffer my singing
> Gipsy of Seasons ere thou go winging;
>   Ere Winter throws
>   His slaking snows
> In thy feasting-flagon's impurpurate glows!
>
> Tanned maiden! with cheeks like apples-russet,
>   And breast a brown agaric faint-flushing at tip,
> And a mouth too red for the moon to buss it
>   But her cheek unvow its vestalship;
>   Thy mists enclip
> Her steel-clear circuit illuminous,
>   Until it crust
>   Rubiginous
> With the glorious gules of a glowing rust.

None of this is anything like as grounded as Aeschylus or
even Browning, or, as in another style contemporary with
Browning's which achieved both the weight *and* the
momentum I was searching for in my own *Oresteia* drafts,
that of Gerard Manley Hopkins, also a Professor of Greek,
who achieves both the sweep and grandeur I have always
found in Aeschylus, and which Hopkins called his 'swell
and pomp', as in these lines, for example:

> Wiry and white-fiery and whirlwind swivelled snow
> Spins to the widow-making unchilding unfathering deep.

'Does this not read like an inspired translation of some
unknown fragment of Aeschylus?' asks D. S. Carne-Ross.
Indeed it does, an inspired *Victorian* translation, and I had
always felt that Hopkins, with his clotted but never clogged

or cumbersome line, and his thorough knowledge of Greek, had everything necessary to render a great translation of Aeschylus, except, perhaps, like most of his contemporaries, a feeling for theatre; and if a translation is not an *acting* translation, and cannot be *played,* it seems to me to fall far short of being a translation of Aeschylus at all. If one turns, however, to an actual, though admittedly extremely youthful, piece of Aeschylean translation from Hopkins (in this case *Prometheus*) the cumulative vehemence of Hopkins' own alliteratively forged verse, with its anglicised versions of Welsh metrical effects from *cynghanedd,* becomes indistinguishable from the lines any Victorian gentleman might have turned out in response to the Greek:

> Sith I loved and lov'd too well
> The race of man; and hence I fell.
> Woe is me, what do I hear?
> Fledged things do rustle near.

Very disappointing stuff from the poet who could come up with English lines like:

> The sour scythe cringe and the bleak share come,

or as Aeschylean a sequence of lines as the following:

> O then weary then why should we tread? O why are
> we so haggard at the heart, so care-coiled, care-killed,
> so fagged, so fashed, so cogged, so cumbered?

or the packed line from 'Spelt from the Sibyl's Leaves':

> Where, selfwrung, selfstrung, sheathe-and-shelterless,
>   thoughts against thoughts in groans grind.

or could himself write a Greek verse with qualities quite recognisably Aeschylean:

> λόγος Ὀρφέως λύραν καὶ δένδρεσιν χοραγεῖν
> καὶ νιφοκτύπαν ὄρεων κορυφαισῖν θαμά, δαμείσαις
> πόθῳ

κελαδοῦντι δ' εὐθὺς ἀνθῆσαι ῥόδοισίν θ' ἁλίου τε γᾶν κὰι
ψακάδος οὐρανίου βλαοτήμασι καλλικάρποις

χιόνος κρύος μεσούσας. πόντιον δὲ κῦμα
τῶν τ'ἐριβρόμων ἀίωστ' ἀνέμων Πνεύματα γαλάνα πέοεν.
κιθάρα δε ταῖς τε Μούσαις ως ἔνεστ' ἐῖπεῖν το
παυσίλυπον
ἀδύνατον κατεκοίμασ' αὐτίκα πάντα λάθα,

which is a version in Greek of the Song from Act III, Scene i
of *King Henry VIII*:

> Orpheus with his lute made trees
> And the mountain tops that freeze,
>   Bow themselves when he did sing:
> To his music plants and flowers
> Ever sprung; as sun and showers
>   There had made a lasting spring.
>
> Everything that heard him play
> Even the billows of the sea,
>   Hung their heads and then lay by.
> In sweet music is such art.
> Killing care and grief of heart
>   Fall asleep, or hearing, die.

Hopkins also manages to make another light Shakespearean
air gravid with compounds we might also find in Aeschylus,
'Tell me where is Fancy bred' (*Merchant of Venice*, III, ii).
What Hopkins is doing in these Greek versions of Shakespearean songs is making them weightier, making them
dance, but dance in Greek clogs rather than ballet slippers.
It is somehow the opposite of what Gilbert Murray does
to Aeschylus. He relieves him of the heavyish clogs in
which he is brilliantly agile and gives him the comfort of
slippers in which, paradoxically, he feels awkward and
gauche. It's not the light fantastic the translation needs to
trip but the gravidly grounded. Browning and Hopkins
give a modern poet *some* feeling for what Aeschylus might

sound like in English, and certainly give more clues than the melodiously Swinburnian versions of a scholar like Gilbert Murray. Louis MacNeice, while translating the *Agamemnon*, wrote in *The Spectator* (1935) that 'a touch of Gerard Manley Hopkins might have helped Professor Murray'. He gives an example:

> Thus if for
>   'Hark! in the gates the bronzen targes groan'
> we substitute
>   'Hark! in the gates the bronze shields groan'
> we improve both rhythm and diction and so make the whole more real.

Murray's verse always comes too trippingly off the tongue and the need to keep metrically light-footed makes him opt for what is, even for his own time, a dated poetic diction. Murray nevertheless, in his use of pronounced rhythms, rhymes and energetic, if balletic, metric, at least gives us an inkling of the momentum I find essential to deliver the dramatic meaning, though much valuable consonantal cargo is thrown overboard to lighten and streamline the skiff. His versions have more feeling for the pace of the drama, even when wallowing in 'melody' and religiose musicality, than Browning.

When I began work on my version for the National Theatre in 1973 I had in mind two basic things: weight and mass on the one hand, and rhythmical energy on the other; the weight never quite so ponderous that the rhythm became clogged or ground to a halt, nor the rhythm so jaunty that the words escaped on the wing. In addition to this, when we take into account at an early stage the masked nature of these plays, which so many scholars, it seems to me, treat only as a by-the-way, a masked nature which makes speeches one block of solid colour rather than the lurches and subtextual twists we associate with Stanislavskian readings of more modern texts, or intimate screen acting, the sense of necessary weight and momentum is linked to a world of primary emotional colours which complicate their palate by accretion and cumulative effects rather than by a prismatic surface.

The early emphasis I'd placed on consonants rather than vowels made me keen to use the kind of actors I'd been working with in *The Passion* – the first part of *The Mysteries*, an adaptation of the Northern heavily alliterative mystery play cycles which came to complete epic fruition at the National in 1985. The work on this Northern classic often betrayed by churchified gentility was also a deliberate reclamation for Northern voices, part of my long slow-burning revenge on the teacher who taught me English at Leeds Grammar School and wouldn't let me read poetry aloud because of my 'common' south-Leeds accent. It was an accent that honours consonants and shortens vowels, ideal for the poetry of *The Mysteries*, written for earlier versions of that accent and, tentatively at this stage, right for the style I was looking for in the *Oresteia*. So the actors I eventually kept trying to insist on were those with accents somewhat like my own with short vowels and a sensuous consonantal quality in their speech. Something also of the style of the medieval plays, written like Greek drama for the open air, influenced my early use of alliteration, which sends dramatic speech like a speeding arrow across large stage spaces, or across the Corpus Christi Day hubbub of crowded medieval streets. Very early in our workshop experiments the instinct for the Northern alliterative style seemed to be right in one important and extremely practical respect: the clarity of language in masks depended more on the consonants than on the vowels, and when vowels were lengthened it caused a vibration in the masks that fogged the language and seriously disturbed the actors' concentration.

The concern for consonantal mass led me to alliteration with its repeated consonants, and its aid to alfresco clarity.

This concern led me to invent a ghostly alliterative metre that owed something to the earliest metrics of Northern poetry, and something to the earliest and most democratic drama in English. The echo of *Beowulf* seemed appropriate enough when we think of the plays of Aeschylus being described as 'slices from the banquet of Homer' and of the parallels often drawn between the heroic world of the *Iliad* and *Odyssey* and *Beowulf*, as in, for example, J. Wight Duff on *Homer and Beowulf: a Literary Parallel*. W. P. Ker in his *Epic and Romance* (1896) says of the epic clan life of early Britain: 'there is no question that the life depicted has many things in common with Homeric life', and 'how much the matter of the Northern heroic literature resembles the Homeric, may be felt and recognised at every turn . . . ' Everywhere Ker finds 'the affinities and correspondences between the Homeric and the Northern heroic world'. and describes *Beowulf as* a 'Northern *Odyssey*'. You can see the translator C. D. Locock in the 1920s making similar connections when he not only offers thirty-two passages from both the *Iliad* and the *Odyssey* but also *Fritiof's Saga*, a nineteenth-century romantic recasting of the Norse saga, *Fritiof the Bold* by the Swedish poet Esaias Tegner (1782–1846), who was also a professor of Greek at Lund University.

What I felt emerging as we experimented was a language that suited the full classical mask, that had an echo of our own 'heroic' clan world, and the Northern energy of our earliest drama, but that would give me the resources I also needed as a modern poet.

One aspect of the style of Aeschylus that Browning tried to reproduce was his compound words and coinages.In *Clouds* Aristophanes mocks Aeschylus as στομφαξ, 'one who speaks mouthfilling words', and κρημνοποιος, which could be translated as 'precipice-spouting' or 'crag-composing', and it is an aspect of his style that has always drawn me to his poetry. W. B. Stanford likens the stylistic device of compounding in Aeschylus to 'kenning', a word derived from medieval Icelandic treatises on poetics to denote those periphrastic, circumlocutory expressions characteristic of Old English and early Teutonic poetry, Old Norse and Icelandic, with typical examples like *oar-steed* for ship and *sword-storm* for battle, or more adventurous and far-fetched ones like *wound-leek* for sword.

That great compendium of 'The Poetry of the Old Northern Tongue', the *Corpus Poeticum Boreale* (1883) of Vigfusson and Powell, singles out Egil Skalla-Grimsson, the tenth-century Icelandic poet, who lived also in Norway and England, as a great creator of 'kennings'. Egil wrote one of his best known poems, 'Hofud-Lausn' ('The Head Ransom'), an end-rhymed *drapa* of twenty staves, composed overnight, with kennings like 'wound-mews' lips' for arrow barbs and 'woundbees' for arrows, to save himself from execution by King Eric Bloodaxe in York about 948. Speaking of Egil's kennings, Vigfusson and Powell say:

> In Egil's vigorous and concise figures we have the noblest examples of this kind [of kenning], often as deeply thought out and as ruggedly true and bold as the tropes of *Aeschylus himself*.
>
> *Corpus Poeticum Boreale*, II, 447

Perhaps my Yorkshire Aeschylus is a descendant of Egil, a skald-kin at least! Egil's style helped the eagle to bark in modern English. And York was also the city where the drama I had in mind and was influenced by was created. The spirit of Egil led me back to Aeschylus and the 'kennings' of Aeschylus back to the saga skald.

> The Greek language permitted great freedom in coining words. Aeschylus made the most of this. Neologisms are used by him with great frequency.
>
> W. B. Stanford, *Aeschylus in His Style* (1942)

Stanford quotes the compound epithet ἀταύρωτος (*Ag.*, 245) used of Iphigenia in the *Agamemnon* and the marvellous αρε˙θυοαυος ('Ares-tasselled'), and comments that they sound 'so grotesque in a literal English version that they are usually mitigated in translation'. Browning looked for the opposite of such linguistic mitigation in his version and I also took to compounding with great relish, happy to associate the 'eagle-bark' of Aeschylus with Egil the Icelander coining his kennings under the threat of King Eric's axe.

One of my favourite Aeschylean neologisms is from *Prometheus Bound:*

ναρθηκοπληρωτος πυρός πηγή
('fennel-filling fountain of fire', *v.* 109)

Old English has a facility for compounding which is characteristic of its poetic style, and I tried to use it not necessarily to match an Aeschylean compound exactly, but wherever I could as a means of also dramatising the tensions and antagonisms of the drama. There was no intention of chauvinistic Saxonising in my echoes, and echoes only, of our 'heroic' world. I wasn't intending to be like Sir John Cheke, the first Regius Professor of Greek at Cambridge, who in Milton's time 'taught Cambridge and King Edward Greek' but whose version of the gospels goes for Anglo-Saxon neologising like *hundreder*, for 'centurion'. Nor was it going as far as William Barnes, who influenced Hopkins with his *English Speechcraft* (1878) which comes up with Saxonising beauties like *push-wainling* for the Latinate 'perambulator', *matter-might* for 'mechanics', while 'laxative' becomes *loosensome*, 'horizon' *sky-sill*, 'embrasure' *gun-gap*, 'emporium' *warestore*; 'forceps' *tonglings*, 'genealogy' *kin-fore*, 'meteor' *welkin-fire*, 'telegram' *wire-spell*. But there is something basic to English and its poetics in such 'kennings.'

In a letter to Robert Bridges Gerard Manley Hopkins called Barnes' work 'a brave attempt to restore English to a sort of modern Anglo-Saxon, 'a vastly superior thing to what we have now'. Both Cheke and Barnes, and, of course, Hopkins were in the back of my mind when I was looking for new compounds, not only to evoke the ghosts of Anglo-Saxon epic and saga, but to help lay bare tensions at the heart of the drama. And those tensions are those of the 'sex-war'. As two eminent scholars have remarked of the *Oresteia*, there is 'continual emphasis on the sexual antithesis' (R. P. Winnington Ingram) and 'the clash between man and woman forms one of the trilogy's pervading themes' (Hugh Lloyd-Jones). Into that clash entered my coined compounds ready to engage.

IV

In April 1979 we had mask workshops and improvisations and, as I had done in the music theatre piece *Bow Down*, another collaboration with Harrison Birtwistle, I made little poems out of the attitudes of the actor to his part of the story, giving to the actor's sometimes strong emotional outbursts a similar rhythmical energy, with my own improvisatory coinings groping towards the style they were helping me to find. As these early workshops included women, the sexual polarisation of the trilogy's matter was made brutally clear. Out of the actor/singer Michael Heath's Apollo, dramatically interrupted by a lightning flash that ran down a pipe into the rehearsal room, and the Clytemnestra of Yvonne Bryceland, Tony Robinson's Cassandra, Jack Shepherd's Orestes, came the frank brutality behind the sex war of the *Oresteia*. I called them 'gloss songs'. They were my way of putting myself into the same vulnerable improvisatory situation as was expected of the even more intrepid actors. These are five examples of gloss songs that survive in my notebooks, though there were many on scraps of paper that I binned as readily as the actors were ready to trash earlier improvisations for something better. I kept a few to register the vehemence and often crude responses the material of the myth seemed to elicit from the actors.

I: ZEUS

Godchamp thought himself so strong
he challenged come-who-may

Godchamp wasn't godchamp long
the son who threw him soon got thrown

Chronos Ouranos the same way
godchamps first and then unknown

so it went on: father/son
father/son again
till ZEUS himself's the champion

ZEUS the stayer sing his praise
ZEUS champion for evermore
Godchamp ZEUS the one who stays

raise the paean ZEUS will reign
with laws for mortals like the law:

AWARENESS comes from PAIN.

2: FURIES

Son of Earth-she-god GAIA
and sky-he-god OURANOS, he,
CHRONOS castrated his own sire
and flung his sperm-bag in the sea.

27

From Sky-he-god's sack of sperm
oozing blood into the brine
came the FURIES whose locks squirm
venomous and serpentine.

Out of Sky's kin-mangled gender
a god now neither she or he
sprang to hound the gore-offender
punish bloodguilt ruthlessly.

Crone-kinder never knowing childhood
she-things with one task to do
snouts pressed to the spoor of shed blood
till the killer gets killed too.

3: APOLLO

Only seven months in the womb!
Couldn't get out fast enough!
Got fattened up on nectar and am-
brosia not papmilk stuff!

Loathed that warm blood-padded cell
that grounded blimp of blood
that gorge of pulsing pinkish gel
that slime of motherhood.

Look at this lot at my feet
all tits and purple clitoris
old vulva-face, foul bitch on heat
not even scorpions would kiss.

That cunt Cassandra got the gift
of APOLLO's prophecy
but when I yanked up her silken shift
she crossed her legs on me!

The gangbag god of muscled air
I rape my crazy Trojan screw
and when she screams out: *Look he's there!*
no one believes it's true.

4: CLYT'S TITS

My suckled he-child made me sore.
He needed just more tits than two
always mewing more more more
and more he got but still not through!

I fed him first with bursting tit
my milk was warm and sweet
ORESTES grew too fond of it
tugged four years at the teat.

I gave him my own breast a queen,
my breasts were ripe and wet
I gave him to a nurse to wean
or he'd be suckling yet!

He stands before me mouth agape
as though he'd suck me if he could,
each breast throbs no no escape
both nipples ooze their motherblood.

V

'Patriarchy means all that is depersonalised, alienated, it means multinational industry, nuclear war, urban isolation, capitalism, as well as rape, the stifling of women's creativity and sexuality. It is a very bad word indeed,' wrote Liz Forgan in *Women's Guardian* (20 March 1979) in an article entitled 'Beware the Bloodthirsty Matriarchs', an account of a Matriarchy Study Group. I was intrigued, and, as there were often days when Peter Hall was forced to abandon rehearsals for industrial diplomacy, I invited these 'bloodthirsty matriarchs' to come into a workshop day to talk and debate sexual politics with the company, and especially what they considered to be the defeat of the Furies at the end of the trilogy. The debate was very polarised.

The *Oresteia* is a sexual battleground. In 1886, just before he started work on *The Father*, Strindberg, whose dramas of the sex-war are almost unbearably raw, had come across an article by Paul Lafargue, the son-in-law of Karl Marx, in *La Nouvelle Revue* (1886), entitled 'Le Matriarcat: Etude sur les Origines de la Famille'. This view of the trilogy sees Orestes as an almost revolutionary initiator of the patriarchal era: '*Oreste est le personnage symbolique qui doit fouler aux pieds toutes les coutumes de la famille maternelle.*' Not only did Orestes kill his mother, destroying the mystique of motherhood, but later married Hermione, the daughter of Helen, sister of Clytemnestra. This would have been incest in early societies. After Hermione he married Erigone, the daughter of his own mother, Clytemnestra, and Aegisthus.

Lafargue was, of course, echoing Bachofen. The rediscovery of Bachofen's *Mutterrecht* by US academic feminists in the 1960s and 1970s had spawned a great deal of pseudo-scholarship about the existence of matriarchal societies before their forceful appropriation by patriarchy. Perverse as much of this was, and unproven as was the historical basis, it had long roots, and most certainly gave a mythological focus to the heated discussions that we also engaged in.

Engels had written in *The Origin of the Family, Private Property and the State* that the defeat of Mother-Right, which he derived from the *Mutterrecht* of Bachofen, which he found dramatised in the *Oresteia*, represented 'the world historical defeat of the female sex'. Freud also found 'still audible in the *Oresteia*' the idea of the matriarchal social order being succeeded by the patriarchal one, but he found the transition

> an advance in civilisation, since maternity is proved by the evidence of the senses while paternity is a hypothesis, based on an inference and a premise. Taking sides in this way with a thought process in preference to a sense perception has proved to be a momentous step.

For Hegel the distinction between what I was to call *bedbond* and *bloodbond* in the *Oresteia* was the basis of the creation of the State:

> The notion, in short, and the knowledge of the substantiality of marital life is something later and more profound than the more purely natural connection between mother and son, and constitutes the beginning of the State as the realisation of the free and rational will.
>
> On Tragedy

But the beginning of the State initiated patriarchy and all its repressions. The 'bloodthirsty matriarchs' – who were, in fact, mild but militant feminists whom I had invited into rehearsals to make the polarisations of the play palpably clear reversed the dictum of Apollo which I gave its stark brutality:

> the womb of the woman's a convenient transit.

This blunt judgement, though it made women in the audience at the National audibly gasp at the affront, has the support of contemporary Athenian science. Aristotle's work links biology and politics:

the female provides the material, the male provides that which fashions the material into shape . . . Thus the physical part, the body, comes from the female and the soul from the male since the soul is the essence of a particular body.

De Generatione Animalium

And in the *Politics* we find:

. . . by nature the male is superior, the female inferior, the one rules, the other is ruled.

The women who came to condemn patriarchy reversed the dictum of Apollo with quotations from Elizabeth Gould Davis, who wrote: 'In nature's plan the male is but a glorified gonad.' Athena, who gives the casting vote to the male, was regarded by radical feminists as a masculine fifth columnist, a status confirmed by her birth (or rebirth) out of the head of her father, Zeus. She is called by Mary Daly, in *Gyn/Ecology: the Metaethic of Radical Feminism* (1978), 'a puppet of Papa', 'a fembot'.

Not all the new feminists were as mildly reproving as those we debated with. There are works which revisit the violence of the world of Aeschylus and relish in a way that does deserve the epithet 'bloodthirsty' the fate of Agamemnon at the hands of Clytemnestra. In Nancy Bogen's novel, for example:

This is what: take his phallus and put the knife to it, and then as I watch the pain spread across his face when he realizes what is going to be said 'This is what you made the child with, this is what you hurt me with again and again, and it is because of this that the people all follow and serve you right and wrong.' And with this draw the blade over it and – 'Now look at it' – fling it in his face.

Klytaimnestra Who Stayed at Home
(New York, 1980)

Reading this we have to remember that Aeschylus uses the word ἐμασχαλίσθη (439) for what Clytemnestra does to Agamemnon and I translate as 'hacked off his cock'.

Interestingly, the actor who became angriest at the feminist revisions of history was eventually cast as Apollo, who is described by Philip Slater in his *The Glory of Hera* as 'the personification of anti-matriarchy'.

One of the results of these discussions and my research and the developing process of rehearsal was that I used the facility for compounding I had allowed myself as a way of linking the clan world of Aeschylus with the Anglo-Saxon, a compounding that helped me clarify these sexual polarities, and underscoring what the aspect of Greek gender can do and English cannot. The choice of a muscular narrative energy of the alliterative line haunted by Anglo-Saxon was then able to carry on it such compounds as *blood-bond* for the claim of kinship, and *bedbond* for the claims of the marriage tie, which sound in this formation like equally matched contestants, and in the court of Athena the final choice of importance has to be made between two other words of equal weight: *bloodright* and *bondright*. So my choices began to throw up words which carried the whole tension of the trilogy. In the same way it enabled me to underline the sexual polarities of, for example, θεος (god) and θεα (goddess) which the Greek gender denotations allow to sound of equal status, whereas the *-ess* suffix of English makes the female form sound diminutive. In the same way I used pairs like *he-child* and *she-child*.

Once I had established the principle, in the course of the trilogy I came up with compounds and coinages like the following:

bloodkin bloodclan blood-due bloodright bloodbond preybirds, nest-theft childloss clanchief star-clans throne-stones godstones chief-stave he-god she-god he-child she-child lust-lode man-hive sky-curse guestright god-

grudge mangrudge manlord life-lot god-sop god-plea
god-seer yokestrap (after Browning) godkin godstone
bondright bloodright bond-true bond-proof bride-snatch
love-gall spearclash shieldclang wavegrave stormflash
waveforce galesqualls blood-price spoil-spouse gut-truth
warcar blood-dew gore-lust grudgehound blood-quag
hackblock (after Browning) dirgeclothes ghostsop god-
sop blood-glut grave-cups gift-glut gore-shots shrinestool
ooze-clots grave-garb brute-clan netmesh blood-smog
spearspoil croprot griefstrings.

Though I was overruled by the management, I had the
feeling that though we shouldn't make the trilogy 'holy' we
could, by segregating the audience into male and female
(like a Greek Orthodox church), electrify the auditorium,
and make those sex-war stichomythia go from the male or
female mask to the divided banks of sexual supporters.

Ironically, the copies of my *Oresteia* text rushed from
the printers for sale at the première came wrapped in old
sheets of a textbook called *Placental Physiology*. On one
page there was the sentence: 'The existence of the mam-
malian ovum was not proved until 1812.' And on another:
'The placenta is the fetal exchange station.'

VI

As there are three auditoria on the South Bank, it means
that there are actors from three plays meeting and ming-
ling. There was some resentment expressed by actresses
about men taking over what seem like brilliant female
roles in Greek drama. I half-promised that I would construct
a satyr play to follow the *Oresteia*, and let the women
play the half-men/half-goats and wear the phalluses as a
mode of comment and redress. It was another enterprise

that floundered because of the industrial disputes at the NT. But I never lost my determination to write about satyrs, as we cannot understand the whole experience of Greek tragedy without them, though they have perished as the divisions between high and low art hardened. I eventually created *The Trackers of Oxyrhynchus* first in the ancient stadium of Delphi in July 1988 then in a revised version for the Olivier in March 1990. But I didn't get to see women wearing the the piano-wire stiffened foam rubber cocks until girls at the University of Durham did a production some years after.

It also led me to conceive an ill-fated trilogy, *The Common Chorus*, for a large cast of women. I also planned it for the Olivier. It was to be the *Lysistrata* of Aristophanes and the *Trojan Women* of Euripides as performed by the women's Peace Camp at the Greenham Common US missile base for the education of the guards behind the wire. The third play was to be a new piece by me about the origins of the machine gun, and the inventors, Hiram and Hudson Maxim. For various reasons the trilogy never happened and history rather marooned the play once the missile base had gone from Greenham.

The Common Chorus, Part One had an energetic performance at Leeds University, but *Part Two* has never been performed and therefore lacks all the kinds of detail and radical revision I always do in rehearsals. All my pieces for the theatre are fundamentally altered and defined in rehearsals and previews. However, the third play became *Square Rounds* (1992), which I wrote and directed for the Olivier for a group of women who played all the male parts, except for two. Only now in retrospect can I see the unity in my theatrical ventures. With its magic, transformations, song, and women munitionettes transformed into top-hat-wearing males like Vesta Tilley, *Square Rounds* drew on the same early experiences of theatre that had led me to my dream of unlocking the energy of 'high' art with the more obviously demonstrable energy of 'low', which launched me into the *Oresteia*.

[2001]

This version of *The Oresteia* of Aeschylus was first produced by the National Theatre Company of Great Britain in the Olivier Theatre on 28 November 1981 and at the ancient theatre of Epidaurus in July 1982 with the following company:

Sean Baker
David Bamber
James Carter
Timothy Davies
Peter Dawson
Philip Donaghy
Roger Gartland
James Hayes

Greg Hicks
Kenny Ireland
Alfred Lynch
John Normington
Tony Robinson
David Roper
Barrie Rutter
Michael Thomas

Director Peter Hall
Music Harrison Birtwistle
Designer Jocelyn Herbert
Assistant Designer Sue Jenkinson
Lighting John Bury
Movement Stuart Hopps
Movement Assistant Lyn Hockney
Staff Director Kenneth Mackintosh
Assistant Director Charlie Hanson
Music Director Malcolm Bennett
Music Assistant Ben Mason
Voice Jane Manning
Production Manager Michael Cass Jones
Stage Manager Rosemary Beattie

Deputy Stage Managers
Courtney Bryant, Brewyeen Rowland
Assistant Stage Managers
Jill Macfarlane, Rebecca Peek, Tim Speechley,
Lesley Walmsley
Sound Ric Green
Assistant Designer (Masks) Jenny West
Assistant Production Manager Mark Taylor
Assistant to Lighting Designer Paul McLeish

Musicians Malcolm Bennett, Simon Limbrick,
Ben Mason (percussion); Helen Tunstall (harp);
Rory Allam, John Harle, Jim Rae (wind)

Instrument Design Arthur Soothill, Brian Ackerman

One

AGAMEMNON

WATCHMAN

No end to it all, though all year I've muttered
my pleas to the gods for a long-groped-for end.
Wish it were over, this waiting, this watching,
twelve weary months, night in and night out,
crouching and peering, head down like a bloodhound,
paws propping muzzle, up here on the palace,
the palace belonging the bloodclan of Atreus –
Agamemnon, Menelaus, bloodkin, our clanchiefs.

I've been so long staring I know the stars backwards,
the chiefs of the star-clans, king-stars, controllers,
those that dispense us the coldsnaps and dogdays.
I've had a whole year's worth so I ought to know.
A whole year of it! Still no sign of the signal
I'm supposed to catch sight of, the beacons,
the torch-blaze that means Troy's finally taken . . .

The woman says watch, so here I am watching.
That woman's not one who's all wan and woeful.
That woman's a man the way she gets moving.

Put down your palliasse. Dew-drenched by daybreak.
Not the soft bed you'd dream anything good in –
Fear stays all night. Sleep gives me short time.

Daren't drop off though. Might miss it. The beacon.
And if I missed it . . . life's not worth the living!
Sometimes, to stop nodding, I sing or try singing
but songs stick in my gullet. I feel more like weeping
when I think of the change that's come over this household,
good once and well ordered . . . but all that seems over . . .

41

Maybe tonight it'll finish, this watching, this waiting,
an end to the torment we've yearned for ten years.

Come on, blasted beacon, blaze out of the blackness!

Sees beacon.

It's there! An oasis like daylight in deserts of dark!
It's there! No mistaking!
Agamemnon's woman –
best let her know the beacon's been sighted.
Time all the women were wailing their welcome!

Troy's taken! Troy's down and Troy's flattened.
There'll be dancing in Argos and I'll lead the dance.
My master's struck lucky. So've I, I reckon.
Sighting the beacon's a dice-throw all sixes.

Soon I'll be grasping his hand, Agamemnon's . . .
Let him come home to us, whole and unharmed!

As for the rest . . . I'm not saying. Better not said.
Say that an ox ground my gob into silence.

They'd tell such a story, these walls, if they could.

Those who know what I know, know what I'm saying.
Those who don't know, won't know. Not from me.

Exit Watchman.

Enter Chorus.

CHORUS

Ten years since clanchief Menelaus
and his bloodkin Agamemnon
(the twin-yoked rule from clan-chief Atreus –
double thronestones, double chief-staves)
pursued the war-suit against Priam,
launched the thousand-ship armada
off from Argos to smash Troy.

Mewing warcries   preybirds   shrilling
nest-theft   childloss   wild frustration
nestling snaffled   preybirds soaring
wildly sculling   swirling airstreams
using broad birdwings like oars
birthpangs   nothing   nestcare   nothing
nothing   fostered nestlings   nothing
crying   mewing   preybirds   shrilling

But one of the god powers up above them –
Apollo   Pan   or Zeus high he-god
hearing the birds' shrill desolation,
birds, guest-strangers in god-spaces,
sends down the slow but certain Fury
to appease the grudge the grieved birds feel.

So Zeus protector of man's guestright
sends the avenging sons of Atreus
down on Paris son of Priam
because of Helen, lust-lode, man-hive,
Helen the she manned by too many hes.

Bedbond   no   not bedbond   spearclash
swordhafts shattered   hacked bones smashed
sparring   skirmish   dustclouds   bloodstorm
Trojans   Greeks   not bedbond   bloodbath

The war in Troy's still in a stalemate
marking time at where it's got to
till the fulfilment that's been fated.
Once the Fury's after victims
no sacrifices   no libations
stop the headlong grudge's onrush.

But as for us   recruiter's refuse,
too old to join the expedition,
shrivelled leafage left to wither,
we go doddering about on sticks.

Neither the nurseling nor the senile
have juice enough to serve the Wargod.
Wargod-fodder's prime manhood.

Argos geezers, back to bairnhood,
ghosts still walking after cockcrow,
old men, dreams abroad in daylight.

She-child of Tyndareos, Clytemnestra,
what news have you had, what fresh reports?
You've given orders for sacrifice. Why?

All the godstones of this bloodclan
earthgods   skygods   threshold   market
look   they're all alight   all blazing

Look here   and there   the flaring firebrands
coaxed into flame by smooth-tongued torch-oils
brought out of store for great occasions

If you can tell us give us some comfort
soothe all that grief that's chewed into our guts.
Hope glimmers a little in these lit godstones,
blunts the sharp chops of gnashing despair.

Gab's the last god-gift of the flabby and feeble –
singing the omens that mobilised Argos:

Two preybirds came as prophecy
blackwing and silverhue
came for our twin kings to see
out of the blue   the blue

The right side was the side they flew
spear side   luck side   War
one blackwing   one silverhue
and everybody saw

and everybody saw them tear
with talon and with claw

44

the belly of a pregnant hare
and everybody saw

and everybody saw the brood
from their mauled mother torn
wallowing in warm lifeblood
and dead as soon as born

blackwing and silverhue
prophesying War
the twin preybirds that cry and mew
hungering for more . . .

*Batter, batter the doom-drum, but believe there'll
    be better!*

Calchas the clanseer cunning in seercraft
when he saw before him the armed sons of Atreus
knew what menfolk were meant by the preybirds –
Agamemnon   Menelaus   battle-hungry hare-devourers . . .

'Hosts commanded by twin birds
soldiers who leave these shores
first Fate will waste Troy's crops and herds
then make the inner city yours

The moment when the iron bit
's between the jaws of Troy
may no skycurse glower down on it
and no godgrudge destroy

Artemis   pure she-god   stung
with pity for the hare
all mothers and their unborn young
come under her kind care

her father's hounds with silent wings
swoop down on that scared beast
Artemis   she loves wee things
and loathes the preybirds' feast.'

Blackwing and silverhue
prophesying War
the twin preybirds that cry and mew
hungering for more . . .

*Batter, batter the doom-drum, but believe there'll
be better!*

Artemis pure she-god   stung
with pity for the hare
all mothers and their unborn young
come under her kind care

Kind even to the lion-pup
you're the one we cry to, you!
Kind to wild beasts at the pap
stop bad signs coming true.

Apollo   he-god   healer   your she-kin
Artemis   intervene   prevent her
sending winds on the fleet from the wrong direction
keeping the armada too long at anchor,

making a blood-debt sacrifice certain,
a sacrifice no one wants to eat meat from,
a sacrifice no one wants to sing songs to,
whetting the grudge in the clanchief's household,
weakening the bond between woman and manlord,
a grudge wanting blood for the spilling of childblood,
a grudge brooding only on seizing its blood-dues.

These omens both fair and foreboding
Calchas the clanseer saw in the birdsigns –

*Batter, batter the doom-drum, but believe there'll
be better!*

So Agamemnon first clanchief of Argos
found no fault in the clanseer's foretelling
and went where the winds of his life-lot were listing,
the Achaian armada still anchored off Aulis.

Wind-force and wave-swell   keep the ships shorebound
men sapped of spirit   supplies running short
foodpots and grain jars   crapping their contents

ship planks gape open   frayed cables and rigging
time dragging   each day seeming two days
the flower of Argos   bedraggled and drooping

Calchas the clanseer   saw into the storm-cause –
Artemis   she-god   goaded to godgrudge

The clans and the clanchiefs   clamour for sea-calm
The god-sop that gets it   makes their guts sicken
The cure for the stormblast   makes strong men craven

The clanchiefs of Argos   drummed their staves on the earth
and wept and wept   and couldn't stop weeping

Then the first he-child of Atreus   Agamemnon
choked back his crying   and finally spoke:

hard   hard for a general   not to obey
hard   hard for a father   to kill his girl
his jewel   his joy   kill his own she-child
virgin-blood   father-guilt   griming the godstone

Can I choose either   without doing evil
leave the fleet in the lurch   shirker   deserter,
let down the Allies   we've all sworn allegiance

They're asking for blood   it's right what they're asking

a virgin's blood only will calm the wind's bluster

So be it then   daughter!   there's no other way

Necessity   he kneels to it   neck into the yokestrap
the General   harnessed to what he can't change
and once into harness his whole life-lot lurches
towards the unspeakable horror   the crime

so men get gulled   get hauled into evil
recklessness starts it   then there's no stopping

so a Father can take his own she-child   take her
and kill her   his she-child   his own flesh and blood

The war-effort wants it   the war-effort gets it
the war for one woman   the whore-war   the whore-war

a virgin's blood launches the ships off to Troy

Her shrillings   beseechings   her cries   Papa   Papa
Iphigeneia   a virgin   a virgin
what's a virgin to hawks and to war-lords?

He says a god-plea   her father   her *father*   then orders
attendants to hoist her   up   on to the godstone

she bends herself double   beseeching Papa   Papa
wraps her clothes round her   making it harder
up   up   she gets hoisted   like a goat to the godstone

a gag in her mouth   her lovely mouth   curbed like
   a horse's
so that this bloodclan's not blasted by curses

her garments stream groundwards   the looseflow
   of saffron
cloth drifting   cloth trailing   she darts them all glances
that go through their hearts   deep into them   wounding

a painting   a sculpture   that seems to be speaking
seeking to say things   but locked in its stone

they know what her eyes say   that gang round the
   godstone

often they'd seen her   at meals with her father
in the place beside his   when they sat at his table
the welcoming table of King Agamemnon

she sat beside him   his innocent she-child
singing the lyresong after libations
the melodious gracethanks   to Zeus   the Preserver

What came next   didn't see   so can't tell you

What Calchas foretold all came to fulfilment

Suffering comes first   then after awareness

The future's the future   you'll know when it's here
foreseeing the future's to weep in advance

The present's enough   and what's going to happen
let it be what we've hoped for   us   the poor remnants
so long the sole bulwark of monarchless Argos

Enter Clytemnestra.

Clytemnestra, we come to you as we would to our
  clanchief
for it's right that we honour the wife of the clanchief
when the manlord himself's not here on the thronestone.
Is it good news and firm news or mere wishful thinking
that makes you sacrifice now on the godstones?

CLYTEMNESTRA
Like mother, like daughter . . . May last night's good news
give birth this dawnlight to a day like her mother.
What I've got to tell you's beyond all you've hoped for.
The Greek armies have taken the city of Priam.

I
CHORUS
Taken Troy? Did my ears hear you right?
CLYTEMNESTRA
Wasn't I clear? Troy was taken last night.

2
CHORUS
My eyes fill with tears, tears of sheer joy.
CLYTEMNESTRA
Then your eyes know it's true our taking of Troy.

49

3
CHORUS
Can you be certain with no news that's concrete?
CLYTEMNESTRA
Yes, unless the whole thing's some he-god's deceit.

4
CHORUS
Or some dream of Troy taken which *seems* to you true.
CLYTEMNESTRA
I put trust in seeming no more than you.

5
CHORUS
Some rumour has reached you the war's at an end?
CLYTEMNESTRA
I'm no simple childwit! Don't condescend!

6
CHORUS
So Troy has been taken *when* did you say?
CLYTEMNESTRA
Last night, she who just gave birth to today.
CHORUS
The news came so fast over such a long way!

CLYTEMNESTRA
Firegod Hephaistos flashed out from Mount Ida
flame after flame bore the beacon's despatches,
jaded flame to fresh flame bearing the firenews.
Ida to Crag Hermes on the island of Lemnos.
From there its third stretch to the top of Mount Athos,
the peak that Zeus favours, then further upwards
and over the ocean dazzling and flaring
luring up fish-shoals to see what the flash is,

a fire-tailed comet transmitting its message
to the watchtowers scanning the sky on Macistos.
They weren't caught napping. They flung the flame
   onwards
and it hurtled over Euripus and watchmen
marked it from their Messapion outpost.
They kindle heaped brushwood and speed the flame further.
It gathers momentum. It doesn't diminish.
It streaks like a meteor over Asopus
and lands on Cithaeron and sparks off the next one.
Again not neglected. So eager the watchmen
they get up a blaze that doubles the last one.
From the bog of Gorgopis to Mount Aegiplanctus
the bright chain of firelinks remaining unbroken,
they spare no effort and heap on the kindling,
the flamehair streaming out over the headland
that faces gulf Saron and then dropping southwards
to the crag of Arachne that borders on Argos
and straight to the palace of Atreus,
the flame that was fathered in Troy's conflagration.

My torchbearers bore all the batons of blazes.

That's the sign, the proof you've been wanting
all the way from Troy, from my manlord to me.

CHORUS
The gods will get all our thanks for their bounty.
But your tale's such a marvel we'd like it repeated.
We'd like all the details. You said first that Hephaistos . . .

CLYTEMNESTRA
Troy's held by the Greeks is the truth you're not grasping.
Pour oil on to vinegar in the same foodpot
they'll never blend in brotherly bloodbond.
So life-lots in conflict cause cries that conflict:
the Trojans all tearful, their arms round their fallen
embracing cold corpses, the widows, the orphans,

knowing their own lives mean only bond-chains,
keen for their bloodkin, their nearest, their dearest;
the Greeks, their whole night spent in harsh skirmish,
famished for breakfast swoop down onto Troy,
no billets allotted, all discipline broken,
each man for himself, the luck of the straw-lot,
they bed themselves down in the houses they've captured,
free of the nightfrost, rough beds in the open,
sleep, for once without sentries, and wake up refreshed.
So provided they don't give Troy's gods provocation
and leave unmolested their sacrosanct seats
there's a chance that the victors will never be victims.
I hope our platoons aren't driven by lootlust
to bring what's tabooed back home here as booty.
They still need some safety on the last lap back home.
And even if the Greeks give grudge to no godheads
the dead that they've slaughtered can't sleep for ever.
Let disaster stop at the place it's reached so far,
the cycle be broken, and hope start to happen.
Let a life-lot that's lucky get crowned with the laurels.

You've heard all my feelings, those of a woman.

   Exit Clytemnestra.

CHORUS

You feel like a woman but talk like a man talks.
Now I've heard all your proofs now I can offer
the gratitude due to the gods who guard Argos.
The joy we feel now seems worth all we've suffered.

Zeus the high he-god with Night as his helper
cast a vast trammel over Troy's towers –
men get meshed in it   women   children
all dragged ashore and beached in harsh bondage.
Zeus cast it   Zeus   protector of guestright.
Zeus got the bullseye when he shot Paris
an arrow that took ten years to its target.

The Zeus-shot they call it   no doubting it either.

Zeus says it   it happens   his plans get accomplished.

So if somebody tells you gods take no notice
when the sacrosanct's trampled on   trod underfoot
point to what's happened   and call him a cretin
point to what's happened   ruin for recklessness
men over-ambitious   treasure-stuffed mansions
measureless riches that can't buy the best things

sufficiency's ample   real wealth is awareness

surfeit   satiety   gold tons are no bulwark
if the godstone of justice gets booted to blackness
true bloodright shattered to atoms of nothing.

Wordpower   temptations   techniques of inducement
soften the wretch up for their master   Destruction

Guilt can't be curtained   it glows through the nightdark

Base battle-bronze battered gets blackened and mottled
so a man's baseness gets clotted with bloodguilt.

The chased culprit's got as much chance of escaping
as a boy has of catching a blackbird bare-handed.

Time spatters the guilty   the blood a man sheds
smears his whole people   his touch clarts his clan.

Now he starts praying   the gods make their ears stone
the deaf gods trample him mid-supplication.

It was like that with Paris   guest-stranger and welcome
at the hospitable table of the bloodclan of Atreus –

his gratitude   guest-thanks   grabbing of Helen

and what did Helen bequeath to her people
spearclash and shieldclang   the massive armada

the dowry she went with to Troy was   destruction.

'A bad day for this house   a bad day for the master
look at the bedclothes   still rumpled with passion'

Menelaus apart   he's brooding his loveloss
stunned into silence   a shadow   a ghostman

statues mean nothing   stone's eyeless and lifeless

his sleep's full of dreamwives   Helen-shaped shadows
that bring ease a moment then vanish away

he tries to grasp her   she slips through his fingers
shadowing off down the flyways of sleep . . .

This is the anguish of the country's chief household

It doesn't stop there though   grief goes all over
each house in Argos sent someone to battle

and gets back for menfolk   jars full of cinders
a plectrum of sorrows plucks women's griefstrings:

'Geldshark Ares god of War
broker of men's bodies
usurer of living flesh
corpse-trafficker that god is –

give to WAR your men's fleshgold
and what are your returns?
kilos of cold clinker packed
in army-issue urns

wives   mothers   sisters   each one scans
the dogtags on the amphorae
which grey ashes are my man's?
they sift the jumbled names and cry:

my husband sacrificed his life

my brother's a battle-martyr

aye, for someone else's wife –

Helen, whore of Sparta!

whisper   mutter   belly-aching
the people's beef and bile: *this war's
been Agamemnon's our clanchief's making,
the sons of Atreus and their 'cause'.*

Where's my father   husband   boy?
where do all our loved ones lie?
six feet under near the Troy
they died to occupy.'

The people's rancour's a terrible burden
the whole clan can curse with one venomous voice.

Night's got something under its dark cloth

listen   dangers hum under its cover
gods see carnage   get the massacre marked –

Furies   the trackers   fulfilling the bloodgrudge
trip the transgressor   tread him into the ground
blown up and bloated   rubbed out into nothing
no one can save you among blurs and shadows.

Rising too high's a danger   it's risky
the pinnacles get the thunder's first flameclap
the cragpeaks feel the first storm-flash

Enough is enough when unmarred by mean mangrudge
Conqueror   captive   don't want to be either
I want to wear neither laurels nor bondchains.

1
Those fires make the rumours fly through the street.
Is it all true, or some he-god's deceit?

2
Who's such a childwit to believe the flame first
then feel despondent when the bubble's been burst?

55

3

Women! Women are always ready to act
before they know if a rumour's true fact.

4

Women are gullible. Minds like dry straw –
one whoosh of belief and then nothing more.

We'll know soon enough what that blaze was about,
those beacons and bonfires, the newfangled flamegraphs,
whether there's anything in it or whether
it's just the wishful thinking women indulge in.

Look, there's a herald coming up from the seashore,
the mud of the trenches caked dry on his tunic.
He's wearing the olive-wreath, and there, look, behind him,
look at that dustcloud. That means that it's real news
not feminine flame-a-phores kindled on mountains,
but words spoken, man to man, and spoken directly.
He'll say rejoice or . . . that mustn't happen . . .
So far, so good. And let it continue . . .
and if there's anyone wants anything else for this bloodclan
I hope that he gets what his malice deserves.

Enter Herald.

HERALD

Homesoil! Argos ground! Clanland! Home!
A ten-year absence ends in this bright dawn.
Most hopes were shipwrecked. One scraped back safe,
the hope that I'd make it back home here to die,
die, and find rest in the earth I most cherish.
Earth Earth Sun Sun!
Zeus godchief highest of he-gods
Apollo godseer Pythian prophet
those arrowshafts shot at us, hold back the volleys,
god-aggro enough on the banks of Scamander.

56

Now be the cure-all, the soul-salve Apollo.
Hermes, he-god, and herald to godclans,
guardian of heralds to men down below,
and heroes under whose gaze we were drafted,
welcome us back, those few spared the spearthrust.
House of our clanchiefs, homes of my bloodkin,
thronestones and godstones facing the sun's glare,
if ever you once did, welcome your king back,
look on him with kind eyes after his absence.
Like a bright firebrand blazing through darkness
to stop us all stumbling, King Agamemnon.
Welcome him warmly. He's earned your warm welcome.
He swung the god-axe, Zeus the Avenger's,
tore Troy's roots up, dug her earth over,
her god-shrines shattered, her altars all gutted,
fruitful earth scorched into futureless dustbowls,
an empire gone putrid and tossed on time's midden.
Troy's neck got his yoke on, your clanchief's,
first he-child of Atreus, most lucky of life-lot,
worthier than any of the honours he's taken.
I doubt raper Paris thought it was worth it.
The town he brought doom on won't boast of his
    bridesnatch.
Branded for wife-theft he lost what he'd plundered,
his ancestral bloodclan razed root and branch.
Priam's sons paid for it. An eye for an eye,
or more like ten thousand eyes for each one.

I

CHORUS

Welcome Herald! You're home. The war's far behind.

HERALD

I kept alive for this. Now death I don't mind.

2
CHORUS
Did you long for your home here back at the war?
HERALD
What else do you think my weeping is for?

3
CHORUS
You could say it was sweet, in a way, your disease.
HERALD
Sweet? A disease! What riddles are these?

4
CHORUS
That longing you had. We caught it here too.
HERALD
You longed for us as we longed for you?

5
CHORUS
So much that our gloom made us groan with despair.
HERALD
What made you so gloomy? Our being out there?

6
CHORUS
It's best for our safety if no more is said.
HERALD
With the clanchiefs away what caused you this dread?
CHORUS
Like you we too wouldn't mind being dead.

HERALD
Suffering. Suffering, only the gods escape it entirely.
If you'd known first-hand our louse-ridden billets,

cramped berths on board, claustrophobic, foul bedding,
what didn't we have to complain of you tell me.
Ashore was no better. Worse. We bivouacked
under the walls with the enemy firing.
Drenched either by drizzle or dew from the ground.
Clothes mouldy with mildew. Locks crawling with lice.

First unbearable cold, snow blowing off Ida,
blizzards killing birdflocks frozen in flight.
Then heat! and even the ocean seemed stifled,
slumped, zephyrless, in unruffled siestas,
slack billows lolling in the deadest of doldrums.

But why go on? What's the point? The pain's over,
and for the dead so over and done with,
they'll never lust after a life-lot again.
The dead are dead. Who wants a head-count?
Why should the living scratch open old scabs.
We've left it behind us. Goodbye to all that!
We're what's left. There's some good for the living.
The pain and the losses don't quite overbalance.
We can shout out to the universe proudly:

The bloodclans of Argos in battle alliance
having mashed into ashes Asia's town Troy
now nail up these god-spoils to Hellas's he-gods.

For all that we'll get the credit and praises
and Zeus the god's whale's share. He made it happen.

That's all. That's all there is for the telling.

CHORUS

Your news shows me that I was mistaken.
But you're never too old to learn a new lesson.
Clytemnestra, she should be first to hear the whole story.
The leftovers and scraps of it satisfy me.

Enter Clytemnestra.

CLYTEMNESTRA

I started my triumph cry some time ago
when the first flame-messenger arrived in the darkness
proclaiming the capture and downfall of Troy.
And what did the men say? 'Just like a woman!
One beacon, that's all, and she thinks Troy's been
     captured.'
Mutterings like that made me feel stupid.
I went on with the sacrifice in spite of their moaning,
then the whole city began 'behaving like women'
raising the triumph cry 'shouting and bawling'
feeding the thankfires almost to bursting.
And why should you tell me anything further?
I'll have the whole tale from the mouth of my manlord.
And it's his welcome now that must be fully prepared.
No day in the life of woman's sweeter than that one
when she flings the door open to welcome her manlord,
her manlord brought safely back from the war.
Go. Tell him come quickly. He's loved by his people.
Tell him he'll find his wife faithful and bond-true
as when he first left her, and, like a good bloodhound,
his loyal servant, and his enemies' foe.
He'll find all his treasures still with his seal on.
Tell him I've accepted no man's attentions.
I'm no more a breaker of bedbond
than, as a woman, I wield a man's weapon.

Exit Clytemnestra.

CHORUS

All the words of the woman are clear enough
if those who are listening give all their ears.

To Herald.

Herald, what about Menelaus our other clanchief?
You haven't said he's home safe as well.

I

HERALD

Falsehood is something fair lies never hide.
The mask of glad messenger just wasn't mine.

CHORUS

Skins can be fair and the fruit bad inside.
Can't good news and truth ever share the same vine?

2

HERALD

Menelaus, he's missing that clan-chief of yours.
He's gone, his ship's gone. And *this* is all true.

CHORUS

He set sail with you though when the force left Troy's shore:
Did a sudden storm blow up and snatch him from view?

3

HERALD

Storm! Yes, you've hit the bull's eye!
'Storm' 's a small word that encompasses hell.

CHORUS

Is he still living, or did the chief die?
Is there anyone there in the fleet who can tell?

4

HERALD

No one knows anything, at least not us men,
only the sun that looks down from the sky.

CHORUS

How did the storm start? Why did it? When?
Was it some godgrudge, and if a grudge, why?

HERALD

A godgrudge! A godgrudge! Don't drag in *those* she-gods!
Some gods preside over pleasures, some pain.
Those she-gods go with the most galling godgrudge.

This day's a homecoming meant to be happy.
When a clan messenger's arrived shedding tears
to announce to his bloodclan what they've been dreading,
the rout of their armies, a mountainous death-toll,
with anguish for all in the rolls of the fallen,
the best lads in their tonloads tangled and landed
and gashed by the flesh-hook, the fish-gaff of Ares,
gaff-flukes and grapnel barbs gory with fleshbits –
if he comes so overbalanced with trouble
then that's the time to start hymning the Furies.
But if the news is good that he's bringing
and the city's wild with relief and success
who wants to be first to get the good curdled
and blurt it all out: 'Shipwreck. Shrewgrudge!
The grudges of she-gods shattered the Greek ships.'

Flame and saltwater are scarcely a bloodbond.
This time they were though, elements merging,
and their bond-proof – smashing our ships into splinters.

Blackness. Waveforce. Sea heaving and swelling.
Fierce thrashing galesqualls whistling from Thrace,
hurricanes blasting, rain lashing and pelting,
ship-prow smashing ship-prow, horned beast goring beast,
beasts with their horns locked butting each other.
You know when a collie not used to its charges
scatters the daft sheep every direction,
colliding, collapsing, that kind of chaos . . .
well that's how the waves were. Next morning
the Aegean had mushroomed with corpses and shipwreck.
Our ship though, amazing, still whole and undamaged.
Some god interceded, got our ship a pardon.
Our helm had been guided by the hand of some he-god.
Our ship was one that didn't get shattered.
Couldn't believe it, escaping that wave-grave,
couldn't believe our life-lot so lucky.

We were shocked in the clear light of morning,
chewing the cud of the nightmare we'd lived through.
If any of the others survived they'll be thinking
we're finished, finished, as we still do of them.
May everything still turn out for the better.
Menelaus, let's suppose that he's made it,
let's hope he's still somewhere under the sunlight.
Zeus can't want the whole bloodclan blasted.
That's the truth you wanted.   You've got it all now.

CHORUS

HELEN wrecker HELEN Hell
the one who first named her knew what was fated –
HEL – a god guided his tongue right – EN
HEL – spear-bride gore-bride war-whore – EN
HEL – ship-wrecker man-breaker Troy-knacker – EN

From silken bowers scented and flowing with curtains
to seas that are breathed on and ruffled by zephyrs,
and after her warhosts bristling with metal,
trail-hounds snuffling the vanishing oar-spoor,
tracking the beached ships up leafy Simois,
trail-hounds scenting the seatracks and bloodslicks.

Godgrudge and mangrudge ganging together
shepherded the blood-bride surely to Troy,
delayed counterblow to the sullied table,
the wrong done to Zeus protector of guestright.
They paid the blood-price, the bridegroom's bloodkin
chanting the bride-hymn, hymning the bedbond.
The new hymn they've learnt in the city of Priam's
not about bedbond but a loud bawl at death
calling Paris the doomgroom, the doomgroom.
War-whore Helen brought suffering, slaughter,
bloodgrudge, futility, childloss and bloodflow.

Story: Man and Lion. This is it –

Lion-cub brought in from the wild
still whimpering for the tit
Man treats it like a child

They dandle it   they fondle   stroke
they sit it in their laps
delight of children and old folk
sits up and begs for scraps

Time passes and the man's cub grows
no more a wean to rock to sleep
suddenly its nature shows
cub savages your sheep

its thankyou for its bed and board
its gratitude for care
your whole flock torn   clawed   gnawed
and bloodflow everywhere

Blood everywhere   blood everywhere
the whole house smirched   defiled
anguish   carnage   and despair
for fostering that child

That harmless orphaned furry beast
greeting for its nurse
was nothing but a fury-priest
a grudge-sent slaughter curse.

Helen to Troy   first windless calm   windless
a priceless treasure   yielding with soft feel
delicate eyeglints   rare orchid with heart-thorns
then abracadabra the nuptials turn nasty,
jinxwoman Helen   wormwood   lovegall
bringing the children of Priam disaster
spurred on by Zeus as protector of guestright,
blood-price   spoil-spouse   connubial Fury.

Wealth-pride never dies childless   never
but always breeds children that go to the bad –
that's half of the story but what I say's this:

Wealth coupled with Hubris   that's the dark pedigree
that sends its black seeds from infant to infant

When bloodright gives birth the children are blotless –

Hubris I breeds Hubris II
O dark ancestral tree
Old arrogance will soon breed new
gory genealogy

Wealth-pride is the furious son
of a fiendish blood-dark mother
Violence is the other one
and dead spit of his brother

Justice shines through hovel smoke
she loves the man who's straight
Justice eats off plates of oak
scorns dainties off gold plate

Hands bespattered with shed blood
raise gilded rafters to the skies
Justice searching for the good
leaves with averted eyes

Justice doesn't kneel to fame
kiss affluence's feet
isn't dazzled by a name
gold-coined but counterfeit

Justice isn't put out of her stride
Justice can't be turned aside

Enter Agamemnon with Cassandra and Trojan spoils.

CHORUS

Bloodshoot of Atreus, destroyer of Troy
what's the best title to give you   what honour
that isn't too high for you or too hackneyed?
What name does you justice   gives you your due?

The world's mostly mummery   sham and not gut-truth.
Someone's wretched and people start sighing;
the griefshow stops a lot short of the heart.
Someone's happy, they act the same hollowly
glum visages forced into grins that are joyless.
But a good judge of livestock knows his own cattle –
their eyes say one thing   he knows the other
their cow eyes may water   he knows it's not love.

I can hide nothing   now I can tell you
when you first marshalled the armies for Helen
your image was evil   I thought you misguided
to wage a long war for one lustful woman
so many cold grave urns for one gadding girl . . .

now though my heart's full   and I greet you
your victory makes everything worth it
the omens I loathed then seem justified now.

And while you were fighting   those who remained here
some have been faithful   and others . . .
but you'll soon sort out the sheepmen and goatmen.

AGAMEMNON

First I greet Argos and the gods of this bloodclan.
They gave me safe passage and helped me smash Priam.
They stopped their ears to Troy's pleas and entreaties.
They cast their votes and pitched all the pebbles
into the bloodpot. Nothing went into the pot for acquittal
Hope hovered round it but hope's got no franchise.
Troy! you can almost see it smoking from Argos!
The rubble and debris still breathe out destruction,

the ashes of surfeited Asia still sighing,
the sickly cachou breath of soft living and riches.
The thanks owed our gods for their bounty's boundless.
Remember them, everyone, now in our triumph,
now that we've got Troy caught in our sweepnet.
They raped one woman. We razed the whole city.
Ground it to powder. Made mincemeat of Troy.
The monster of Argos, the horse-monster did it,
chock full of shock-troops, clearing Troy's bulwarks
just when the Pleiades were starting to wane,
leaping the battlements the ravening lion
glutted its bloodlust on Troy's royal children.

What you said about praising and joy I agree with.
Not many can look on success without mangrudge.
Grudge gangrenes the gut. The suffering's twofold:
one's own lack of luck, another's good life-lot.
I know what I'm saying, knew only too well
how men can dissemble, make friendship a sham.
Most of my comrades were shadow men, shadows.
Only Odysseus, first reluctant and cussèd,
once into harness pulled his weight beside me.
And whether he's dead or alive isn't certain . . .

As for the matters of bloodclan, clan-rite and clan gods
we'll call the clan council to meet in full conclave.
Emergencies needing immediate attention –
drastic surgery. Cauterise. Cut out the canker . . .

Now into the palace, my household hearthstone,
to give the thanks due to all my great godkin.
They sent me out. They brought me back safely.
I've won this once but I have to keep winning.

Enter Clytemnestra.

CLYTEMNESTRA
Kinsmen, old men of Argos gathered before us
I'm not ashamed to confess in your presence

my love for my manlord. Time removes shyness.
I don't need to hear stories, I suffered first-hand.
I suffered greatly with my man at the warfront.
For a woman to sit alone at home waiting
with her man at the war's a terrible burden.
There's no end to the rumours she has to keep hearing.
News-runners arriving in rapid succession
bawling the worsening news to the bloodclan.
If my manlord received the wounds rumour gave him
he'd gape open now like a sea-fisher's grabnet.
I was driven distracted . . . rope round the rafters . . .
neck in the noose . . . getting tighter . . . half-throttled . . .

   To Agamemnon.

that's why our child isn't here now in Argos,
our child, our bed-bond's first bloodshoot,
our *he*-child, Orestes.   No need for suspicion.
He's in Phocis with Strophius, our ally and friend.
Strophius warned me of possible troubles,
the threat to your life in the perils of warfare,
the likelihood here of popular rising.
When people are down they get trampled further.
My words have no wiles, and no guile to gull you.
Now my eyes are pumped dry. No more tears to
   squeeze out.
Eyes bleary with weeping and sleepless night-vigils
hoping the beacons from you would get kindled.
If I slept, *if*, a mere gnat-whine would wake me,
loud as a bugle bray, wake me from dreaming.
And what did I dream of? Your danger. Your deathwounds.
Ten years of tight corners crammed into a catnap!
All that I suffered but no longer feel fettered,
I'm free to say welcome, my lord, to your house,
welcome as the watchdog is in the sheepfold,
mainmast of our vessel, chief central rooftree.
Like an only child to its father you're welcome,

welcome as land is to those on the ocean,
welcome as dawn is after long nightsqualls,
as a spring is to travellers thirsting for water.

The release! Yanking necessity's yokestrap off!

Now, my great manlord, come down from your warcar.
But don't let those feet that have trampled Troy under
step on mere earth.

To Slaves.

Why are you waiting?
Carry out my commands for strewing the pavestones,
drag the dark dye-flow right down from the doorway.
Let bloodright, true bloodright be the king's escort.
No sleeping for me till the gods get their pleasure.
The she-gods of life-lot, I'll be their she-kin,
the female enforcer of all they have fated.

AGAMEMNON
She-child of Leda, my household's best bloodhound,
your words, like my absence, lasted too long.
Our praise-singers spout out such paeans for payment.
We are a warhawk, no woman wanting such welcomes.
Such prostrations, such purples suit pashas from Persia.
Don't come the Khan's courtiers, kowtow or cosset.
Don't grovel, suck up, salaam, and stop gawping!
Such gaudy displays goad gods into godgrudge.
Give honours to humans more meant for mankind
than such stuffs even skygods won't scorn to be swathed
in.
The mortal who blackens such silks with his bootsoles
best beware of bad trouble, best look to his life-lot.
My fame's managed so far without fancy footmats.
The greatest of godgifts is canniness, caution.
Luck has to last the whole length of a lifetime.
If happiness fails in the last lap it's futile.

Fortune can only be first. All after it's failure.
Good luck gets the champion's laurels or nothing.
Runners-up in the race are degrees of disaster.
My stride's strong and steady till disaster's left standing.

1
CLYTEMNESTRA
Then stride 'strong and steady' on what we have strewn.
AGAMEMNON
No, it smells baleful. No blessing or boon!

2
CLYTEMNESTRA
Is 'great' Agamemnon godstruck, afraid?
AGAMEMNON
No, but I stand by the statement I made.

3
CLYTEMNESTRA
And potentate Priam? Would *he* tread it or not?
AGAMEMNON
That Trojan satrap? Traipse over the lot!

4
CLYTEMNESTRA
Are you afraid of what the people might say?
AGAMEMNON
The voice of the people exerts its own sway.

5
CLYTEMNESTRA
Mangrudge is proof that a man's reached great heights.
AGAMEMNON
And only he-women go looking for fights.

6

CLYTEMNESTRA
Give way from the grace of your great victory.
AGAMEMNON
Would that give you joy, that gesture from me?
CLYTEMNESTRA
Let me win a little, great manlord. Agree!

AGAMEMNON
If it means so much . . .

To Slaves.

here, help get these boots off.
Campaign comrades, loyal old leathers.

Keep godgrudge off me as I tread on this sea-red.
I'll feel that I'm walking the women who wove it.
Mounds of rich silver went into its making.
So much for me . . .

Indicates Cassandra.

This stranger needs looking after.
The gods like some kindness from those who have
    triumphed.
Be kind. Nobody wants to end up in bondage.
Pick of the booty, the Trojan spoil loot-pearl,
this girl's the men's gift to grace their commander.

Well, since I've yielded, I'll do what you ask me,
and tread on your red path into my palace.

*Agamemnon begins walking on the cloth towards the
palace doors.*

CLYTEMNESTRA

The sea's there for ever. No one can drain it.
And it oozes for ever the dyes of dark sea-red
to stain all the garments this house has a wealth of.
The gods have made sure that we've never been lacking.
And if gods had prescribed it as a rite for his safety
I would have trampled each inch of rich raiment.
If the treeroot's living the house gets new leafage
spreading cool shade at the time of the dogstar.
Your return's like a rare spell of sunshine in winter,
like Zeus when he ripens the sour grapes for the vintage.
A master's presence then 's the finishing stroke.

O Zeus, Zeus who brings all things to fulfilment
my fulfilment lies in serving your purpose.

Exit Clytemnestra.

CHORUS

Fear whirs its wings round my heart
my soul flies into the future
the songnotes darken with prophecy.

Certainty's thronestone's deserted
nothing says go to my panic
Can't spit out the gobbets of nightmare
Sand's silted over the marks of the hawsers
Time's covered up the chainchafe of anchors
where the dogships strained at their leashes for Troy
and they've returned   my own eyes can see them
and still I'm uneasy   terrified   why?

Listen   a dirgesong nobody's strumming
Listen   the Furies' monotonous humming
Listen   strings tuned to the terror that's coming.

Enter Clytemnestra.

CLYTEMNESTRA

You too, Cassandra. Cassandra, come in!
Zeus can't be angry. He wants you to join us
to share in the household's ritual washing
taking your place among all the slave-girls
at the godstone to one who keeps this house wealthy.

Come down from the warcar. Why be so haughty?

If it has to happen, enslavement,
they're lucky to fail to hereditary masters.
The ones who suddenly come into a fortune,
get rich by a windfall, they're brutal to slaves.
We'll treat you kindly according to custom.

CHORUS

It's you she's addressing, Cassandra, no savvy?
You're fast in the fate-net, the shackles of life-lot.
You can't scramble out. Best do as you're bidden.

CLYTEMNESTRA

Sparrowbrain! What does she jabber in, ba-ba gibberish?
I'll try her again. Go inside! Go inside!

CHORUS

Go. It's best. And you haven't much choice.
Do as you're bidden. Come down from the car.

CLYTEMNESTRA

I don't have time to stand about waiting.
The sacrifice. It's standing now at the godstone.
The victim's prepared. My dreams reach fulfilment.

If you want to partake in our worship, then come.

To Chorus.

Nothing gets through. Try her in dumbshow.

CHORUS

An interpreter's needed. Somebody clever.
She's like a wild animal caught in a net.

CLYTEMNESTRA

Maniac, more like, listening to voices.
Her father's city's caught fast in the net.
She'll go champing her chops on the chainbit
until her mettle and madness froth off as blood.
I'm not staying here to be sneered at by slavegirls.

Exit Clytemnestra.

CHORUS

I pity the creature. She needs understanding.
Come down, poor woman, down from the warcar.
Necessity. Neck into the yokestrap!

CASSANDRA

otototoi popoi da!
Apollo   Apollo!

CHORUS

Apollo? Then that *otototoi*'s all wrong!
Apollo hates death-notes and dark sorts of song.

CASSANDRA

otototoi popoi da!
Apollo   Apollo!

CHORUS

Listen! Again. Apollo hates the sort of note
that comes strangled and anguished out of her throat.

CASSANDRA

Apollo   Apollo   waygod   destroyer
Again you're Cassandra's appalling destroyer!

CHORUS

She's in a trance, about to prophesy.
Even in bondage her gift doesn't die.

CASSANDRA

Apollo   Apollo   waygod   destroyer
where have you brought me   what house is this?

CHORUS

The house of Atreus. That much *I* know.
It's a poor prophetess asks me questions though!

CASSANDRA

ah   ah   ah
god-shunners   kin-killers
child-charnel   man-shambles
babe-spattered abattoir

CHORUS

She's like a bloodhound nose to the ground
tracking the kill that's got to be found.

CASSANDRA

I track down the witnesses
children   babes   shrieking butcher
barbecued childflesh wolfed down by the father

CHORUS

Your prophetic powers none of us doubt.
But that kind of vision we can well do without.

CASSANDRA

I see   somebody   evil   something
agony   agony   more   more   more
no one can bear it   no one can stop it
help's far away over the ocean

75

CHORUS

Now I'm lost, though till now the tale was clear.
We breathe *that* story in our atmosphere.

CASSANDRA

husband   bed-mate
body washed in your bath-trough

hand over hand   hauling the catch in

CHORUS

Now it's got worse. I can make no sense
of these dense riddles that grow more dense.

CASSANDRA

net   hell-net
she-snare   bed-mate   blood-mate
the deathpack howls over its victim
the fiendswarm surrounds it for stoning

CHORUS

Don't rouse the Furies. Don't start them humming
you make me feel hopeless. Don't drag them in.

The heart loses blood as cloths lose dyestuff
and the sun oozes light at its setting.

Death moves in fast. I can feel his shadow.

CASSANDRA

Look there   there   look
bull   cow   bull   cow   don't let them grapple
he's caught in the robe-net   she gores him and gores him
butting and butting   with blood-crusted horn
slumps into bathblood   bloodsplash

CHORUS

I'm no good at oracles telling the future
but I recognise evil in what she keeps saying.

76

Evil's all men get out of oracles.
Her words spell out terror, and smell of the truth.

CASSANDRA

him   me   him   me   him   me
woecups   mine slops over the brim
what have you brought me here for?
to die beside you   what else?

CHORUS

Sing your own deathdirge, nightingale.
You're like the brown bird shrilling your grieftrills
warbling insatiably Itys O Itys!

CASSANDRA

Wings   wings   no weeping   no wailing
Cassandra   bloodblade and hackblock

CHORUS

This nightmare, this maelstrom, where does it come from?
Strange cries, shrill shriekings! Where will they end?

CASSANDRA

Paris   blood bridals   kin-doom
Scamander   Scamander   Cassandra's Scamander
I was a youngster on your riverside once

Griefstreams of Acheron   I'll sing beside you.

CHORUS

That's clear enough. A child couldn't miss it.
Your death songs pang me and pain me like snakefangs
Your anguish tears me in two just to listen.

CASSANDRA

Troytowers tottering   Troytowers destroyed
sacrifice   sacrifice   beast after beast
all father's cattle   utterly useless
the Troy of my father   ashes   all ash

I'm on fire too   come crashing to earth.

CHORUS

What is it wringing these cries from your body?
These painpangs and griefsongs? Don't understand.

CASSANDRA

Off with the brideveil then. Look into truth's pupils
The truthgust. It's rising. Blowing fresh headwinds
sweeping sea-ripples into dawn's molten cauldron,
then building a woe-wave as big as a mountain.
Riddles are over. Keep close on my track now
as I scent out the spoor of ancient transgression.
Listen. The rooftops. Monotonous humming
that drones on forever and means only terror.
The blood-bolstered fiend-swarm holds its debauches,
cacophonous squatters that can't be evicted,
chant over and over the crime where it started
cursing a bedbond a bloodkin defiled
trampling all over the flowing bed-linen.

Have I shot wide or am I on target?
Swear I know all the curse of this bloodclan.

CHORUS

And if I did swear, what good would it do,
what would it alter? But it's a wonder
a stranger like you knows the truth of our story.
It's as if you'd witnessed all you're describing.

I

CASSANDRA

Apollo the seergod put this power in my head.

CHORUS

A god, and so lovesick he'd bribe you to bed?

78

2
CASSANDRA
I've always thought it too shameful to tell.
CHORUS
Shame's a luxury for when life goes well.

3
CASSANDRA
He got me flat on my back. I felt his breath. Hot.
CHORUS
And did the he-god get what he wanted, or not?

4
CASSANDRA
I told him he could then later said no.
CHORUS
You've already been given the god-vision though?

5
CASSANDRA
I foretold Troy's downfall, the Trojans' defeat.
CHORUS
And didn't Apollo make you pay for your cheat?

6
CASSANDRA
Yes, no one ever believed me, not one single word.
CHORUS
But we have believed all we have heard.

CASSANDRA
ah   ah   ah   ah

truthpangs   truthpain   tornado and maelstrom
doomfever   doom-ague   shakes my body again

look on the rooftops   dream-shadows   children
killed by their bloodkin, their hands full of *ugh*
offal and giblets   their very own innards
held out to their father as succulent morsels.

The lion plots vengeance   the lion that's gutless,
the lion that lolls in my master's own chamber
waiting to welcome my homecoming master
(master, that's what as his slave I must call him)
Commander of triremes, crusher of Priam,
but blind to cabal, the insatiable hell-bitch,
licking his hand   ears pricked in welcome
furry and cur-like concealing a Fury
red-blooded, intrepid, the man-slaying woman
what name of monster's best to describe her?
Blood-sucker   basilisk   two-headed shark-hag,
rock-trog skulking for sailors to wreck them,
hell-dam fire-breathing war   war   at her husband,
boundless in brazenness, hear her hosannas
like battle-cries raised when the victory seems certain.
But how well she dissembles that so wifely welcome.

Whether I'm believed or not doesn't matter
Whatever you do the future will happen.
Through pity and tears you'll know the true prophet.

CHORUS

Thyestes eating his children, that I got, yes.
I sicken and tremble at truths so unfeigning.
The rest I can't fathom. I'm lost I'm afraid.

I
CASSANDRA

Agamemnon. He's the one you'll see dead!
CHORUS
Ssshh! Such things shouldn't even be said.

2
CASSANDRA
Even unspoken this sore won't heal.
CHORUS
It will if the he-gods hear our appeal.

3
CASSANDRA
And while you're appealing your king's being hacked.
CHORUS
I don't know the man who'd commit such an act!

4
CASSANDRA
If you say *man* then you don't understand.
CHORUS
I don't know the man, nor how it's been planned.

5
CASSANDRA
And yet it's your language you're hearing me speak.
CHORUS
No oracle's clear, though they all speak in Greek.

CASSANDRA
ah   ah   fire in me   Apollo's

Two-legged lioness tupped by the wolfman
when the great lion's gone she'll kill Cassandra

brewing the witchbane   her bubbling grudge-broth
into the cauldron   death-dose for Cassandra

She sharpens the swordblade to hack down her husband
a hacking he earned by bringing me with him.

Why do I wear these garments that mock me,
the trappings of prophetess, rod, garb and raiment.

Cassandra tears off the regalia of prophetess.

I'm going to die but you'll go before me.
It's some satisfaction to trample these trappings.
Go and bestow these 'gifts' on another.

ah Apollo Apollo clawing my clothes off.
He grabs the prophetess garb off my body.
He mocked me, Apollo, though dressed as his prophet.
He wanted me scorned and derided by bloodkin,
called vagabond, mountebank, gypsy and starveling.
The god-seer casts his prophetess to disaster.

My father's own priestess now mere beast oblation
lifeblood flowing hot off the hackblock.

We won't die forgotten. Gods always notice.

He'll come our avenger, our bloodgrudge-fulfiller,
he'll come, motherkiller, wanderer, exile,
setting the copestone on this bloodclan's corruption,
the father's corpse drawing the son back to Argos.

Why these tears? These eyes saw Troy levelled.
And those who destroyed her doomed also to die.
Now it's for me to die . . .

Cassandra approaches the palace.

                              the doorway to death
I pray for a clean blow, no painful convulsions,
my blood ebbing gently, closing my eyes.

CHORUS

Such suffering, child, such pain in your wisdom.
If you can foresee death then why do you go to it
so meekly like a god-destined goat to the godstone?

THE ORESTEIA

I
CASSANDRA
There's no escape now. No more delay.
CHORUS
'While there's life there's . . .' you know what they say.

2
CASSANDRA
No hope for me though. It's pointless all flight.
CHORUS
How bravely you seem to face up to your plight.

3
CASSANDRA
Yes only the doomed are ever called brave.
CHORUS
But isn't it noble to face up to the grave?

4
CASSANDRA
You mean like my father and brothers all died.

Cassandra moves towards the palace and recoils.

CHORUS
What is it? Fear? Was that why you shied?

CASSANDRA
Ugh! Ugh!

5
CHORUS
What was that cry for? What sickens your brain?
CASSANDRA
The palace! It stinks like an abattoir drain!

6

CHORUS

It's the sacrifice made for our clanchief's return.

CASSANDRA

It stinks like the gas from a burial urn.

CHORUS

It's only the incense the priests always burn.

CASSANDRA

I'll go inside, wailing our deaths, mine, Agamemnon's.
Enough of life! Friends, I'm no frightened fledgling
flinching with fear when the bushes get shaken.
From you what I beg's the bearing of witness,
when woman for woman my killer's killed also
and the man mated to doom gets killed for your clanchief.
I beg this favour as a stranger going to die now.

CHORUS

I pity you, so open-eyed about dying.

CASSANDRA

A few last words, a requiem dirgesong
I ask the sun whose last rays I'm addressing
that when the avengers cut down the assassins
one stroke's for the slavegirl butchered defenceless.
Man's life! Luck's blotted out by the slenderest shadow.
Trouble – a wet sponge wipes the slate empty.
That pain's also nothing makes life a heartbreak.

Cassandra enters palace.

CHORUS

Human beings in their pride
restless and dissatisfied

No palace dweller bars his door
to opulence and cries: *No more!*

the gods let our great king destroy
the topless towers of Priam's Troy

vanquisher conquistador
crowned with all the spoils of war

now the blood that Atreus shed
falls on Agamemnon's head

he's to die but what's the good
his death too cries out for blood

AGAMEMNON
(*within*)

Ah!

CHORUS
Whose was that voice screaming in terror?

AGAMEMNON
(*within*)

Ah!

CHORUS
That was the king unless I'm in error.
Now we should take council and every man
should say what he thinks is the safest plan.

1
In my opinion we ought to bring
the whole city here to help the king.

2
And I say rush in, break down the door
catch them with swords still dripping with gore.

3
I'm also for action. I'll second that.
Any action at all's better than chat.

4

It's quite clear, I mean quite clear to me
their action's a prelude to tyranny!

5

They don't discuss, they do, and while we prate
they stamp their boots on all debate.

6

But I haven't a plan and no one can
go into action without a plan.

7

Agreed! Hear, hear! There's no way talk
can make a dead man get up and walk.

8

Just to save our skins shall we stand by
let murderers rule us, our clanchief die?

9

No. Never! As for me I'd sooner die
than live two seconds under tyranny.

10

But can we, from the cries we heard,
infer that murder *has* occurred?

11

We should have proof before we act.
Guesswork's not the same as fact.

12

I think the meeting as a whole's agreed –
conclusive evidence is what we need.

*The palace doors swing open and reveal Clytemnestra
standing over the bodies of Agamemnon and Cassandra.*

CLYTEMNESTRA

I've spoken many words to serve the moment
which I've no compunction now to contradict.
How else but by lying and seeming so loving
could I have plotted my enemy's downfall?
How rig the net so it can't be leapt out of?
This is the bloodgrudge, the grudge's fruition
something I've brooded on quite a long time.
I've done what I meant to. I wouldn't deny it.
Over his head I cast a vast trammel
the sort that hauls in whole shoals at each casting.
He couldn't get out of his rich, flowing doom-robe.
Twice I struck him. He screamed twice, then crumpled.
Once he'd fallen I struck him a third blow,
one struck for Zeus in his role as corpse-keeper.
He lay there gasping and splurting his blood out
spraying me with dark blood-dew, dew I delight in
as much as the graincrop in the fresh gloss of rainfall
when the wheatbud's in labour and swells into birthpang.

So that's how it is, old men of Argos.
Cheer if you want to. I revel in glory.
He's had his libation, spurts from his bloodvein.
He poured woe and bitterness into our winebowl.
He's got the last goblet and laps up the lees!

CHORUS

Your words revolt me. How can you trumpet,
so unlike a woman, over your manlord?

CLYTEMNESTRA

Still you can treat me like a woman who's witless?
My heart's made of steel, and as I have stated,
whether you like it or not, there's Agamemnon.
This is the swordhand that brought him to bloodright.
I hacked down my husband. That's how it is.

CHORUS

Woman! Some earthbane's driving you crazy.
To brave the damning voice of the people!
You've sown and you'll reap. Banishment. Exile.
Driven out of the country. Cursed at and spat at.

CLYTEMNESTRA

O *now* you're ready with banishment, exile,
the people's hatred and public damnation.
And how did you punish this murderer here?
Meant as little to him as slaughtering cattle.
His sheepfolds were bursting, he butchered his she-child,
the she-child I laboured to launch on her life-lot,
as some specious god-sop to settle the stormsquall.
You should have banished *him* for pollution,
but it's now that you start to play at stern judges.
Banishment! *If* you can make me. *If* you enforce it.
If I prove the stronger I'll teach you some wisdom.
You'll go back to school and learn some hard lessons.

CHORUS

You're maddened by powerlust, raving.
Your brain's beweevilled with blood-deeds.
Your eyes have red bloodflecks for pupils.
Your doom's to be honourless, friendless, defenceless
and stabwound for stabwound you'll reap retribution.

CLYTEMNESTRA

Then listen to this, the oath that I'll swear by.
By bloodright exacted on behalf of my she-child,
by Iphigeneia whose bloodgrudge has roosted,
by the Fury for whom Agamemnon's the booty,
I swear I'll never let fear to my fireside
as long as the hearth's kept alight by Aegisthus,
loyal friend always, my shield, my protector.

Look at him, Shaggermemnon, shameless, shaft-happy,
ogler and grinder of Troy's golden girlhood.

Look at her, spearprize, prophetess, princess,
whore of his wartent, his bash back on shipboard.
They've got their deserts the two of them now.
There he lies. She's sung her swansong and lies
as she should do stretched out alongside him,
his 'dear' 's death a side-dish to the banquet of his.

CHORUS

Please send me my end now, but not too painful,
let me lurch gently out of my life-lot
now that our king's been dragged under the death-yoke.

Two women made him suffer then die:

Wild Helen causing the death-throes of thousands
now you've won your garland of glory,
a blood-wreath whose redness can't be rubbed off.

CLYTEMNESTRA

Don't call on death or surrender to torment.
Don't turn your hatred on Helen my she-kin.
Don't think she alone brought the Greeks to their ruin
as though only she were the cause of their anguish.

CHORUS

As far back as Tantalus the grudge-demon started,
harried this bloodclan from those days to these days,
harries it now in the shapes of these she-kin,
Clytemnestra   Helen   those carrion crows
cawing discordantly over our gables
maws crammed with corpseflesh and carrion gobbets

CLYTEMNESTRA

Better to blame the blood-guzzling grudge-hound
battening on us for three gorgings of gore.

He kindles the gore-lust in the guts of our bloodkin.
As one sore scars over new pus starts spurting.

CHORUS

Insatiable bloodgrudge, gore-ogre, flesh-glutton
goes on and on plaguing and galling
but what isn't godsent?   Zeus is behind it.
Nothing occurs but the gods make it happen.

King Agamemnon, how can we mourn you,
how give a voice to bereavement and loveloss,
there in the spider's web spewing your life out
the impious weapon swung by the spousefiend?

CLYTEMNESTRA

Spouse? No! Wife? No! What swung the swordblade's
the semblance, the shape of this corpse's spouse only.
Wielding the weapon was no wife and no woman
but his family's phantom, Atreus the flesh-chef
offering flayed these fully fledged victims
one for each butchered and barbecued babe.

CHORUS

You guiltless? You guiltless? and who'll be your witness
though some god must have helped you fulfil the
   bloodgrudge.
Black Ares amok, wading deep in the blood-bog –
the bloodgrudge that goads him the cold joints of children.

King Agamemnon, how can we mourn you,
how give a voice to bereavement and loveloss,
there in the spider's web spewing your life out,
the impious weapon swung by the spousefiend?

CLYTEMNESTRA

His death's no worse than the one he inflicted
when he forged his own link in this house's doom-chain.
He suffered the fate he made others suffer –
lphigeneia still wept for, sweet flower, his she-child.

Don't go boasting in Hades, steel-slinger, sword-brute,
you got back your stabwounds, all you inflicted.

CHORUS

My mind's off its moorings. Its foundations are shaking.
No longer a drizzle, a hammering bloodstorm,
Fate strops its blade for more and more blood-bouts.
Earth   Earth   Earth   why didn't you take me
rather than let me live to see the king humbled
sprawled out in his blood in a bathtub of silver?
Who'll bury the body? Who'll sing the gravedirge?

To Clytemnestra.

You wouldn't surely first kill our clanchief
then pour specious tributes over his tombcairn?

Who'll mourn him with real grief and not a mask only?

CLYTEMNESTRA

That's not your business. I hacked him down and the
   sword hand
strong enough to strike him can dig him a ditch.
No mourning. From no one. All that's forbidden.
Iphigeneia   she'll greet him by the waters of sorrow
flinging her arms round her father to kiss him.

CHORUS

Choler for choler, bloodgrudge for bloodgrudge,
while Zeus the high he-god is still the gods' clanchief
the law for the living is killers get killed.
Blight's in the bloodstream, curse in the corpuscles,
the feet of this clan bogged down in the bloodquag.

CLYTEMNESTRA

The future, the truth, you're beginning to see them.
I'll make a bond with this palace's bloodfiend.
What's happened so far I'll accept and fall in with,
hard though that is, I'll do it, provided
the fiend leaves this house and finds other quarters
to ravage the people and goad them to murder.

Riches mean nothing. A little suffices
if only this frenzy of kin-killing ceases.

*Enter Aegisthus from a side entrance with a silent
bodyguard, an 'anti-chorus', the same number as the
chorus.*

AEGISTHUS

A great day when bloodright comes into its own.
This proves there are gods who see crimes and punish.
I'm happy, so happy to see this man tangled
in robes of dark red the Furies have woven,
fulfilling the bloodgrudge caused by his father.
This man's father, Atreus, once king of Argos,
there being some dispute as to who should be clanchief,
drove my father (his brother) Thyestes away.
Thyestes came back as a suppliant begging
at least his life sparing, the minimum mercy,
no son's blood staining his father's own threshold.
But this man's father, Atreus, Atreus the godless,
whose mask of warm welcome kept hatred hidden
threw a great banquet as if for Thyestes
and dished up his children as the daintiest titbits.
The fingers and toes he chopped off to disguise it
and my father alone of the guests got this childstew.
Not being aware what it was he was eating
he bolted the banquet that blasted this bloodclan.
When he knew what he chewed, he choked on the
    childstew,
shrieked, reeled backwards, spewed out the offal,
turned over the tables and cursed the whole bloodclan
grinding the meat into mush with his boot-heel.

And that's why your clanchief's lying there murdered.
And I wove the net we got him ensnared in.
Third son of Thyestes, I plotted for bloodright.
Driven out with my father while only a baby

as a man I've returned escorted by bloodright.
In exile I had all the threads twisted ready
biding my time for the trap to be fashioned.
Now I'd die happy, happy now bloodright's
got Agamemnon caught fast in fate's trammel.

CHORUS

Aegisthus, gloating on carnage. Revolting!
You did it, plotted it, *you*, single-handed?
The people will stone you. You don't stand a chance.

AEGISTHUS

Pretty grand talk to come out of the galleys!
We've got the tiller. Get on with the rowing.
Old as you are, you still can learn lessons
though you'll find wisdom a tough course to take in.
Prison. Starvation. They motivate scholars,
make even dodderers like you get good totals.
Don't push on the horse-goad. You'll get yourselves hurt.

CHORUS

Woman! Waiting at home for the menfolk
wallowing, befouling a warrior's bedbond!
How could *you* bring down a great soldier?

AEGISTHUS

Whinny like that again and you'll rue it.
The songs of Orpheus may have tamed creatures,
yours work on me in the other direction.
A dose of the strongarm will soon get you docile.

CHORUS

You, rule Argos? You, who let a mere woman
murder the king when you hadn't courage.

AEGISTHUS

Deception, that was the work for the woman.
I, with my bloodgrudge, was under suspicion.
Agamemnon's gold will buy off his people.

And those who won't be bought will be broken.
No colts without collars. Hunger and darkness
they teach the mettlesome quieter manners.

CHORUS

Couldn't kill the king with your own hands could you?
Let a woman get her clan and her clangods corrupted,
the gods of Argos. But I tell you . . . Orestes . . .
if he's alive (and luck guide his life-lot)
he'll kill this couple, our bloodgrudge-fulfiller.

1

AEGISTHUS

You want your first lessons already, I see.

CHORUS

Comrades, you're needed. Stand firm with me.

2

AEGISTHUS

Draw your swords out. Ready. Stand by.

CHORUS

Stand by. Not one of us here's afraid to die.

AEGISTHUS

I'm glad that you told me   So go ahead, die!

CLYTEMNESTRA
(*interrupting*)

No!   No, my dear, no more blood-letting.
There's been enough. Enough. Old men of Argos,
go home now quietly before you regret it.
We did what we had to. Let it rest there.
The fiend's hooves have galloped over our spirits.
Let it rest there. Take advice from a woman.

AEGISTHUS

But they, they gibe at me, mock me.
You're pushing your luck you old foulmouths.
I'm your new ruler. Don't you forget it.

94

I
CHORUS
Argives don't grovel to your evil sort.
AEGISTHUS
Then Argives like you will have to be taught.

2
CHORUS
Not if Orestes comes back to his own.
AEGISTHUS
Exiles eat hope, all gristle and bone.

3
CHORUS
Grow fat on injustice. Shit on the state!
AEGISTHUS
I'm warning you, old fool, before it's too late . . .

4
CHORUS
Cock-a-doodle-doo, the dungheap lord,
crow a bit louder, your hen will applaud!

CLYTEMNESTRA
Let the terriers yap, all bark and no bite!
You and I, we'll rule this house, and set it right.

*Exit Clytemnestra with Aegisthus, into the house
of Atreus. Chorus disperses silently.*

End of Part One.

Two

CHOEPHORI

Orestes and Pylades at the grave of Agamemnon.

ORESTES

Hermes, he-god, who can go in and out of the ground,
he-god still wary to keep power with the fathers,
now I have need of you, back home from long exile.
This is the gravemound of Agamemnon, my father.
Help my cries through the ground to his ghost.

Cuts off two locks of hair.

I lop off one lock and so move into manhood.

And this one for your mound as a mark of my mourning.

Your son and heir wasn't here to salute you
no final farewell as the earth was flung over.

Look! There! What's that? That procession of women,
wending this way, all dressed in drab dirge-clothes.
What's it in aid of? More doom? More disaster?
They're carrying jars, jars full of libations.
I suppose that they're sops for my father's sore spirit.
It must be! There, among all the mourners
is my she-kin Electra, wasted by weeping.

Zeus! High he-god! Help it to happen,
the vengeance I want to take for my father.

To Pylades.

Pylades, you and I stand aside, keep out of eye-shot
till we're sure of the meaning of the rites we're to witness.

CHORUS

Coerced into keening by Queen Clytemnestra
for King Agamemnon as if for our bloodkin
we carry these ghost-sops out to his gravemound.
Lashed out to lament the lost lord of Argos
we Trojans trench flesh ruts into our faces.
There's no need to coerce us, we cry anyway.

Our lives have been one long meal of mourning,
one life-long banquet, one blow-out of bale.
We claw our clothes open, mad in our mourning.
Our ripped pap-wraps shriek as we shred them.

This bloodclan's doom-demon disguised as a dream
crashed through into Clytemnestra's calm midnight
and squeezed from the queen's throat a throttling shriek,
a cry that re-echoed through each recess and corner
and pounded for entry to the coops that we're penned in.
The whole household heard it. Our hair stood on end.
Then spoke a clanseer whose knowledge was nightmares:

'The bitter dead below bellow for blood-dues.'

So godsops she sends, empty gifts and libations
meant to ward off what gnaws her at night-time,
sends me out here as soon as the dawn breaks
that woman hated and loathed by the he-gods.
The grave-charms she wants get choked in my gullet.
What godsop or bribe makes spilt blood unspilt?
Shed blood's shed for ever. The dead stay dead.
This bloodclan, this house, what hasn't it suffered?
Murk, man-shunned and sunless, smothers the bloodclan
when the clanchief, its light, is stifled by death,
death-doused, mouldering under his gravemound . . .
He counted for something, the king of this bloodclan,
battle-proof power, both strife-proof and plot-proof.
The lips of his people respected that power,
their hearts honoured their hero and helmsman.

Now all honour's usurped by terror the tyrant.
Success gets sucked up to. The god is good life-lot.
All grovel to that as to godhead or greater.
But to those who loll in the luck of their life-lot
the justice of bloodright's the bolt from the black –
some netted at noontide, others at night-time,
daylight or darkness, both nourish their doom.
When the earth's gullet's choked on the gore it has gulped
the bloodglut clots rock-like and can't reach earth's gut.
Guilt in the guilty likewise stays clotted
the cankers of guilt craze the culprit and kill him.
The blood of the killed, the bed blood of virgins
(both dooms we endured in the downfall of Troy)
is worn by the guilty like gauntlets of gore.
All the world's waters forced through one funnel
and sprayed at the bloodspot as much good as spittle!
Necessity! That brought us to where we are now,
hauled from our homeland, dragged here as drudges,
lugged into a life-lot, unloving and loathly,
brought into bondage, doom's dragnet round Troy,
we bite hard on the horsebit, gulp down our gall,
and go through these griefshows as she commanded.
But our grief is no shamming, the tears shed are true,
mourning our helplessness under harsh masters,
our massacred menfolk, the mass-graves of Troy.

ELECTRA

Women, Troy's warspoils, now palace work-slaves
whose work gives the palace its appearance of order,
since you've been sent to attend me, give me advice.
What graveside grace goes best with these griefcups?
What address would my father find even decent?
'To the man from the woman, to the loved from the loving'!
Call Clytemnestra, my mother, a woman who loves!
I don't have the nerve, the effrontery for that.
What to say as I pour honey, then milk, wine and then
    water? –

What's usually intoned here 's useless, insulting.
'*To those who send grave-gifts, send the good they deserve.*'
The good they deserve's the same fate as my father's.
No words, but a silence the way he was slaughtered
pouring the griefcups as if they were slop-pails.
Friends! Serfwomen, freeborn, both fettered to fate,
shackled to shame we share the same hatreds.
Between us there need be no sort of secret.

CHORUS
I swear by the cairn that keeps the king's dust
I speak all my secrets, and you have my trust . . .

I
ELECTRA
Speak then. I swear the same oath you all swore.
CHORUS
For those you can trust pray as you pour.

2
ELECTRA
Those I can trust. Who near me 's still true?
CHORUS
Yourself! Those who hate Aegisthus are too.

3
ELECTRA
Then myself! And you? Do you count on my side?
CHORUS
Judge only my words, then you can decide.

4
ELECTRA
Who else can be counted? Consider and say . . .
CHORUS
Orestes! *Orestes!* Though still far away.

5
ELECTRA
Orestes! Orestes! The best thing to say!
CHORUS
For those you can't trust, the killers, pray . . .

6
ELECTRA
Pray what? Tell me, I'm eager to learn . . .
CHORUS
Pray that a man or a god will return.

7
ELECTRA
Return to reckon the guilt of those two?
CHORUS
No! Kill them. That's all. *Blood for blood.* That will do.

8
ELECTRA
Demand gods to deal death! Is that right or good?
CHORUS
Right and good! Right and good! Blood demands blood.

ELECTRA
God-guide and ground-god, god-go-between, herald,
linking upper and nether, the dead and the living,
Hermes, he-god, help me and get them to hear me,
the spirits I pray to, that prosper this palace,
and get her to hear me, the greatest of she-gods,
EARTH who pushes all beings out of her belly,
suckles her creatures, and swells with their corpses.
Get her to listen. I pour the libation
and pray to my father:

'Pity! For me! For Orestes!'

This bloodclan's benighted and he's its bright beacon.
We're both dispossessed, deprived of our bloodright.
She bartered her bairns and bought as her bed-mate
Aegisthus who shares in the guilt of your killing.
Electra's a bondslave, and Orestes an exile.
Clytemnestra and Aegisthus, basking and idle,
loll in the luxury made by your labours.
I pray Orestes returns with luck in his life-lot
and my life-lot unsullied, not marred like my mother's,
heart and hands blameless, unblemished by blood.

These prayers on our part. And for them we oppose
I pray the bloodgrudge-fulfiller will soon be appearing,
the butchers be butchered, and pay blood for blood.

Agamemnon, come up at the head of the ground-gods.
Agamemnon, come up with Earth the great she-god,
bring blessings and bloodright blazoned with laurels.
These are my prayers, and I pour your libations.

   To Chorus.

You water the seed of my prayer with your wailing.
As I pour deliver the dead a due grave-dirge.

CHORUS

Tears drop on your dark head
drop by drop the way you bled

Your grave holds both bad and good
what we beg is 'blood for blood'.

Agamemnon, mind in murk,
hear our words, make them work –

Bloodgrudge-fulfiller
Come   kill the killer

big   bow   bent   back
sword   in   slash   hack.

ELECTRA

Gulped by Gaia the drinks have got through
through to my father . . .

Sees lock of hair.

> . . . but here's something new!

1
CHORUS

Fear makes my heart jig. What have you found?

ELECTRA

A lock of hair has been laid on the mound.

2
CHORUS

A man's or a woman's? Who put it there?

ELECTRA

It looks like a bloodkin's, this lock of fine hair.

3
CHORUS

A bloodkin's? I don't understand. Don't leave me to guess.

ELECTRA

It's mine or it's no one's this mystery tress.

4
CHORUS

Your mother, the murderer, she wouldn't dare . . .

ELECTRA

Yet I've a feeling I know it, this hair.

5
CHORUS

Whose is it then, if you say it seems known?

ELECTRA

Whose I don't know, but it's so like my own.

6
CHORUS
Orestes! Orestes has sent us this secret sign.
ELECTRA
It can only be his hair, if it's not mine.

7
CHORUS
Orestes in Argos? Too risky if that's what you meant.
ELECTRA
No, for the sake of his father he had the lock sent.

CHORUS
Only *sent*! The more cause to weep for him then.
Orestes will never see Argos again . . .

ELECTRA
A surge of choler and grudge sweeps over my spirit,
spitted on pain like a stabwound or spearthrust.
Drops like the spindrift spat off a seaswell
break from my eyes at the sight of this curl.
Who else from Argos would this lock belong to?
Never hers, the murderess, my mother. My *mother*!
She's stifled and smothered all motherly feelings.
How can I know it's Orestes for certain.
Only hope makes us so foolish and stupid.

If this hair had a voice and was sent as a herald
then I wouldn't waver or be so distracted
and I'd know by its clear-spoken message
that either it came from a head I detested
or was the bloodkin's I longed to believe it,
a grace to my grief, a grace to this gravemound.

The gods I've invoked are wise to what seaswells
we're whirled on, like sailors in shipwreck.
If we were meant to, then scrape home we will.
A great oak can sprout from the tiniest acorn.

I call on these gods for my prayers to be answered.

Enter Orestes and Pylades.

ORESTES
They're answered, those prayers. The gods favour you.
Now pray that our future is fortunate too.

1

ELECTRA
Our future? Prayers answered? What do you mean?
ORESTES
You prayed to see something. Now you have seen.

2

ELECTRA
How do you know what it was that I prayed?
ORESTES
For your much-loved Orestes to come to your aid.

3

ELECTRA
Then how can you say that the gods favour me?
ORESTES
You've got what you prayed for. Look! I am he!

4

ELECTRA
Stranger, you're weaving some net or some snare.
ORESTES
If you are entangled, I'm also trapped there.

5

ELECTRA
You mock my misfortune, make it a game.
ORESTES
I mock my own then, my misfortune's the same.
ELECTRA
Orestes! Orestes! Is that really your name?

ORESTES

You look at me and still can't recognise
your bloodkin, your brother before your eyes.
Yet when you looked at the lock I had laid
you gasped as if gazing straight into my face.

Indicates lock of hair.

Look that's where I lopped it from. Match it with mine.
Look how alike, how akin the two locks are.

Produces a piece of weaving.

Look at this weaving your fingers once fashioned,
the stroke of your batten, the patterns of beasts.

Electra excited.

Easy! Still! Keep all emotion masked within.
Our 'nearest and dearest' would like us destroyed.

ELECTRA

Beloved, beacon of this blacked-out bloodclan,
the seed of deliverance watered by weeping.
The love of four bloodkin belongs to you only –
loathed mother, lost father, sacrificed sister
and brother, the bloodkin I truly believe in.

Brute force and bloodright and Zeus the high he-god
be your protectors in pursuing our bloodgrudge.

ORESTES

ZEUS, high he-god, steel us to the struggle,
fledglings left fatherless when the great eagle
got snarled in the shuffling coils of the she-snake,
fatherless fledglings, famished orphans too feeble
to carry the quarry off back to the eyrie,
fledglings and fatherless, Orestes, Electra,
both outcasts alike and blocked from their bloodright.

Eagle Agamemnon gave the he-gods a gift glut.
The godstones of Argos bubbled with bloodflow.
Cut down his egrets, your guts will go goatless.
With the bole of the bloodclan blasted no bull's gore
will gurgle down godstones on sacrifice days.
So nourish the nestlings, build up the bloodclan
though now it looks much too low to be lifted.

CHORUS

Quiet, if you want your bloodclan rebuilding.
The whole space of Argos whispers with spies.
It only needs one to report to our rulers.
One day very soon I hope we'll be watching
their flesh spit through flames and bubbling pitch.

ORESTES

Apollo stays close till all gets accomplished.
His oracle told me to push through our bloodgrudge.
And if I flinched from fulfilling the bloodgrudge
by killing those guilty of killing our father
he warned me my heart's blood would harden and freeze.
By not taking their lives my own would be taken
but not before tasting great torture and torments.
He detailed disease, malignant malaises
the unappeased dead demand as appeasement –
skin-canker, skin-scabs, flaying the flesh raw,
crusted with fungus sprouting white bristles,
the perpetual prowling of the black pack of Furies
whose dark nightly saltlick's the blood of my father,
darts from deep darkness, shafts shot from below
for the killing of bloodkin who bay for their bloodgrudge.
Frenzy and mania, phantoms at midnight,
venomous shadows that slink into his sleeptime.
He blinks, rubs his eyes. They're still at his bedside.

Harried and hounded out of his homeland,
a palsied pariah, scarred over by scourges,

flayed by brass flail-rods, a leprosied carcase.
Such scapegoats share in no wine-bowl libations.
No one spares him bed, bread, or broth-bowl.
All godstones are barred him, and, gobbled alive
by bubos and fleshblight, he perishes friendless.

When that god says *do it* no one says no.

Without any god-goad I've still got my grudges,
Still got my grief for Agamemnon, my father.
Dispossessed, I need no spurs to my spirit.
And these men of Argos, whose glory is greatest
who braved long war boldly and battered down Troy,
now sheepish and slave-like to a woman and she-man
who queens it beside the real clanchief, his consort.
This weapon I wield will unmask the woman.

CHORUS

She-gods of life-lot
ZEUS   high he-god

only gods can stop the rot
drag good up out of bad

Bloodflow for bloodflow
deathblow for deathblow

blood-debt for blood-debt
keeping the blades wet

bloodshed for bloodshed
keeping the blades red

What you do gets done back
you/him   him/you

hack   slash   slash   hack
three generations through

She-gods of life-lot
ZEUS   high he-god

ORESTES

Father, father doused in doom
kept immovable by death
what can grope through your grave-gloom
unbreachable by light or breath?

What words can worm their way
through the sour soil of sorrow
what beacon of bright day
burrow your dark barrow?

From all the bloodclan's grave-rites
they barred and blocked your bones,
never-budging, held by night's
death-heavy anchorstones.

CHORUS

The gnashing jaws of fire gnaw
only the corpse's rotten flesh.
His bloodgrudge goes on craving gore
and doesn't crumble into ash.

When bloodkin keen the killer feels
their dirges haunt him like halloos.
The hounds of grief bay at his heels,
the dead demanding their blood-dues.

A bloodkin's dirge is a keening net
its trammels trawl for guilt
mourning spreads its mesh to get
guilt netted   gaffed   and killed.

ELECTRA

Now it's Electra your she-child
who mourns and beats her breast.
The wailing comes out rushed and wild
long cooped up and repressed.

Now listen to your she-child's dirge
he-child, she-child both in turn,

both exiles, outcasts urge
your spirit from its urn.

bout one   bout two we lost to fate
the same fate that threw you
unless your spirit lends its weight
bout three will be lost too.

CHORUS

Gods can make a gravedirge glad
dragging good up from the bad.

Instead of dirges we might sing

Welcome home, new clanchief, king!

ORESTES

I wish that you had lost your life
to a Trojan in the War
not netted by a treacherous wife
your bathtrough grimed with gore.

Then hero's honour you'd bequeath.
We could have borne it if your bones
were still in Asia and beneath
a tomb of towering stones.

CHORUS

A hero in a hero's grave!
A tombcairn like a tower!
The comfort of the clanchief's stave
still wielding its old power!

A monument, a glorious mound
Dignity   no shame
Agamemnon underground
with still unblemished name!

ELECTRA

No hero's cairn, not killed, not dead!
No mass-grave by Scamander.

I want fate standing on its head
the goose hacked by the gander!

As your killers hacked you, hack,
hack down your killers first.
I want time to be turned back
my father's fate reversed.

CHORUS

North of the North Wind lives a clan
spared the mortal lot of man

but this is South, a man cannot
turn back the tide of his life-lot.

Gold comes cheaper than new blood
but you are young and dream of good.

When you two drum your palms together
the pulse gets passed down to your father.

If those with bloodguilt beat the ground
their gloves of blood will dull the sound

but the dead respond to you
the guiltless tone of your tattoo

underground the dead decide
Agamemnon's on your side.

ORESTES

The bloodgrudge! ZEUS! It's been asleep.
Drag it up from its earthen bed.
The bloodgrudge bond that I've to keep
's to strike my mother dead.

CHORUS

Aegisthus, Clytemnestra killed
I'll shout a joyful shout.
My heart's been bursting ages, filled
with all the hate I now let out.

ELECTRA

ZEUS your great steel fists one two
crunch their skulls with all your might.
Our country needs new trust in you
bloodwrong to yield a new bloodright.

CHORUS

The law's the law: when blood gets spilled
there's no rest till the killer's killed.

Bloodflow for bloodflow the doomsong goes –
blood shrieks for the Fury as it flows.

The Fury forges the long bloodchain –
the slain that link the slain that link the slain . . .

ORESTES

Grudges of the dead below
look we're the dregs of a royal race,
the bloodclan of Atreus brought so low.

ZEUS! Which way leads us from disgrace?

CHORUS

My heart-strings snap, my heart goes black
it darkens if you weaken,
but when I see your strength come back
hope blazes like a beacon.

ELECTRA

Our strength's that we've survived the trials
the one who bore us brought us.
I'll bare my wolf-fangs when she smiles.
Wolf mothers breed wolf daughters.

CHORUS

As in Persia both fists pound
a dervish-like delirium,
till the skull's blood-pulses sound
like a battered battle-drum.

ELECTRA

Wolf mother murdering your man!
Agamemnon got no graveside
lamentation from his clan,
dumped in a ditch you dug dry-eyed.

ORESTES

A ditch! The wolf-bitch dug his shame
I'll hack my mother down to save
Agamemnon's blood-grimed name
then gladly go to my own grave.

CHORUS

To stop his bloodgrudge in its tracks
she hacked off his cock, his hands, his feet,
cleavered the king with her man-axe
and jointed him like butcher's meat.

ELECTRA

And I imprisoned in a poky pen,
cooped and kennelled like a rabid cur.
Let all the grief I poured out then
become the rage you pour on her.

CHORUS

Yes, let it fire the rage you feel.
Two bouts are lost. The bout to be
depends upon your fire and steel,
hot heart, cool head to win bout three.

All addressing Agamemnon's tomb.

ORESTES

Be in my corner, help me win.

ELECTRA

Father, all my tears say fight!

CHORUS

All as one cry: back your bloodkin,
come up, come up into the light.

ORESTES

Bloodright versus bloodright! Ours or theirs?

ELECTRA

Gods, make it ours the juster cause.

ORESTES

It scalds my skull to know your prayers
unlock doom's long-barred doors.

CHORUS

This clan's got ruin in its veins,
its blood-strung lyre's cacophonous.
The chords it strums are death-black strains.
Its wounds don't scab. They spurt out pus.

The only way such sores get better
's keep the cure within the clan.
The clan's its own leech, own blood-letter,
its medicament's: man murder man.

Groundgods down below it's you
all our prayers are going to.
Back Agamemnon's child-bloodkin
and will with god-wills that they win.

ORESTES

You, the great clanchief, were killed like a cur.
I pray for your help to be lord of your bloodclan.

ELECTRA

I pray for escape from the bondage I've suffered
but not before shedding the blood of Aegisthus.

ORESTES

Then only then, in accord with clan custom,
can a fitting funeral be offered with feasting,
or, when fate and gore on the sacrifice crackle,
Agamemnon alone gets no goat to his glory.

ELECTRA

And, from what you bequeath me, your burial barrow
will be overflowing with bridal libations.
On the day that I marry your mound will mean most.

ORESTES

Earth, she-god, let my father back me.

ELECTRA

Persephassa, she-ground-god, grant victory.

ORESTES

Remember the bathtrough where you were struck dead!

ELECTRA

Remember the net-thing cast over your head.

ORESTES

In silk stuff not steelware you spewed out your blood.

ELECTRA

Humbled and hacked down under a hood.

ORESTES

Don't taunts such as these torment you down there?

ELECTRA

Shove your head through the earth to show us you care!

ORESTES
(to Agamemnon's grave)

Bloodright! I want it to back me in the bout that's to be.
I want the headlock on them that they got on you,
flatten them to the floor as they flattened you.
They outwrestled you, but I'll best them this bout.

ELECTRA

This last, then no more. Eagle Agamemnon
your egrets call you from your grave-eyrie,
fledglings and fatherless, he-child and she-child.

ORESTES

Don't let the seed of Pelops perish for ever.
Death's no death when the blood-kinder flourish,
blood-kinder, cork-floats that keep the net buoyant,
when the flax-strings get sodden they keep it from sinking.
For the sake of your spirit we've spent this time pleading
Grant us your grace and your ghost's the first gainer.

CHORUS

Since his grave has been given no clan lamentation
the length of your mourning was right and becoming.
Now you've gorged on your grave-dirge, go into action,
and find out where fate and your life-lot will lead you.

ORESTES

So I will but before I do battle I want to be told
why she sent out this crowd of you carrying cups,
libations so late for a crime past all curing.
Neither the honey, the milk, the wine nor the water
have savour or solace for skulls without senses.
What you pour may be precious but paltry as godsops.
The grave-gifts so meagre, the crime so immense.
A man can daub tombs with all his hives' honey,
swill all his winestores over the stones,
empty his flocks' and herds' udders daily,
waste all his water, and still smell of murder,
so what do they mean, Clytemnestra's libations?

CHORUS

I know what they mean. Clytemnestra had nightmares.
Shaken by shadows that slunk into her sleeptime.
Now, though she's godless, she sends gifts to his gravestone.

I

ORESTES

Is there more to the dream you can tell me about?

CHORUS

She opened her legs and a serpent crawled out.

118

2

ORESTES

Tell me the rest if you know how it goes.

CHORUS

She swathed her snake-baby in swaddling clothes.

3

ORESTES

This baby, this snake-thing, how did she feed it?

CHORUS

She says that it sucked at her very own tit.

4

ORESTES

And did it not pain her to give a snake suck?

CHORUS

Bloodclots came out with each mouthful it took.

ORESTES

No dream, mother, here's your snake-baby. Look!

CHORUS

She shrieked out in her sleep and woke with a start.
All the doused torchlights made eyeless for night-time
blazed out of their blindness to comfort the queen.
At dawn she despatched us with the dead man's libations
to lance the pus-bloated source of her sorrows.

ORESTES

Then by the earth and the grave of my father
I pray I'm this vision's fleshly fulfiller.
The snake came out of the same womb as I did
swathed in the same swaddling clothes as myself,
sucked at the same breast I sucked as a baby,
got bloodclots mixed in, as it sucked the sweet milk out,
so that she who gave suck screamed out in a panic.
Same womb, same swaddling clothes, same breast to
   suck on,

blood and milk, all point to me, and to murder!
the son in the snake-scales sent as her slayer.

CHORUS

My reason tells me that you read the dream rightly.

Now give your instructions to those on your side,
who should work with you, who should be watchers.

ORESTES

Simple.   My sister must stay in the palace
keeping the bond struck between us a secret.
By cunning they killed.   By cunning they'll die
caught in the same net they caught Agamemnon.
Apollo commands it and Apollo's a prophet
whose habit has never been falsehood before.

I, like a stranger with backpack and bundles,
will come in this guise to the gates of the courtyard,
with Pylades here, son of Strophius of Phocis
bound to our bloodclan by handclasp and spearbond.
We'll both of us speak like they do in Parnassus
assuming the accent of the folk back in Phocis.
If the gateman's ungracious and treats us with gruffness
on the grounds that this house is afflicted by fate
we'll stay so that passers-by stop and start saying:
'Aegisthus goes against all god-ordained guestright
by keeping these wanderers waiting unwelcomed.'
But once past the gatelodge and into the palace
if I find that creature on the throne of my father
before he gets chance for looking me over
and asking 'Where does the stranger hail from?' I'll strike.
My answer to him will be straight to the point,
straight to the swordpoint, guts on my skewer.
The Fury that squats in this clan's never famished,
never gone short of its gore-shots to guzzle.
This third and last cup's to quaff undiluted.

ORESTES

Electra, keep watch on what happens within
so that the details all dovetail in neatly.

To Chorus.

Keep quiet where you can, or take care when talking.

To Pylades.

And Pylades, my companion, keep close to me.
See I wield my sword well in the fight that's to follow.

Exeunt Orestes, Pylades, Electra.

CHORUS

What Earth breeds is appalling.
Monsters rock in the arms of the sea.
Fearful sky-flames flare and fall
through terrible void territory.

Monsters, meteors, sea, soil, space,
things that fly, creep, crawl,
of all these horrors the human race
is the terror that tops them all.

Male boasting, pride in being HE
only one thing's got that beat
bursting the bedbond bestially
the female bitch on heat!

I

When Althaia was brought to bed
with Meleager, fate
prophesied he'd soon be dead
if a log burnt in the grate.

Plucked from flames, under lock and key,
the half-burnt brand's the boy's life-charm.
Safe with his mother, except that she
will be the one who does him harm.

Her son killed two of her bloodkin
and murderous mother Althaia
flung the half-burnt log back in
the life-devouring fire.

2

King of Megara, Nisos,
his life-charm was on his head,
one strangely purple lock whose loss
would mean he would be dead.

She knew this, she-child Skylla,
another bitch on heat,
she lopped the lock, foul father-killer
for the sake of the king of Crete.

The king of Crete had dangled gold
before her greedy eye.
For a paltry chain she sold
Megara and watched her father die.

Megara burnt, her people slain,
Minos keel-hauled her by her feet,
dragged her from his anchor chain
the whole way back to Crete.

This bloodclan too. A bedbond void
of love by which a man's destroyed.

The plot against your manlord's life,
you the cunning killer wife.

Against a man his enemies revered
and all his spear-foes justly feared.

You prized a fireless hearth instead
a spearless she-man in your bed.

3

LEMNOS! Its very name is vile
Clytemnestra should have been

of that murderous and manless isle
the killer queen.

Queen of women who wield knives
or slaughtered husband's sword.
The Lemnos husband-killing wives.
LEMNOS – name to be abhorred.

The swordpoint pricks against the skin
ready to be driven in.

Bloodright pushes at the hilt
to broach the gory springs of guilt.

The transgressors, those who trod
down the laws of ZEUS, high he-god.

Bloodright's the whetstone where fate whets
the blades demanding old blood-debts.

Bloodgrudge leads the son at last
to purge the bloodspill of the past.

Enter Orestes and Pylades as Phocians.

ORESTES

Gateman! Gateman! Can't you hear all this knocking?
Anyone there? Gateman! Gateman! Is there no one
    on duty?
This is the third time of knocking. Is nobody there?
Are the good laws of guestright ignored by Aegisthus?

GATEMAN

I hear you. I hear you. Where you from, stranger?

ORESTES

Go tell your masters there's someone with tidings.
And quick. The warcar of night drives on the darkness.
Time travellers were thinking about dropping anchor
in a place that makes all wayfarers welcome.
Fetch someone out in authority here.

Fetch the mistress. No, maybe the man would be fitter.
With women words have to be guarded and careful.
But man to man I can say what I mean and no hedging.

Enter Clytemnestra.

CLYTEMNESTRA
Stranger, all you've to do is declare what your need is.
Such a house can supply every kindness and comfort –
warm baths, beds that are balm to limbs worn by travel,
honest eyes that watch over your wishes and wants.
But if what you've come for is weightier counsel
that's work for the menfolk, and I'll see that you meet.

ORESTES
I'm not from these parts but from Daulis in Phocis.
I was trekking to Argos, my gear in this backpack
when I meet with a stranger who asks where I'm off to.
I tell him Argos, and, when he hears that, this stranger,
Strophius a Phocian (that's who the man turned out to be)
says to me: 'Since you're, in any case, going to Argos
you could save me a journey and take me a message,
a message concerning a man called Orestes.
Announce to the parents in Argos the death of Orestes.
Then ask if they want him fetched home, his ashes,
or if he's to lie here in Phocis for ever an exile.
A good bronze urn guards his ashes at present.
His ashes got tears shed. The man got some mourning.'

I pass on his words as he spoke them, not knowing
if whom I'm addressing's directly related.
It seems proper to speak to a parent in person.

CLYTEMNESTRA
Your news brings the whole house down on our heads.
Ungrappleable bloodgrudge that bullies this bloodclan,
possessing the piercing sharp eye of the preybird

takes aim from safe ambush to send its sharp shafts home.
You strip me of near ones, leaving me naked.
And now Orestes . . . who seemed to tread surely,
who kept clear of the clay this bloodclan gets stuck in.
He was the one hope we still held for this household,
the balm we all banked on for the bloodgrudge's orgies.
Orestes, our hope, must be crossed off the rollcall.

ORESTES

With hosts such as you here so favoured by fortune
I'd more gladly be a guest whose tidings were good ones.
Between host and guest there's no goodwill greater.
But the bonds that I've given both bind me to truth,
my bond to Strophius, my guest-bond as stranger.

CLYTEMNESTRA

Your words won't make you the less warmly welcomed.
If you hadn't brought them someone was bound to.
It's time now that travellers who've spent the day trekking
should cease feeling footsore and seek out their comforts.

To attendants.

Take them to where the man-guests get quartered,
him and the man who's his travelling companion.
Supply them with comforts this palace is famed for.
Serve them in all things or answer to me.
Meanwhile I'll convey your news to the clanchief
and along with all our true loyal supporters
we'll hold a clan council and consider the case.

Exeunt Clytemnestra, Orestes, Pylades.

CHORUS

Loyal supporters of the true bloodkin
when can we let our pent feelings out,
when snatch out the galling gag of grief
and give Orestes the victory shout?

125

Earth she-god, high gravemound
dumped on the lord of the seas
send help up from underground
prosper these prayers and pleas.

Word-guile, word-guile gets things done
and ground-god Hermes who can throw
dust in the eyes of everyone
pushes the blade in from below.

It seems our fake Phocian is working already.
I see the old nurse of Orestes walking here weeping.
Cilissa! Where are you going to through the gateyard
with woe the unwanted one walking beside you.

Enter Nurse.

NURSE
Queen Clytemnestra says 'Quick fetch Aegisthus!'
to meet man to man with some strangers who've come,
confront them in person and hear the new tidings . . .
In front of the serfs she faked grief on her features
but her eyes through the mask wore nothing like mourning.
Nay they blazed like joy beacons at what had befallen.
The news that's been brought's a great bane for this
    bloodclan
but for Aegisthus a just cause for rejoicing.
This household's caused me perpetual heartache.
No bane to this bloodclan ever beat this one.
Death shook the house and I shrugged – but now
    it's Orestes,
my little Orestes, who I wore out my life for.
Came straight off his mother and got clapped to my paps.
Got these very breasts as a baby, Orestes!
Trouble! That lad gave me trouble in tonloads!
Led me a dance he did, demanding, demanding,
getting me up from my couch with his crying,
and when I was with him there was nothing he wanted.

They're like puppies, aren't they though, babies?
Still in their nappies what can they do? Nothing!
While they lack language they just keep you guessing –
is it hunger or thirst pangs or wanting to piddle,
their little bellies just do it regardless.
You have to read minds, keep one jump ahead
or else you get caught with their crap to clean out.
Wet nurse and washerwoman I was to Orestes.
Had him entrusted by King Agamemnon.
Now I hear that he's dead, my dear little baby.
I'm off to Aegisthus, the bane of this bloodclan.
When he hears of the death, he'll be glad and delighted.

I

CHORUS

How is he to come? Does she say how, the queen?

NURSE

How? Don't get you. Don't know what you mean.

2

CHORUS

I mean does she tell him to come armed or not?

NURSE

O armed and attended! His spearmen! The lot!

CHORUS

Then tell him there's no need of his combatant gear.
Tell Aegisthus there's joy in what he's to hear.
Tell him come quickly the man we all hate.
'The messenger's mouth sets a twisted tale straight.'

3

NURSE

Are you trying to tell me this news makes you glad?

CHORUS

Why not? If ZEUS will make good out of bad.

4

NURSE

But Orestes, our one hope, he's gone as you know.

CHORUS

Only a blind seer would say that was so.

5

NURSE

What are you saying? Is there more to be known?

CHORUS

The gods will do their work. You do your own.

NURSE

I will. I'm off with my message. I've no doubt
the gods in their wisdom will sort it all out.

CHORUS

Chief of the godclans, ZEUS, now send
this house a balanced end.

Let the lovers of good law
get the bloodright they've longed for.

Let the man who's gone within
meet with his enemies and win.

If you help him your godstone
will get more goats than it's ever known.

The colt of one dear to your heart
's coupled to disaster's cart.

Now that he's nearly won his race
see he keeps up his winning pace.

Don't let him slacken off so late
and falter halfway down the straight.

Gods of this clan's rich stores
the feelings that we have are yours.

Let fresh bloodflow now wash clean
all the bloodflow that has been.

Dry old murder's loins make barren
the teeming womb of this blood-warren.

APOLLO, healer, whose light even
makes the deep dark cave a haven.

Let this bloodclan's latest one
lift his eyes up to the sun.

Let the beacon of bright freedom blaze
through the veils of murk and haze.

HERMES, guile-god, if you choose,
those you champion can't lose.

You blind their opponents so
they can't see the coming blow.

Those you help see through the dark
and shoot their weapons at the mark.

Their targets can't see. All they feel
's their hearts pierced suddenly by steel.

Then sing this bloodclan brought to land
out of the wild sea, beached on sand.

Like the women of fishermen who wail
until they glimpse the first white sail.

The wind drops, the dark sky clears
the women's wailing turns to cheers.

Cheers as the laden ships reach shore
and loved ones suffer storm no more.

And when the deed is to be done
courage when she calls you SON.

Shout back MY FATHER'S, call his name
do the blood-deed with no blame.

Be like Perseus, one who slew
a monster woman as will you.

Those below the earth and those above
want their bloodgrudge not son's love.

Plunge your sword up to the hilt
in the cause of this bloodguilt.

Enter Aegisthus.

AEGISTHUS
Here I am as the messenger summoned.
I'm told certain strangers have brought baleful tidings,
news most unwelcome, the death of Orestes.
The beast's back's already rubbed raw by its burdens
and now it gets plagued by another sore pack-gall.
Am I to take this as fact and as proven
or is it mere women's talk starting a panic,
words flying and burning themselves out for nothing?
Who knows any more to make it all plainer?

CHORUS
We heard the same story as you, but we're only women!
You don't need to listen to second-hand hearsay,
go inside straightaway and question the strangers.

AEGISTHUS
Yes, I want to have the messenger questioned
if he himself witnessed the death of Orestes
or whether he's simply passing on rumours.
I'm too open-eyed to be gulled or outsmarted.

Exit Aegisthus.

CHORUS
Both bloodblades are now drawn out
for the final killing bout.

Either Clytemnestra's cleaver
finishes the clan for ever

or Agamemnon's son can light
the beacon, freedom, in black night.

In the blood-bout two to one,
back up Agamemnon's son.

*A cry from the palace. Should be identical to cry
of Agamemnon.*

AEGISTHUS
(*within*)

Aaaaggghhh!

CHORUS

Listen! Whose was that cry? The clan's in the balance.
But better we women withdraw till it's settled.
Whatever the outcome we must seem to be blameless.
One way or another the battle's decided.

Enter Servant.

SERVANT

He's killed. The master! He's killed. The master. Aegisthus.
Open the door to the women's apartments . . .
A strong arm's needed, though he's past help, Aegisthus.

Help! Help! Everyone's deaf, there's no point in shouting.
Deaf or asleep. But where's Clytemnestra?
Her head's the next one due for the hackblock.
The axeshaft's poised in the clenched fist of bloodright.

Enter Clytemnestra.

CLYTEMNESTRA

Who's that shouting for help in the palace?

SERVANT

The dead, the dead are hacking the living down

CLYTEMNESTRA

Ah, your riddle's by no means baffling to me.
We're to be killed by the same guile we killed by.
Get me my man-axe, my king-cleaver. Quick!

Exit Servant.

We'll put to the test who's victor, who's vanquished.

Enter Orestes and Pylades.

ORESTES

It's you I'm after. He's had enough the one inside.

CLYTEMNESTRA

Ah, dead, dead! My shield, dear Aegisthus.

ORESTES

Your *dear* Aegisthus? Then into his grave-bed.
Continue your coupling as cold stiffened corpses,
carry on tupping under your tombcairn.

CLYTEMNESTRA

Orestes! Have pity! These breasts you nestled on
and nuzzled the nipples for their nourishing milk.

ORESTES
(to Pylades)

Pylades! What shall I do? Shame, pity, awe,
all make me shrink from killing my mother.

PYLADES

Remember Apollo and all that you swore
Give grudge to mankind but not the godclan.

ORESTES

I remember. You were right to remind me.

To Clytemnestra.

Inside! I want to kill you on top of his body.
Since you preferred him (when alive!) to my father.

132

Aegisthus greater than King Agamemnon!
The one you should have showered love on not hatred.

Sleep beside your dear one even in death.

1
CLYTEMNESTRA
I want to grow old with the son these breasts fed!
ORESTES
My father's murderess eating my bread!

2
CLYTEMNESTRA
The she-god of Fate, son, she played her part.
ORESTES
The same she-god then drives my sword through your
heart.

3
CLYTEMNESTRA
Your mother's bloodgrudges, don't they make you scared?
ORESTES
Would a mother throw her son out if she had cared?

4
CLYTEMNESTRA
Not thrown out, sent to an ally when Argos got hot.
ORESTES
Sold! A chief's son, a free man, and sold for what?

5
CLYTEMNESTRA
Yes, if I sold you, what was my pay?
ORESTES
Too shameful to think of, let alone say.

6

CLYTEMNESTRA

What of your father? What of his shame?

ORESTES

He suffered. You sat here. Spare him your blame.

7

CLYTEMNESTRA

A woman suffers with her man at the wars.

ORESTES

But his toil supports her while she sits indoors.

8

CLYTEMNESTRA

So you'll condemn me, your mother, to die.

ORESTES

Your own actions condemn you, mother, not I.

9

CLYTEMNESTRA

Your mother's bloodgrudges like dogs will hunt you.

ORESTES

I'm hunted by my father's so what can I do?

10

CLYTEMNESTRA

Deaf as the gravehole my son pays no heed.

ORESTES

When my father was murdered *you* started to bleed.

11

CLYTEMNESTRA

You! You were the snake crawled out of my womb.

ORESTES

Your nightmare was true. It showed you your tomb.

You killed my father. I kill my mother.
One blood-wrong gives birth to another.

Orestes and Pylades take Clytemnestra off.

CHORUS

I spare some pity for this fallen couple,
but better Orestes surfs over this bloodcrest
than the eye of the bloodclan is shuttered for ever.

Time brings bloodright to blast Troy.
Agamemnon's house next call.
Two lions enter and destroy
the house, and now the lions fall.

Orestes, guided by Apollo
comes home and hacks them dead.
The distant exile has to follow
the god-goad in his head.

At last this house is freed,
restored to its old health.
Dead the ones who let it bleed
away its wealth.

The killer had to be concealed.
He counterfeited then attacked.
Bloodright, Zeus' she-child, steeled
his right hand as he hacked.

At last this house is freed
restored to its old health
dead the ones who let it bleed
away its wealth.

APOLLO cries from deep cleftshrine
guile crushes guile, deceit deceit!
We've got to trust whatever divine
power helps us to our feet.

The beacon's relit
light's in the halls
harsh chain and bit
cause no more galls

House of Atreus stand
get up off the ground.

Time brings it all about,
scrubs the blood off the bricks,
drives the bloodgrudge squatters out.
Now all three dice say six!

The beacon's relit
light's in the halls
harsh chain and bit
cause no more galls

House of Atreus stand
get up off the ground.

> *Palace doors open. Orestes with bodies of Clytemnestra
> and Aegisthus. The tableau repeats the stance of
> Clytemnestra over Agamemnon and Cassandra.*

ORESTES

Here they are, the two tyrants who crushed you.
They killed my father and blasted the bloodclan.
Puffed up with pride they were, up on their thronestools,
and still in love, look, still clinging so closely,
carrying their bedbond into the grave-hole.
The pledges they gave have both been accomplished –
kill my father together, together to fall.

> *Shows robe.*

Now look again, you who are here to bear witness.
This contrivance they fangled to fetter my father
both his hands and feet held fast and hobbled.
Spread the thing out. Gather round in a circle,

display the great cloak-shroud so that the father (not mine
but the sun who sees all things I mean by the father)
can see the crime of my mother in all its true grimness,
so when I stand trial the Sun will bear witness
that Orestes was right to go through with this killing.
Right to kill his mother. As for Aegisthus –
he got the just death all adulterers deserve.
What of her who hatched this horror up for her husband,
whose children she carried under her girdle,
a burden apparently loved but really abhorrent,
what about her? If she'd been shark-hag or viper
just the mere feel of her, without any fang-marks
would turn her poor victim purple with poison,
make him all stiff and all swollen with blood.
Her spirit alone spurts out putrefaction.

Shows robe again.

What shall I call it? What name gives it status?
Net to snare animals, shroud for a corpse,
drape for a bath-trough. No, net's the best name.
Call it a hunting net, trip-rope, a trap-robe,
an ideal device for roadside desperadoes
who lurk by the highway waylaying wayfarers.
With one of these they'd snare them in thousands.

Rather than end up with a wife like my mother
I'd rather die without heir, without he-child.

CHORUS
In that net you bled to death
a butchered carcase bathed in blood.
For the one who still draws breath
suffering bursts into bud.

ORESTES
Did she do the deed or not? This is my witness,
the cloth all becrimsoned by the sword of Aegisthus.

The embroidery rotted by time and by bloodstains.
Wailing over this web gives my father his gravedirge.
My dirge is for all the deeds done by this bloodclan.
I've won this bout but the laurels are blood-smirched

CHORUS

No man's life-lot ever goes
painless till the post is passed
Man gets preyed on by his woes
from his first day to his last.

ORESTES

I've got to tell you. The whole thing's unending.
My chariot races. I rein my team in as they're charging.
The uncontrolled horses crash into the trackrails.
They gallop my mind off, dragging behind them.
Fear squats in my mind, plays music for scaring.
But while I still have some grip I say to the Argives,
I was right to kill Clytemnestra, my mother,
daubed in my father's blood, hated by he-gods.
Apollo's voice was my chief provocation:
*Do what you have to, and go away guiltless.
Don't do it and* . . . The pains that he promised
were out of all range of man's usual troubles.
Look at me now with this olive, this garland.
I go as a suppliant to Apollo's great godstone
where purifying fires are forever kept burning,
exiled for shedding the blood of my bloodkin.
Apollo said I should only seek help from his godstone.
I beg men of Argos now and in future
to bear witness as to how these horrors happened.
I go as a wanderer, exiled from my bloodright.
Living or dead, I leave you my memory.

CHORUS

The memory will be of a man who did well.
Don't burden your mouth with any bad omens.

You've brought freedom back to the city of Argos
by lopping the heads off two serpents at once.

1
ORESTES

Ah! Look! Coming! Gorgons. Garb black, entwined
with snakes for hair. I've got to run.

CHORUS

It's nothing, Orestes. It's all in your mind.
Fear nothing. Your father's pleased with his loyal son.

2
ORESTES

These aren't in the mind. They're real and they're near.
My mother's grudge-dogs close at my heels.

CHORUS

Orestes, it's fresh blood on your hands makes you fear.
It's only blood-frenzy your spirit feels.

3
ORESTES

Apollo! Look at them. More! More! More!
Through black blood-ooze their eyes stare straight at me.

CHORUS

Apollo's the one god to cleanse you of gore.
The touch of Apollo will set you free.

ORESTES

You can't see them. I can though.
They're baying for my blood. I've got to go.

Exit Orestes pursued by Furies.

CHORUS

Then let the god you go to give
you sustenance and help you live.

This, the third stormblast to buffet this bloodclan.

One: the banquet of babes, the bane of Thyestes.

Two: the Achaean warlord hacked down in his
 bath-trough.

Three: the deliverer . . .
                          or new doom in disguise?

When will the blood-grudge be weaned
off blood,
          when will it sleep,
                              the fiend?

End of Part Two.

Three

EUMENIDES

Temple of Apollo at Delphi.

First in my prayers, Earth, Gaia, great she-god,
primeval prophetess and eldest diviner.
Then after her mother came Earth's she-child Themis
who handed it on to the Titaness Phoebe,
who bestowed it in turn on Apollo as birthgift.
Leaving rocks and bog on the island of Delos
Apollo made landfall on Attica's shoreline
where Pallas has harbours bristling with ships' masts
and then pushed on upwards as far as Parnassus
escorted by offspring of Hephaistos the smithgod
who laid roads for Apollo to lead him to Delphi.
Those Athenians made the whole wilderness docile.
When Apollo arrived, the people and Delphos,
Delphos of Delphi, state-pilot and steersman,
greeted the young god with all welcome and worship.
Zeus gave Apollo divine inspiration,
made him fourth prophet here, and here he still is.
Apollo's the mouth of Zeus, the high he-god.

These prophet gods take first place in my prelude.

Next Pallas Athene who stands before god-shrines.
I honour the nymphs in the Corycian caverns,
hollow, where birds swoop, patrol place of spirits.
Dionysus too has a presence in Delphi
since the god headed his horde of Bacchantes
and got Pentheus hunted and trapped like a hare.
The spring of Pleistos, the power of Poseidon
and Zeus the Fulfiller, the highest of he-gods!

143

Now on the shrinestool, inspired and prophetic
I hope that my powers are as strong or are stronger.
Any Greeks here, come forward. Draw lots and enter.
I'll give you the answers the god sends in trances . . .

Priestess enters the shrine. Silence. Then a scream.
Then Priestess comes out again on all fours like a dog.

PRIESTESS

Terrible things to clap mortal eyes on
have made me bolt out of the house of Apollo.
Sapped of all strength my feet can't support me.
I scrabble on all fours. My legs have gone liquid.
A scared old woman crawling, worse than a baby.

Entering the innermost shrine with its garlands
I set eyes on a man at the shrine's central stone,
an abomination to gods in the suppliant's seat.
His hands dripped blood. He had his drawn sword out.
He held an olive-branch tipped with white wool tufts.
In front of this person, a strange group of she-hags
sighing and snorting, asleep on the thronestools.
Not women really, but more like the Gorgons.
I call them Gorgons but they weren't that exactly.
I once saw a picture of Harpiae, Graspers,
unflaggingly swooping on Phineus the Thracian,
keeping the blind king in perpetual tension,
filched his food off him or left it beshitten,
splattered their bat-bowels over his platters
and kept him terror-stricken and starving.
These were black like Harpiae but they were wingless.
The snorts from their nostrils would keep you a mile off.
Their eye-sockets glued with sickening ooze-clots.
Their grave-garb's all wrong for the statues of godheads
nor would it seem right in the houses of mortals.
Don't know what brute-clan this brood belongs to,

what region would want to boast that it bred them
and didn't wish now that their birth had aborted.
What happens now depends on the master of Delphi,
Doxias Apollo, sign reader, all powerful, healer.

He purifies others' homes, let him cleanse his.

Exit Priestess.

The inner shrine revealed with Apollo and Orestes.

APOLLO

No, I'll never desert you. I'll guard you for ever,
either close by you, or if not, at a distance.
Towards all your enemies, like those pursuers,
I'll never show mildness, nor ever mellow.
I've put them to sleep, these creatures men spit on,
blood-battening bat hags, shrivelled but virgin,
crone-kinder no kind caresses, covers or couples.
Who'd tup these terrors? No god, man nor brute beast!
They're born to brew bale. They're evil for ever.
Their abode's the bottomless void black abyss,
abominations both to men and Olympian he-gods.

But still you must run. Don't flag and don't slacken.
They'll hound you through the whole length of the
    landmass,
tracking you over the well-beaten foot routes
then across seas, through cities lapped by the ocean.
Don't surrender. Don't let your step falter
by brooding on all the pain that you'll suffer.
When you come to the city of Pallas Athene
sit down in safety, embracing her image.
There we'll find judges and words of appeasement
and means to release you from this burden for ever.

I moved you, I, to murder your mother!

ORESTES

Lord Apollo, you know about justice none better,
and since you know don't forget how to use it.
Apollo's potency goes without question.

APOLLO

Remember that then! Don't give way to panic.

Invokes Hermes.

And Hermes, my brother, kin through one father
(and what bloodkin exists any closer than that?)
watch over Orestes, be Hermes Escorter.
Shepherd my suppliant. Guide him to Athens.
Zeus ever respects the rights of the outlawed.

Exeunt Apollo, Orestes.

*Enter Ghost of Clytemnestra who speaks to the still
unseen Chorus of Furies within.*

CLYTEMNESTRA

You're supposed to be Furies and I find you sleeping!
When Furies need naps they're no longer Furies.
Dishonoured, defamed by the dead that I dwell with,
I walk underground through a gauntlet of ghost-cries,
catcalls that brand my phantom with blood-guilt.
Slaughtered though I was by the hand of my he-child
not one spirit's incensed at the sore fate I've suffered.
Look here at my heart with hackmarks all over.
Remember too all those midnight libations,
not winebowls, but liquor much redder and thicker,
poured at the hour when there's only you stirring
while mortals are sleeping, gods in god-spaces.
But you trample and spurn all my spendthrift libations.
He's given you the slip the quarry you're hunting
like a nimble deer clearing the spread of your net-mesh
belling his beast-taunts as he bounds off for freedom.
Listen! It's for my after-life that I'm pleading.

Wake up, she-gods of underneath spaces.
The Clytemnestra you're dreaming calls you from sleep.

Furies are heard within, moaning in their sleep.

O make your cow noises! Your quarry's escaped.
He's lucky in *his* friends. At least they aren't Furies.

Furies are heard again moaning.

Snoring and sleeping! Does my pain stir no pity?
Mother-killer Orestes got out of your clutches.

More Fury noises.

Sleeping and whining! Whining and sleeping! Wake up!
Aren't Furies supposed to make people suffer?

More Fury noises from within.

Fagged out by fatigue it sleeps off its labours
the she-snake, whose fangs have been syphoned of venom.

Furies whine louder and higher.

CHORUS OF FURIES
Get him! Get him! There he goes!

CLYTEMNESTRA
Dreaming of hunting, like dogs, but not doing!
Baying like bloodhounds that track in their slumbers.
Dreaming not *doing*! Get up and get going.
Sleep only blunts your rage at my bloodwrong.
My bloodgrudge should boost you back into action.
Bloodgrudge is a goad to upholders of bloodright.
Let your breath billow round him its gore-reeking gases.
Shrivel his flesh with hot blasts from your bowels,
fart fire through your flues till he flops like a fruitrind.
Hound him and hunt him till he sags like a skin-bag.

*Exit Ghost of Clytemnestra. Enter Chorus of Furies
one by one.*

CHORUS

Wake up! Wake up your she-kin as I woke you.
Still asleep? Then shake off your stupor.
Make certain the chase here wasn't for nothing.

Chorus searches for Orestes.

All for nothing! Pointless, pointless pursuit!
Running till we dropped. A little nap.
All for nothing. The blood-guilty brute
still wide-awake leaps out of our trap.

Calling into Apollo's sanctum.

Apollo, Apollo, thief of a he-god!
we she-gods have the ancientest rights,
that you, a young he-god ride over roughshod.
Strutting young upstart! We spit on such slights.

You pamper this suppliant you hide,
and he's a mother-killing son.
A god condoning matricide!
Who'd see right in what you've done?

Grudge gored my gut like a goad in a racehorse.
Felt on my flesh like the flail of a flogger
sharp, vicious, whistling like pliable ice.
They do things like that the new era he-gods,
get their way only by forcing the feeble.

Look at his thronestool sticky with bloodspill.
His navelstone's only a blood-sodden hackblock.
Prophet Apollo pollutes his own godstone.
Of his own accord gets his stone caked with bloodclots.
He's breached all the godbonds to bolster up mortals,
poaching the preserves of she-fate and life-lot.
That abomination Apollo's protecting Orestes!

Has he crawled into the ground? Let him.
Wherever he is the FURIES will get him.

148

He brings his blood-guilt. Next in the chain's
the bloodgrudge-fulfiller who beats in *his* brains.

Enter Apollo.

APOLLO

Get out! Get out! Out you go! Out you go!
Leave the prophet's earthcleft free of pollution
or a serpent with wings on and venomous fangbane
shot from gold bowstrings will go through your gutbag!
You'll spew up black slaver of gobbled-up goreswill,
gore-clots your crones' gobs sucked out of corpses.
Not a finger of yours should befoul my own hearth-fane.
You belong where heads go splat off the hackblock,
eyes get gouged out and lugged from their sockets,
where bloodright's castrations, boys' bollocks battered,
men spitted on stakespikes screaming for mercy.
Your bat-snouts go snorting in society's bloodtroughs.
It's the food you get fat on makes you hated by he-gods.
All your appearance says blood food and filth baths.
You hags should live in the beast dens in jungles.
dark lairs all larded with shit and chewed gristle,
not here, contagious to all you come close to.
Get out! Out you go! You goats with no goatherd!

CHORUS

Thank you, Apollo! Now may we reply?
Apollo, how can you pose as a simple abettor
when you and you only bear all the bloodguilt?

I

APOLLO

How? At least explain that charge. But then you must go.

CHORUS

He killed his mother, because you said so.

149

2
APOLLO
To avenge his dead father as any son should.
CHORUS
You harboured him here with his hands red with blood.

3
APOLLO
I told him to come here to be purged of bloodstains.
CHORUS
And we drove him here, but get abuse for our pains.

4
APOLLO
You're not fit to set foot here, such hags as you.
CHORUS
We did only the work that we're destined to do.

5
APOLLO
And what 'special mission' have you ever had?
CHORUS
The mission of driving matricides mad!

6
APOLLO
And if it's her manlord a woman has killed?
CHORUS
That wouldn't be bloodkin's blood that has been spilled!

APOLLO
So you'd scorn bondright, the man–woman bedbond?
Hera, high she-god and Zeus, the high he-god,
they even swore vows and were coupled in bondright.
So you'd dishonour and cast on the midden
the she-god of love, Aphrodite of Cyprus,

she with whose help men form bonds of the closest?
That bedbond's sanctified by the she-gods of life-lot
and needs no other oath if the guardian's justice.
So if one murders her mate in the bedbond
and you slacken your rigid rule against slaughter
then it's unjust your pursuit of Orestes.
One crime you come down on, the other pass over.

Athena must judge between bloodright and bondright.

7

CHORUS
He'll never escape. I'll go on pursuing.

APOLLO
Do, by all means, it's your own bale you'll be brewing.

8

CHORUS
You can't belittle our rights for all your abuse.

APOLLO
I wouldn't take them, for nothing, even from Zeus!

9

CHORUS
Yes, we've heard you're well in with the throne!
But with shed mother-blood blazing the trail
I'll keep on pursuing till the end of the hunt.

APOLLO
You do your 'duties'. I'll do my own –
which is protecting my suppliant. If I fail
his rage will cause men and gods great affront.

Exit Apollo.

Exeunt Chorus sniffing for the trail.

*Scene changes to Athens. Before the image of Athena.
Orestes clasps the image.*

ORESTES

Athena, high she-god, I was sent by Apollo.
Look on me kindly. I'm cursed and an outcast.
Though still a cursed outcast there's no need of more
   cleansing.
My bloodguilt's been blunted enough by my contact
with places and peoples who helped my purgation.
All this was decreed by Apollo at Delphi.
I've crossed land and sea to your house and your statue.
Until the issue's decided I stay beside you.

Enter Chorus, one by one, still sniffing the bloodtrail.

CHORUS

Here! He's left a very clear track behind him.
We don't need his cries but only these bloodclues.
Like hounds tracking down a deer that's been bleeding
we bound between blood-drips till our quarry's cornered.
This manhunt's a killer. I pant with exhaustion.
We've combed the whole land, the coastline, the ocean,
swift flotilla of Furies, wingless sea-eagles.
My nostrils say here he's cornered and cowering.
The glad smell of gore smiles its warm welcome.

Seek   seek   scour the ground
the mother-killer's got to be found.

Sniff at the trail. The blood's still wet.
Don't let him flee from paying his debt.

He's there! And once again, look, begging protection,
this time his arms are wound round a she-god.
He won't pay his blood-dues. He wants to 'stand trial'.
What rubbish *trials* are when the blood shed's a mother's!

A mother's blood has run away
into the earth it goes to stay.

The blood that trickles on the ground
's not balls of thread to be rewound.

Trial! This is the trial your trackers intend:
first suck red libations from limbs while they're living,
browse on your blood, all over your body,
broach you all bloodless, haul your husk off below,
a morsel of torment for your own mother's murder.
Down there you'll see all those who've offended
a god or a guest or the parents who got them,
get the blood-doom their deeds have duly deserved.

Hades, death-god holds assize
on a man's deeds when he dies

death-god Hades won't forget
the deed of blood and the blood-debt.

ORESTES

I've been through them all, the forms of purgation,
rites which used speech, rites which used silence.
Here my wise mentor says words are in order.
The blood on my hands has already grown drowsy;
it lowers its eyelids. The stains have stopped staring.
It was washed off with pig's blood by Phoebus Apollo.
My hosts came to no harm by giving me housing.
So the mouth's unpolluted that pleads with Athena,
god-queen of the country, to come to my rescue.
She won't need her spear to make long-lasting allies
of me and my country, and the people of Argos.
Whether she's now in the Libyan deserts,
or by Lake Tritonis, her Libyan birthplace,
seated and skirted to receive men's obeisance,
or booted for battle, as brave as a he-god,
siding with her friends on the Phlegrean flatlands –

As a she-god she'll hear me over great spaces.
Come, Athena, come now to my rescue!

CHORUS

Neither the power of Apollo, nor the power of Athena
can save you from perishing spurned and abandoned,

even forgetting that joy had a meaning,
broached of blood, banqueted on, flesh pod, shadow,
a shrivelled-up fruitrind squeezed dry of its juices.

Won't answer! Spits what we say back in our faces!
Our little sacrifice all ready for slicing!
No need of godstones, we'll eat you still living.
It will swaddle you helpless, our 'lullaby', listen –

She-kin, show our force. Join hands!
Dance the doom-dance steps, display
through our grim music that our band's
a power over men that gets its way:

Our mission's bloodright, we're not sent
ever to harm the innocent.

Show us your hands. If they're not red
you'll sleep soundly in your bed.

Show us your hands. Left. Right.
You'll live unhunted if they're white.

Show us *your* hands. There's one we know
whose hands are red and daren't show.

With men like him whose hands are red
we are the bloodgrudge of the dead.

Our band of witnesses pursues
the bloodkin-killer for blood-dues.

NIGHT, Night, Mother Night
who bore us to uphold bloodright,
Leto's he-child takes away
the rights you gave us to our prey,
this cringing beast, his cowering whelp
evades us with that he-god's help.
Apollo's foiled us of the hide
of our allotted matricide.

Victim! Victim!
Listen! Our song!

The Furies' lyreless lullaby's
music maddening men's mind

Victim! Victim!
Listen! Our song!

It binds man's brain and dries
man's fruity flesh to rind.

The she-god of life-lot gave us these powers,
Ours, ours, for ever ours.

Those who kill their kin I hound
until I've got them underground.

Even dead they don't go free,
I torment them endlessly . . .

Victim! Victim!
Listen! Our song!

The Furies' lyreless lullaby's
music maddening men's mind

Victim! Victim!
Listen! Our song!

It binds man's brain and dries
man's fruity flesh to rind.

When we came into being, they were marked out,
    the confines.
We and the Olympians have no intimate contacts.
Food's offered to either but not both together.
We don't wear white robes, they don't wear black ones.

Family strife, domestic pet
born in the wild and won't forget

When bloodkin kills bloodkin
that lets the Furies in

Into the household keen-scented hound
blasting the building back into the ground

After the victim; hot on his trail
tracker Furies that never fail

He tries running. O let him try
a bloodkin's blood will never dry.

He tries running. Fresh wet gore
keeps the Furies hot on his spoor.

We'll snatch back our prey from this she-god's protection.
There should be no question of such gods interfering
or muddying issues by setting up 'sessions'.
Zeus, the high he-god finds murderers hateful,
he bars that blood-dripping breed from his precincts.

Family strife, domestic pet
born in the wild and won't forget

When bloodkin kills bloodkin
that lets the Furies in

Into the household keen-scented hound
blasting the building back into the ground

After the victim, hot on his trail
tracker Furies that never fail

He tries running. O let him try
a bloodkin's blood will never dry

He tries running. Fresh wet gore
keeps the Furies hot on his spoor.

The pomp and proud carriage a man's puffed up with
above
moulders to nothing when he's dragged off below.

He sees the drab black we're draped with to dance in,
hears the feet pounding the pulse of the bloodgrudge.

Down, down, down I dive from a great height
and fall on him with all my weight

Down, down, down I dive, my leaden tread
cracks the bloodkin-killer's head

Down, down, down he goes with sickening thud
slipping in his bloodkin's blood.

Down he falls, and falling knows nothing, nothing.
A smother of madness clouds round the victim.
The groans of old murders thicken the bloodsmog
that billows all round and blacks out his household.

Down, down, down I dive from a great height
and fall on him with all my weight

Down, down, down I dive, my leaden tread
cracks the bloodkin killer's head

Down, down, down he goes with sickening thud
slipping in his bloodkin's blood.

That's how it is, and that's how it's staying.
We've got all the skills. We get things accomplished.
We memorise murders. We're never forgetful.

We terrify mortals. We spit on their pleadings.
We relish our office, though spurned by the he-gods.

We're despised, we're rejected. The light we work by
is nothing like sunshine. Sharp and sheer-sided
our tracks are a peril to blind and to sighted.

So show us the man who can stop himself shaking
when he hears me lay claim to my titles
ratified by fate, and never, *never* rescinded.
My honours are ancient and in no way diminished

though I work underground, in the earth wnere it's
   sunless.

   Enter Athena.

ATHENA

I heard far away someone crying: ATHENA!
I was on the banks of the Trojan Scamander
taking possession of my portion of spearspoil,
land won by the Achaeans, then awarded to me
and offered by me to the children of Theseus.

And summoned I sped here, the scales of my aegis
whipped by the winds as my feet raced me onwards.

   Sees Chorus.

I see a strange breed here, new to my country.
This breed doesn't scare me but causes me wonder.

   To Chorus.

Who are you? You and you, all here assembled?
The stranger prostrated before my own image,
and you, like nothing engendered by means that are
   normal,

neither like the she-gods that consort with the he-gods
nor like the humans in shape and appearance.

But since we've been made to share the same earthspace
it's wrong to abuse you as monstrous and shapeless.

CHORUS

She-child of Zeus, we'll tell you all briefly.
We are the children of Night, and we're ageless.
Below ground where we live we're known as the Grudges.

I

ATHENA
So now I know your mother and what to call you.
CHORUS
And soon you'll know also the work that we do.

2

ATHENA
I will, provided it's clear what you say.
CHORUS
Kin-killers, we hunt them. They are our prey.

3

ATHENA
Where do you land him when you've netted your fish?
CHORUS
Where all words for joy sound like gibberish.

4

ATHENA
Are his deeds the reason that you're in full cry?
CHORUS
He murdered his mother in cold blood, that's why!

5

ATHENA
Was he goaded or forced to against his own will?
CHORUS
Forced! It was his mother this man dared to kill!

6

ATHENA
There are two parties present. I must hear them both.
CHORUS
He won't let us swear ours, nor swear his own oath.

159

7
ATHENA
It's not justice you want but the mere outward show.
CHORUS
How? You're the she-god of wisdom, say why that is so.

8
ATHENA
Sworn oaths would unfairly favour your cause.
CHORUS
You question him then. The decision is yours.

9
ATHENA
The decision is mine. You'll give me you trust?
CHORUS
Knowing your father it seems that we must.

ATHENA
(*addressing Orestes*)
Stranger, now it's your turn to speak and make answer.
Tell me your country, your bloodkin, what's happened
then make reply to the charges they've levelled.
Belief in your case brought you here to my godstone
clasping my image like the suppliant Ixion,
first man to kill, first cleansed of his killing.
Answer my questions and answer them clearly.

ORESTES
She-chief Athena, let me remove the misgivings
implied in the last words you addressed me.
Unlike Ixion, *I* need *no* blood-absolution.
My undefiled hands cause no smirch to your image.
And this is the proof I can give of my cleansing:
the law is that one who's been guilty of bloodshed's
debarred from all speech until sprinkled with pig's blood

by one who's empowered to perform the purgation.
Long since and elsewhere I was purged in that manner
by sucklings with throats slit, streams with their currents.
So dismiss your alarm at likely pollution.
As for my bloodkin that's also told quickly –
I'm Argive, and when you ask me who is my father
I'm proud to reply that he *was* Agamemnon,
commander of all Achaia's great ship-force
with whose help you crushed Troy into nothing,
one of those clanchiefs who won you your spearspoil.
After Troy he returned to a death most unworthy.
My black-hearted mother, she killed my father.
She swaddled him first in a devious dragnet –
its red eyes still stare at the blood in the bath-trough.
Coming home after exile I killed my mother.
I killed her because she killed my dear father.
In all this Apollo was my god-accomplice.
Apollo jabbed sharp spurs into my spirit
and promised great pains if their guilt went unpunished.
Just or unjust? You must give judgement.
Whatever your verdict I'll take it as binding.

ATHENA

A hard matter, this, to judge for a mortal,
and even for me it's too hard to pass judgement
when retribution runs so close behind bloodguilt.
It's made all the harder since you've come to my godstone
a suppliant cleansed by all rites and procedures.
Still blood-stained I'd have you barred from my city.

Indicating Chorus.

But these too have a cause which must be considered.
They have certain duties it's pointless dismissing
and if the verdict frustrates them of victory
they'll disgorge their grudge-venom into the ground
and blight all the land with eternal diseases.

I let them stay or I drive them away –
That's the dilemma, my desperate decision.

I'll swear in a tribunal to be judges of murder
a tribunal for this case and all such for ever.

To Orestes and Chorus.

Gather your witnesses, gather your evidence,
your sworn support in the cause of true justice,
I'll pick and bring back the best men of Athens
to judge the facts fairly without any falsehood.

*Exit Athena. Orestes and Chorus remain. Scene
changes to Acropolis.*

CHORUS

All right's destroyed by this new dispensation
if the wrong cause of this killer's allowed to succeed.
One murderer's freedom gives licence to all,
makes murder the norm not merely the nightmare
that gnaws at the sleeptime of fathers and mothers.
They'll be wide awake now when the wounds get inflicted.

We Furies were once mankind's sleepless watchdogs
inflicting transgressors with vehement madness.
Our anger and grudge have been put out to grass now
and all forms of death have the run of the world.
When he sees trouble looming over his neighbour
a man starts to wonder when his own turn will come
and asks someone else how to stop the contagion
and he offers philtres for safety. All futile!
And don't let someone smitten cry out the old cry
on bloodright or bloodgrudge or us, the *deaf* Furies.
Some father, some mother, their pain new upon them,
might weep and might wail with such piteous appeals.
Bloodright! Like Troy it's all rubble and ashes.

Fear's a good gateman to stand guard of the passions.
Often men suffer to win some small wisdom.

Those men and those cities where fear has no franchise
will never show justice the slightest respect.
A life with no rules, a life of repression
anarchy, tyranny, you must respect neither.

Somewhere between's where the god plants his banner.
Out of two forces he makes a new fusion.
Going beyond bounds, overstepping the limits
that comes about where the gods get degraded.
The mind that is balanced, and keeps within confines
gets the happiness men struggle and pray for.
Above all respect the godstone of bloodright.
Don't besmirch or befoul it with impious bootsoles
just because loot looms in front of your goldlust.
Blemishing bloodright makes catastrophe certain.
Honour mother and father, and welcome guest-strangers.
And the man who does right without fear's compulsion
he's the one who won't find his life-lot unlucky
or himself and his bloodkin blasted entirely.
But the man who scorns all and does what he wants to
and caring for no one heaps up his wealth-spoil
and believes his snatched freight's assured a safe voyage,
will be forced to strike sail when the stormwaves start
    swelling,
his prow and his spars all pulped into splinters.
He shouts as he feels himself tugged by the tide-race.
He shouts to deaf ears. The gods' laughter mocks him,
the hothead who boasted that this couldn't happen,
helpless, aghast, as he's hurled at the headland,
and leaves on Right's reef the wreck of his life-lot,
and is lost, and unwept for, wiped out, forgotten.

Enter Athena, Jury of twelve Athenians, and a Herald.

ATHENA

Sound the trumpet, keep the people in order.
Let the shrill battle-horn the Etruscans invented

163

change mortal breath into blares from its metal.

Sound of trumpets.

This is a court now, and crowded with people.
We must have strict silence and closest attention
so the laws I lay down can be learnt by the city
and these hear their case decided on merit.

Sound of trumpets.

Now hear the laws I lay down, my Athenian people,
brought together to try the first case of bloodshed.
For the children of Aegeus, father of Theseus,
this council of judges will sit here for ever,
on this hill of Ares, the Amazons' camp-site
when they came to make war through their grudge
    against Theseus.
They erected great turrets to overlook Athens
and sacrificed cattle to Ares the War God,
hence the name: Areopagus, rock-hill of Ares.
The people's reverence and the fear that they're born with
will restrain them day and night from acts of injustice
as long as they don't foul their own laws with defilement.
No one should piss in the well they draw drink from.
Anarchy! Tyranny! Let both be avoided
nor banish fear from your city entirely.
A man without fear abides by no law-forms.
If you justly cherish this new institution
you'll have a bulwark known to no other humans
from Scythia down to the Peloponnesus.
This established tribunal will be totally bribe-proof.
The watchdog stays wakeful to let you sleep soundly.
This long address I intend for you and the future.

Enter Apollo.

ATHENA

Lord Apollo, you are out of your precincts.
Explain your presence here at this meeting.

APOLLO

I come as a witness. The man they're accusing
came as a suppliant and I gave him shelter.
I also purged him of the blood he had shed.
I'm his advocate too as well as a witness.
I share the blame for the death of his mother.

Begin the proceedings, that you preside over.
And make use of your wisdom to help us to judgement.

ATHENA
(to Chorus)

The trial is now open. First, prosecution.
Speak, and put before us complete information.

CHORUS

We may be many, but on this we're united.

   To Orestes.

Answer the question each one of us asks you . . .

1
CHORUS

You killed your mother. Say yes or no.

ORESTES

Yes, I can't deny it was so.

2
CHORUS

First fall to us! We win with two more.

ORESTES

Don't crow too soon. I'm not on the floor.

3
CHORUS
Now *how* did you kill her? (Judges take note!)
ORESTES
I drew my sword and gashed open her throat.

4
CHORUS
Who was it drove you to dare such an act?
ORESTES
Apollo, and Apollo will witness that fact.

5
CHORUS
You killed your mother at Apollo's behest?
ORESTES
I did, and still think it done for the best.

6
CHORUS
I doubt if you'll think so once pinned by your doom.
ORESTES
I have faith in my father's help from the tomb.

7
CHORUS
Your mother's among them so don't trust the dead.
ORESTES
My mother, she had two guilts on her head.

8
CHORUS
Explain to the judges how you make two.
ORESTES
Her husband, my father, that's two men she slew.

9

CHORUS

She paid by her death. You still have to pay.

ORESTES

When she was alive did you make her your prey?

10

CHORUS

He wasn't her bloodkin, the man that she killed.

ORESTES

And you say that it's bloodkin's blood that I've spilled?

CHORUS

How could it not be? How else could the mother
you murdered have fed you inside her body?
Dare you disown the bloodbond that's closest?

ORESTES
(to Apollo)

Now be my witness. Explain to the judges
whether I killed my mother with justice.
That I did the deed there's no point denying
but done rightly or wrongly, Apollo decide
and help me to state my case with the judges.

APOLLO

To you the high tribunal sworn in by Athena,
I, Apollo, the prophet, who can't utter falsehood
say that Orestes here acted with justice.
Whenever I speak to man, woman or city
from the oracle shrine-throne I sit on at Delphi
it's always as mouthpiece of Zeus, the high he-god,
so if I plea for justice, I speak for the Father,
Zeus, the high he-god, whose will you must bend to.
No oath has more power than the oath of the Father.

CHORUS

So Zeus, you say, was behind your instruction
that Orestes avenge the death of his father?
Does Zeus disregard the rights of his mother?

APOLLO

It's not the same thing the death of a man, though,
a man also honoured with Zeus-given chief-stave,
a *man*, moreover, killed by a *woman*
and not by war weapons, an Amazon's arrows,
but in a manner you'll hear, you, Pallas Athena,
and you sitting here to vote on this issue –
The man came home after ten years' campaigning
(and a fair judge would say that he'd gained himself glory)
came home from the wars to a 'womanly welcome'!
And as he was stepping up out of his bathtrough
she pitched her dark doom-tent over his body,
she hacked down her husband while he was helpless,
fastened and feeble in the maze of its meshes.
A fine death for a man, clanchief, commander!
I show you the woman just as she was
to goad you to just grudge when weighing this issue.

CHORUS

So Zeus thinks a father's death more important?
Yet Zeus was the one bound Kronos, *his* father!
Doesn't this act show a slight contradiction?

To *Judges*.

Consider this fact when reaching your verdict!

APOLLO

Animals! Beast-hags hated by he-gods!
Chains, fetters, locks can all be unloosened.
There are many means to burst bonds and shackles,
but once a man's dead and earth's lapped his blood up,
the blood drains away and never returns.

Though Zeus can reverse all other conditions
he's never come up with a charm against dying.

CHORUS

So then supposing this man *is* acquitted,
will the man who has shed the blood of his mother
live in the house of his father at Argos?
Who will want *his* hands griming the godstones?
What clans will want *him* at their ritual cleansing?

APOLLO

I'll answer that, and this answer's decisive! . . .

The mother of what's called her offspring's no parent
but only the nurse to the seed that's implanted.
The mounter, the male's the only true parent.
She harbours the bloodshoot, unless some god blasts it.
The womb of the woman's a convenient transit.
I've got proof here at hand to back up my statement
that the male can father with no help from the female.
Here is the she-child of Zeus, the high he-god,
who was nurtured in no womb's watery shadows.
Such an offspring no she-god could bear on her own.

To Athena.

And I, Pallas, will do all that Apollo is able
to make them both great, your city, your people.
I sent him a suppliant here to your godstone
so that you'd have him as a true friend for ever,
a spear-friend and ally, his people, your people,
loyally bound in a bond that is lasting.

ATHENA

So, as both sides have spoken, I order
the judges to come to the justest decision.

I
CHORUS

All the shafts in our quiver, they're all of them shot.
We need only your vote to make our word law.

APOLLO

You've heard what you've heard. Let each cast his lot.
Remember the god-bond that each of you swore.

2
CHORUS

Beware that in no way you dishonour our band.
If we're dishonoured we'll poison your grass.

APOLLO

Fear the oracles, that's my command.
My oracles, Zeus's, they must come to pass.

3
CHORUS

Your oracles will never be free of the blot
from dabbling in blood-deeds more than you should.

APOLLO

So you say Zeus the Father was wrong or was not
to purge Ixion first man to shed blood?

4
CHORUS

Words! Words! But if I don't get the bloodright that's due
I'll come down on this country with all of my force.

APOLLO

What young god or old god cares about you?
The case will be mine as a matter of course.

5
CHORUS

You cheated old she-gods, the Fates, once before
when you saved Admetus from a funeral pyre.

APOLLO

We have to help suppliants, and all the more
when he comes at a time when his need is most dire.

6

CHORUS

You befuddled the ancient she-gods with wine!
You made the old dispensation mere jest.

APOLLO

And that's all you'll be when the victory's mine.
You can spew all your venom. We won't be impressed.

CHORUS

You new he-gods trample the she-gods of old.
When I hear the verdict then I'll decide
whether or not this country gets blasted.

ATHENA

It's my duty to come to a final pronouncement.

I add my own vote to those for Orestes!

I myself was given birth by no mother.
I put the male first, although I'm unmarried,
and I am the wholehearted child of my father,
so I can't count the death of a woman
of greater importance than that of her manlord.

If your votes turn out equal Orestes still wins.

Now turn the urns over and reckon the ballots,
those of the judges assigned to this duty.

I

ORESTES

O Phoebus Apollo, what will it be?

CHORUS

O Night, our dark Mother, are you here to see?

2

ORESTES

Now for the end, a noose or new day.

CHORUS

Either honour, or ruin, if he gets away.

ATHENA

Count the pebbles you've shaken out of the vote-pots.
Make sure there are no mistakes in your tally.
The slightest error could lead to disaster.
One vote could renew the strength of a bloodclan.

The votes are counted.

This man stands acquitted of the charges of murder.
The votes on each side turn out to be equal.

ORESTES

Pallas Athena, you give my clan back its lifeblood!
You've given me back the fatherland barred me.
Once more Greece can say: Orestes of Argos,
restored to his bloodright by Pallas Athena,
by Apollo and by Zeus the Preserver.
Zeus saw my father's death in all its true grimness.
Zeus saw clearly that I needed preserving
from these terrible grudges who champion my mother.

Before I go to my country, I give you this god-bond –
this land and its people, now and for ever,
no clan-chief of Argos will ever attack you,
or I'll come as a ghost if they've broken my god-bond,
and mar all their marches, make journeys joyless,
until they repent their rash expeditions.
But so long as they honour this city of Pallas,
stay loyal in peace, and in war keep their spear-bond,
then I'll come as a ghost more gracious and kindly.

Farewell Athena, and people of Athens.

Get a good headlock on whoever you wrestle.
Come from all bouts with the victory laurels.

Exit Orestes.

CHORUS

You upstart gods
you've ridden down
the ancient laws
snatched my honours
out of my hands.

My rancour's roused,
my heart will ooze
black venom out
over the land
until it's waste.

Bloodright! Bloodright!

Womb-blight, crop-blight,
the earth all scorched,
the people starving.

The people mock me,
my wrongs are too much!
Daughters of Night
degraded and crushed.

ATHENA

Listen to reason. Don't take things so badly.
You're not defeated. The votes came out equal.
There was no dishonour to you in the verdict.
Luminous proof came from Zeus the high he-god
and he who had spoken the oracle witnessed
that Orestes should not be condemned for his action.
So why do you ravage the land with your rancour?
Don't let your rage scorch all our fields cropless,
your dewfalls of acid shrivel the seedpods,

and I will make you the solemnest promise
that you shall be given a cavern for refuge
with glittering thronestools next to your godstones
held in great honour by all here assembled.

CHORUS

You upstart gods
you've ridden down
the ancient laws,
snatched my honours
out of my hands.

My rancour's roused,
my heart will ooze
black venom out
over the land
until it's waste.

Bloodright! Bloodright!

Womb-blight, crop-blight,
the earth all scorched,
the people starving.

The people mock me.
My wrongs are too much.

Daughters of Night
degraded and crushed.

ATHENA

You're *not* dishonoured, so don't use your godhead
to blast this country of mortals with earthblight.
That would abuse your position as she-gods.
I have access to Zeus, and what's more have access
alone of all gods, to Zeus' munitions,
the mighty high he-god's missiles of thunder!
But this isn't a case for desperate deterrents.
I'd rather you yielded to gentler persuasion.

Take back your threats, don't spit spiteful poisons
over the fruitcrops, so that harvests don't happen.
Lull the black swell of your billowing bloodgrudge
and have half of my honours here, half of my worship.
The land's a broad land. It has people in plenty.
As the Furies you'll be favoured with sacrificed firstfruits,
propitiations preceding childbirth or bedbond.
You'll only have praise then for my persuasions.

CHORUS

The ancient conscience
pushed underground.
The ancient conscience
dishonoured, despised!

My nostrils snort
with rage at my shame.

Terrible anguish
bores under my ribs.

Night!   Mother!
Listen!   My cry!

The new he-gods
with their fouls in the ring
have robbed me of honour
making me nothing.

ATHENA

I'll allow you your anger since you are older.
Your years in the world have given you wisdom
and though yours may be greater, Zeus gave me insights.
If you leave this land for an alien bloodclan's
I tell you that you will learn to love this one.
Time in its passage will honour my people,
and you, enthroned by the shrine of Erechtheus,
will get more in the way of rites and processions
from my men and women than from the rest of mankind.

On this land, my land, goad no one to bloodshed,
or let them strop their grudge on your whetstones,
our youth up in arms and drunk with aggression
battling like bantams in the strife between bloodkin.
Let them battle abroad if they need to gain glory.
I want no cocks fighting in my country's farmyard,
birds of a feather I forbid to do battle.

Such, if you'll have them, are the honours I offer.
For the good *you* do, good returns and good god-gifts,
a share in this country the gods above cherish.

CHORUS

The ancient conscience
pushed underground.
The ancient conscience
dishonoured, despised.

My nostrils snort
with rage at my shame

Terrible anguish
bores under my ribs.

Night!   Mother!
Listen!   My cry!

The new he-gods
with their fouls in the ring
have robbed me of honours
making me nothing.

ATHENA

I'm making you offers which I'll go on repeating
so that you'll never have any grounds for complaining
that you, an old she-god, were spurned and dishonoured
by me a young she-god, nor cast out by my people.
But if you have any respect for persuasion
and feel its soothing charm as I'm speaking,

and the linctus of language can placate you and lull you,
you'll decide to remain. But if you don't want to
it wouldn't be right to bring down on this city
your grudge or your anger, or harm to the people,
when you've been offered a share in the land here
with a full portion of honour now and for ever.

I

CHORUS
What kind of shrine did you say I'd possess?

ATHENA
One free from suffering. Will you say yes?

2

CHORUS
And if I say yes what powers will I wield?

ATHENA
You'll make them flourish, flock, family and field.

3

CHORUS
Would you entrust such powers to *me*?

ATHENA
Yes, and prosper the fortunes of each devotee.

4

CHORUS
These powers, will you pledge they'll endure?

ATHENA
I'd make no offers if I weren't sure.

5

CHORUS
You're beginning to charm me. My anger subsides.

ATHENA
Live in this land and win more friends besides.

6
CHORUS
What charm for this land would you like me to chant?
ATHENA
Nothing where darkness is dominant.

Bring blessings from earth, sea-billows and sky.
Let the wind warm the land as sun-filled sou'westers,
let farm-fields and flocks always be fruitful
and never fail folk who will farm them in future,
and as the land prospers so will the people,
especially those who give gifts to your godstones.
Like a green-fingered gardener tending his garden
I let the good grow, and nip the bad as it's budding.
I see that the good's wants get well enough watered,
protect their green life-lot from all blight and croprot.

Your part's to prosper my people in peace-time,
and mine, when the time comes for war-cries and weapons,
is to make certain my city's triumphant.

CHORUS
I'll share in the homeland of Pallas Athena
and not degrade a city
that all powerful Zeus and Ares the War God
make guardians of godstones,
Greece's great glory.
I pray the golden sun
make the earth burst open,
the ground gush with good life-gifts
harvest after harvest.

ATHENA
I act on behalf of a people I cherish
and instal among them these implacable spirits
whose province has been and is to manage mankind.
A man feels their onslaught but not where it comes from.
Crimes from the past get him hauled up before them.

And though he bursts his lungs with loud shouting
their silent grudge grinds him down into nothing.

CHORUS

And no searing winds strip bare the orchards,
no scorching heat burn the new buds dry.
May Pan prosper the sheepfolds
doubling the increase at lambing
and Hermes of windfalls and godsends
disclose the rich streaks of silver.

ATHENA

Listen to what the Furies, the *Furies,* are pledging.
The Fury's a force both with the high he-gods
and with the powers beneath the earth's crust.
Anyone can see how they work among mortals –
one man's life-lot's as bright as a ballad,
another's life is one blinded with tears.

CHORUS

I ban the death that descends too early
and cuts down a man who's barely reached manhood.

Grant good bed-bonds to girls that are graceful,
you she-gods of life-lot, sisters and she-kin,
both beings the offspring of one mother, Night.
You are present in every household,
at the family's feast-rites for death and delivery,
at the birth, and the death and the bedbond.
You are the most rightfully honoured of she-gods.

ATHENA

These she-gods of all gods willing such good things!

How grateful I am that Persuasion was guiding
my tongue and my lips when they were resistant.
The Zeus of debates and assemblies presided
turning a battle to a debate about blessings,
the rivalry now only vying to bless best.

CHORUS

May faction, sedition
for ever flesh-hungry,
civil disturbance,
cycles of slaying,
never bray in this city,
its dust never gulp
the blood of its people,
the state get ripped open
by the rages of bloodgrudge,
a chainlink of murder.
Let the linking be love-bonds,
common likes, common hatreds,
a group bond against
the troubles men suffer.

ATHENA

Listen!   They're learning to bless, groping for goodness.
I foresee great future good in these fearful faces.
If you show them the kindness they show you,
your city's set fair on the straight road of justice.

CHORUS

Fare well, fare well, grow wealthy, grow great,
fare well, citizens so close to Zeus,
favourites of his favourite she-child.
Under the wings of Athena grow wise
with her father looking on you with favour.

ATHENA

Fare well to you too.   Now I'll lead the way
to show you the chambers in the deep cavern
by the light of the torches of those who'll escort you.
Now, sped on your way by the savour of godsops,
go to your underground shrines in the rock-hill
and there keep what will harm Athens imprisoned
and set free only what will help her to victory.

Children of Cranaus, who reside on the rock-hill,
escort on their way these welcome guest-strangers,
and give them the good will that they'll give to you.

CHORUS

Fare well, fare well, mortals, immortals,
all of you here in the city of Pallas.
Only give grace to your new guest-strangers
and you'll never lack any luck in your life-lot.

ATHENA

I endorse all you pray for on behalf of my city.
And now by the light of the blazing torch-beacons,
I'll escort you to your underground chambers
along with those who tend to my godstone,
the flowers of Athens, once land of Theseus,
the women of Athens, girls, mothers, old women,
will come as a glorious group in procession.
Drape our honoured guest-strangers in robes of deep
    sea-red
and lead then with torchlight held up before you,
so that these Furies, who turned out so kindly,
will reside and show love, and bless Athens for ever.

PROCESSION OF WOMEN

Go to your home, children of Night,
honoured with music and torchlight.

Silence while the Kind Ones pass.

Go to your home, underground and primeval
honoured by sacrifice and libation.

Silence while the Kind Ones pass.

Grave powers, gracious and kindly,
attended by torches, follow us home.

Now echo our chorus, raise your own cry!

Peace between the Kind Ones and Athens!
ZEUS/FATE, high he-god and she-god
together helped all this to happen.

Now echo our chorus, raise your own cry!

THE COMMON CHORUS

Introduction

HECUBA TO US

The one performance, the unique occasion, of an ancient Greek play may strike us now as an almost reckless encounter with the inexorability of transience, yet in its very uniqueness lies the secret of the glory of the continuously passing present of performance. We know, in proscenium terms, that once the curtain has risen it has to fall. The current obsession with televising and videoing stage performances almost inevitably undermines the true nature of the theatrical. But the play published here, conceived as it was for the National Theatre's Olivier stage, entered oblivion rather as unlucky players of *Monopoly* enter jail without passing GO. It entered the stream of oblivion without ever having been buoyed on it for even the brief unique performance that most Greek tragedies and comedies were designed to have.

My previous piece, *The Trackers of Oxyrhynchus*, although it later found a brief life on the same NT stage, had been originally conceived in this spirit, for one unique performance in the ancient stadium high up the slope of Delphi, a site considered by the ancients as the centre of the world. How differently the energies of performer and audience are concentrated if they know there is only one chance to give or receive the occasion. It was in this spirit too that the papyrus of the ancient play was in that version literally destroyed by fire, and it was in this spirit that the company prevented three rather peeved TV crews from filming what we all thought then would be the first and final performance, so that everything was committed to the care of memory, that last resort in the ruins of time. As Spenser wrote:

For deedes doe die, how ever noblie donne
And thoughts of men do as themselves decay,
But wise wordes, taught in numbers for to runne,
Recorded by the Muses, live for ay . . .

And elsewhere, in 'The Ruins of Time':

For not to have been dipt in Lethe Lake
Could save the sonne of Thetis for to die:
But that blinde bard did him immortal make
With verses, dipt in deaw of Castalie.

All of us in the *Trackers of Oxyrhynchus* company drank literally the 'deaw of Castalie' before the performance at the sacred spring beneath the towering, red-hued Phaedriades at the beginning of the Sacred Way in Delphi. It was to give inspiration for that one occasion. But then surprisingly the play, although in a form altered for the specifics of the South Bank, was given more performances, and what was intended to have been the last took place, again with local textual additions, in Carnuntum near Vienna, Austria, on 19 May 1990. Carnuntum was a former frontier post of the Roman Empire and the military base of three emperors, as commemorated on the label of the local Grüner Veltliner, wine grown by Josef Köck, the *Dreikaiserwein,* emblazoned with the heads of Marcus Aurelius (161–180), Septimis Severus (193–211) and Diocletian (284–305). Marcus Aurelius, when he was in Carnuntum in AD 173, during his campaign to keep the marauding Marcomanni and Quadi respectful of the imperial border and stay on their side of the Danube, wrote, in his quieter moments, what became Chapter Three of his *Meditations* in Greek. My original intention for the one performance in Delphi had been extended to Carnuntum, and on both sites there were associations of transience, in the spirit of which I had originally conceived the unique performance. At Carnuntum Marcus Aurelius was thinking about the inexorability of time and he wrote:

Hippocrates, after curing many sicknesses, himself fell sick and died. The Chaldean astrologers foretold the death of many persons, then the hour of fate overtook them also. Alexander, Pompeius and Julius Caesar, after so often utterly destroying whole towns and slaying in the field myriads of horse and foot, themselves also one day departed from life. Heraclitus, after many speculations about the fire which should consume the Universe, was waterlogged by dropsy, poulticed himself with cow-dung and died. Vermin killed Democritus; another kind of vermin Socrates.

Around that same time Pausanias, the physician from Asia Minor who wrote a guide to Greece in the second century AD, saw the ancient stadium of Delphi, where we had played our first performance. It must then have just been refurbished with marble from Mount Pentelicus by Herodes Atticus, who died around the same time as Marcus Aurelius. All that is left of that marble refurbishment is the chisel marks in the quarry from which the marble was taken. When Sir James Fraser, who edited Pausanias and checked on his descriptions at the end of the nineteenth century, stood on the site of the stadium he reflected that the marble had 'probably gone in the way of so many other ancient marbles in Greece into the lime kiln'.

Whenever I work at the National Theatre I usually walk to the South Bank from Clapham Common, and every morning as I walk along the Thames from Vauxhall I pass groups of Japanese tourists doing the same thing, taking pictures of each other from a position that gives them a shot of Big Ben in the background. The succession of clicks like an orchestra of clave-wielders tuning up always makes me go forward to rehearsals committed to the essential transience of theatre. Theatre can only celebrate its presented moments by embracing its own ephemerality. In that is the glory of performance. Theatre has to be given and received at the moment of delivery. This is its essence. The mythologies of fame are mere yellowing calling cards. When the world-famous conductor Herbert von Karajan died in 1989 his fellow conductor Sir George Solti observed: 'This year everyone talks about him. Next year it'll be 50 per cent less. The third year no one will say anything. This is the human fate, to be forgotten.' Heinrich Heine was appalled by the vision that he had of his *Book of Songs* being used by the grocer for packets into which to pour tobacco and snuff, rather as Ragueneau's wife, Lise, uses the manuscripts of her husband's poetic friends to wrap pastries and tarts in, in Act Two of *Cyrano de Bergerac*. Addison, reviewing a show at Drury Lane for the *Spectator* in 1711, wrote of 'a dozen showers of snow which, I am informed, are the plays of many unsuccessful poets artificially cut and shredded for that use'. At the National Theatre stage door I came across a rehearsal draft of *The Trackers of Oxyrhynchus*, torn into three-inch squares, being used to write telephone messages on. And Jack Shepherd, who played Grenfell/Apollo in the production, told me that when he had been filming a legal drama the brief that his lawyer character carried was made up of old pages of a script of mine for a film/poem about death in Naples called *Mimmo Perella non è piu*. None of these fates is quite the indignity that Lord Chesterfield mentions in his letters of 1747 where, advising his son not to waste time, he cites the good example of a gentleman who purchased 'a common Horace, of which he tore off gradually a couple of pages, carried them with him to that necessary place, read them first, and then sent them down as a sacrifice to Cloacina'. The Egyptian *fellaheen* employed by Grenfell and Hunt in the excavations in *Trackers* used the papyri of Plato and Euripides as compost for their greens, and in the final version for the NT in 1991 the rubbish tips of the South Bank contained the poster, programme and text of the play being performed.

The play contained the rubbished version of itself. Sometimes, walking from rehearsals, either via Covent Garden or via Waterloo, I came across other emblems of the ephemerality of theatrical endeavours I had been associated with. Walking past the now padlocked, dilapidated Lyceum I look up and take wry note of a piece of flapping poster saying 'The Best Show in Britain, no less' of the National's *Mysteries* that transferred there in 1985. Or walking through Cardboard City to catch the Underground at Waterloo I see the now scarcely recognisable features of Edward Petherbridge and Sian Thomas and the fragmentary letters ON . . . IS of my own name on what was once a poster for my version of *The Misanthrope*, revived at the NT in 1989. On a concrete pillar in front of the crates and cartons that are the refuge of the homeless is the already disintegrating papyrus of a *Trackers* poster: . . . CKERS, it says. It is also heavily graffitied, and in one place in smaller writing, to accommodate the message to the medium, the phallus of the leaping Silenus has been pencilled *Mrs Thatcher* – who has herself now entered the stream of oblivion meditated upon by Marcus Aurelius.

This contemplation of the ruins of time is a common theme in all literature and thought. As the philosopher George Santayana wrote:

> The spectacle of change, the triumph of time, or whatever we may call it, has always been a favourite theme for lyric and tragic poetry, and for religious meditation. To perceive universal mutation, to feel the vanity of life, has always been the beginning of seriousness. It is the condition of any beautiful, measured, or tender philosophy.

It is to find the meaning of suffering in such a context that Greek tragedy exists. And out of the same source comes the laughter of comedy and the celebration of the satyr play. Closer to our own precarious days the theme of transience was taken up by one who certainly helped us to become more fearfully aware of it. The 'father' of the atom bomb, J. Robert Oppenheimer, was thinking perhaps of a vista longer than the one his own invention shortened when he wrote:

> Transience is the backdrop for the play of human progress, for the improvement of man, the growth of his knowledge, the increase of his power, his corruption and partial redemption. Our civilisations perish; the carved stone, the written word, the heroic act fade into a memory of a memory and in the end are gone; this house, this earth in which we live will one day be unfit for human habitation as the sun ages and alters.
>
> *Uncommon Sense* (1984)

Certainly Oppenheimer's invention, unleashed upon the world in 1945, made a great many people feel that we did not have to wait for the ageing of the sun for the earth to become unfit for human habitation. The American psychologist Robert Jay Lifton, who studied the survivors of Hiroshima, showed that when our sense of 'symbolic immortality' is undermined and threatened, as it was in the Cold War after 1945, then our 'confidence in the overall continuity of life gives way to widespread death imagery'.

It was into this new context of the old idea of transience experienced in the worst times of the Cold War nuclear confrontation that I chose to put the *Lysistrata* of Aristophanes and *The Trojan Women* of Euripides together as *The Common Chorus*. I imagined them played and performed by the women of the peace camp at Greenham Common for the benefit of the guards behind the wire who were defending the silos where the weapons of our ultimate extinction were stored. Nuclear weapons gave mankind what Hannah Arendt called a 'negative solidarity, based on the fear of global destruction'. Their presence also made us stare into the face of oblivion in a way unlikely to be redeemed in the memory of those whom Hecuba addresses as 'later mortals', and into whose hearts and songs she commits the suffering of her women at the end of *The Trojan Women*. As my Lysistrata is made to say in the text published here:

> In the Third World War we'll destroy
> not only modern cities but the memory of Troy,
> stories that shaped the spirit of our race
> are held in the balance in this missile base.
> Remember, if you can, that with man goes the mind
> that might have made sense of the Hist'ry of Mankind.
> It's a simple thing to grasp: when we're all dead
> there'll be no further pages to be read,
> not even leaflets, and no peace plays like these,
> no post-holocaust Aristophanes.

And no post-holocaust Euripides either! No Hecuba entrusting her story to the future. That moment in *The Trojan Women* was central to my understanding of how the tragedy and comedy produced within four years of each other might be played together. When everything has been taken away from the women of Troy, with their city in flames, the death of all their menfolk, the execution of the child Astyanax, it is left to the one who could be said to have lost most to seek for one last redeeming idea. Hecuba says:

> εἰ δὲ μὴ θεὸς
> ἔστρεψε τἄνω περιβαλὼν κάτω χθονός
> ἀφανεῖς ἂν ὄντες οὐκ ἂν ὑμνηθεῖμεν ἂν
> μούσαις ἀοιδὰς δόντες ὑστέρων βροτῶν

(1242–5)

If we hadn't suffered we wouldn't be songs for 'later mortals'. The song for later mortals is the tragedy being performed. Hecuba addresses the Athenian audience of 415 BC across time from an already mythical and long-ruined Troy. They are the very 'later mortals' whose songs

are Hecuba's redemption. Every time the play is played
through history in all its versions the 'mortals' become
'later'. And we are the latest mortals now. We are in that
long line of 'later mortals' first addressed in 415 BC as if
from the present suffering of the Trojan Women of
centuries before. We are the latest mortals who guarantee
that the suffering was not in vain, and that the chain of
commemorative empathy is unbroken. The Trojan women
exit into the imagination and memory of each audience
whenever the play is played. Hecuba leads her women into
theatricality and into the only redemptive meaning known
to the pre-Christian world and, I might add, to our
post-Christian world. The pathos of her address to us in
our lateness in mortal history is all the more precariously
and transiently poised when it is made outside the base
where a destructive force is housed that will undermine
history and human memorialisation permanently. It becomes an appeal for the past not to be betrayed along with
the present and the future. As Lysistrata says:

> Since 1945 past and present are the same.
> And it doesn't matter if it's 'real' or a play –
> imagination and reality both go the same way.
> So don't say it's just a bunch of ancient Greeks.
> It's their tears that will be flowing down your cheeks.

In order to place the tragedy in this context I had to use
the contemporaneity of comedy to first establish the parallels and allow the play to pass from Greenham to Greece
and back in a fluid way.

If I am a serious witness of mutability and the ruins of
time I have to confess that I believe that versions of
ancient plays have to be redone for each new production.
There exists the basic culturally deciduous network of
stems and branches of the original, which itself changes
shape through growth and atrophy, and there is also the
foliage for each new season's versions. I live on yet

another border of the Roman Empire, and often walk on the wall built by the Emperor Hadrian to divide the Romans from the barbarians. It has survived, or not, in various ways, ways that affect all monuments whether physical or spiritual. There are portions that have survived pretty well and can give a reasonable idea of the scale of the original enterprise. Then there are the bits of it – stones, milestones, altars, columns – from the wall and adjoining camps that have been recycled to become barns, farmhouses, pig-troughs, gateposts, even church fonts and church pillars as at Chollerton. And there are sections – like the marble hewn from Mount Pentelicus to make the stadium seats in Delphi – which have gone into the lime-kilns, some of which you can still see, to become mortar for building new structures in a modern style, or fertiliser for depleted fields. Representing an ancient play uses all these processes. Sections can be revealed intact. Some are cannibalised as elements of modern structures, some transformed into bonding or fertilising matter, generating new growth here and now.

Twenty years before I embarked on *The Common Chorus* I had done another version of the *Lysistrata* of Aristophanes for a group of student actors and village musicians in northern Nigeria in collaboration with the Irish poet James Simmons. The text is unperformable outside Nigeria and was responsive to the tensions that later erupted into a devastating civil war. Contemporaneity is essential to the serious comedy of Aristophanes. The political situation has to be mortally serious. His play was written in the twenty-first year of the Peloponnesian War that eventually destroyed Athens. And neither his play nor that of Euripides prevented it happening.

A women's peace magazine produced from Brighton in the 1980s called itself *Lysistrata,* and there was in its pages a reaching backwards to the suffering of the past, meeting, if you like, the hands held out by Hecuba to the 'later mortals' from the ruined city of Troy. There was a sense expressed by these women and the women of Greenham that 'we are all interdependent, we are all responsible for each other, how delicate the strands, how strong the web'. Their historical empathy with the suffering of the past and their concern for the very existence of mortals later than themselves gave me the essential spirit to allow the play to move between Greenham and Athens in 411 BC. If the tragedy I had wanted to perform with the comedy declared that remembrance was the one human redemption, then the comedy, in the spirit of the peace women's banners at the Cenotaph, declared that REMEMBRANCE IS NOT ENOUGH, and all their effort in the play is to prevent that dark, soul-rending effort of remembrance from becoming necessary once again in human history – if remembrance itself could survive the ruins of time in any Third World War. In that spectacular photograph of Greenham women dancing hand in hand in a circle on top of a missile silo I like to imagine both Lysistrata and Hecuba.

As Jeffrey Henderson tells us in his study of Aristophanic sexual imagery, 'of several words used to indicate the cunt whose basic notion is that of an opening or passageway, θυρα [= gate] is the most popular'. And it is outside the gate into the missile base that the Greenham women pitched their benders. On one notorious occasion the women padlocked the main gate. The hilarious sequence of soldiers and police trying to re-open the gate can be seen on the film *Carry Greenham Home*. I use the action to represent the occupation of the Acropolis in the ancient original and symbolically to represent the women closing the entrances to their bodies. As Henderson also points out, the most notable use of θυρα is in the *Lysistrata*, where it is used to mean the gate of the Acropolis and the gates of love.

Leaflets inviting women to come and demonstrate at Greenham by linking arms and forming a chain around the perimeter fence declared that 'we will turn our backs on it. Turn our backs on all the violence and destructive power it represents . . . ' In theatrical terms, by turning their backs on the base the women turn themselves towards the audience. Thus they are continually 'presented', as they would have been in the masks worn in the original ancient production. Also the Greenham women faced forwards in order to scrutinise those who passed by the base on foot or in cars for signs of support. In this way I could find a ready motivation for the actors to face outwards and play out to the audience. The Cruise missile bunkers had three metal shuttered openings, like the back of the Olivier stage. I had intended these to be raised at the end of the second play, *The Trojan Women*, to let out the headlights of the convoy bearing the missiles, blinding the audience before the final blackout.

I imagine the first play, the comedy, the *Lysistrata*, played with all its robust Aristophanic language as a direct response to the sexually abusive language that was continually directed at the women, especially when trying to sleep, by the guards at the wire. I spoke to Greenham women about this, and it is recorded by Caroline Blackwood in her book on Greenham, *On the Perimeter* (1984):

'I am so tired,' said Pat. 'We had such an awful night with the soldiers. They shouted at us all night. They just couldn't stop. It was sexual, of course. It's always sexual.'

Apparently many of the soldiers were under the impression that all the peace women were only camping round the base because they wanted to sleep with them. This was such a vain and deluded assumption, it was comic. Never had any group of men seemed less sexually desirable than the defenders of the Cruise missile when seen from the peace camps.

What is the matter with these soldiers, I wondered when I later heard them bellowing their horrible obscenities. Presumably they didn't carry on like dirty-minded schoolboys at home. Yet the peace women brought out everything that was sadistic and infantile in these men. The sex war that was raging on the peri-meter was a very ugly and cruel one.

And, of course, behind these British guards, in the heart of the base, were the USAF personnel, recreating the comforts of the USA and singing the kind of songs that appeared for sale in a publication from the USAF 77th Tactical Fighter Squadron at Upper Heyford. The following are typical fare:

I fucked a dead whore by the roadside
I knew right away she was dead
The skin was all gone from her tummy
The hair was all gone from her head.

And as I lay down there beside her,
I knew right away I had sinned.
So I pressed my lips to her pussy
And sucked out the wad I'd shot in.

Sucked out, sucked out.
I sucked out the wad I'd shot in, shot in,
Sucked out, sucked out,
I sucked out the wad I'd shot in.

Or:

I love my wife, yes I do, yes I do, I love her truly.
I love the hole she pisses through,
I love her ruby lips and her lily white tits,
And the hair around her asshole.
I'd eat her shit gobble, gobble, chomp, chomp,
With a rusty spoon, with a rusty spoon.

Not all the songs are of masculine sexuality. There are battle cries also:

Phantom flyers in the sky
Persian pukes prepare to die,
Rolling in with snake and nape.*
Allah creates but we cremate.

North of Tehran, we did go
When FAC said from below
'Hit my smoke and you will find
The Arabs there are in a bind.'

I rolled in at a thousand feet,
I saw those bastards, beating feet,
No more they'll pillage, kill and rape
'Cause we fried them with our nape.

I imagined such songs spluttering through the walkie-talkies of the British guards at the wire, songs with a Budweiser slur, coming from close to the silos where all the mod-cons of Milwaukee were available so that the Americans didn't have to feel they were actually abroad. We shall be glad to be rid of such songsters and the weapons they brought with them.

Unfortunately the Quick Reaction Alert – which involved at least one flight of nuclear-armed missiles being permanently in readiness – is not a common category in the world of theatre, as opposed to the theatre of war. There is no QRA at the RNT! By the time various managements had lingered over this text, the tension of a topical present and a tragic past had leached away into oblivion. Thankfully the Cold War has ended and my play has been marooned in its moment. The 'text', as Tarkovsky said of the film script, gets 'smelted' into performance. This text never went through that essential smelting process. If I wanted to do *Lysistrata* now, I might have to begin again with a third and totally different version. To recognise

---

*nape = napalm

197

that a performance text has to be done again and again is to acknowledge the transience, the flow, the ephemerality of all theatrical realisation. And it is in that spirit that I have to acknowledge also that the time for this particular version of the *Lysistrata* of Aristophanes has passed, with the thankful ending of the fearful Cold War that produced it. However, in July I received from friends in Dubrovnik *An Appeal for Peace in Croatia*. It was written on the opening night of a play: 'In these times of deafness in which the word that cries for peace and understanding has become inaudible, our company is playing *Hekuba* by Marin Džić – the tragedy of a mother at the end of an absurd war.' Hecuba is once more committing herself to later mortals, aware of their imminent mortality. And where Hecuba is then Lysistrata isn't far behind.

[1991]

Part One

ACT ONE

Darkness. Last part of the night. USAF Greenham Common. Spot illuminating a large letter C woven in the perimeter wire out of rags, biscuit wrapping, coloured papers.

> GUARD 1
> *(standing behind the letter C)*

Cock!

Spot illuminates a letter N woven into the perimeter wire.

> GUARD 2
> *(standing behind letter N)*

Nob!

Spot illuminates a letter D woven into the perimeter wire.

> GUARD 3
> *(standing behind letter D)*

Dick!

Pause.

> GUARD 1
> *(to Guard 2)*

Can't spell, you young uns of today.
Don't yer know that KNOB begins with a K.
NOB's got a K there in the front.

> GUARD 2

Nah, daft ha'porth, K's for Kunt.

GUARD 1

Cock!

GUARD 2

Nob!

GUARD 3

Dick!

GUARD 1

Christ, but I could do with a screw.
Too long on this job, my balls are turning blue.

GUARD 3

I tell you, mate, doing this patrol
doesn't give a bloke much chance of hole.

GUARD 1

And if you spend too long on this fucking wire
you'll find someone's been at home poking the wife's fire.

GUARD 3

Back there the cunt's all Yankie and it's booked
so as far as fucking fucking goes you're somewhat
    fucking fucked.

GUARD 1

Ay, back there in the base there's bags of US pussy.

GUARD 2

Who cares where it comes from. I'm not fussy!
I'm a shagaholic, me. Hey I saw a real beaut
in a Buick, Dolly Parton tits, cute, real cute.

GUARD 1

Cock!

GUARD 2

Nob!

GUARD 3

Dick!

*One of the walkie-talkies at the hips of the Guards
begins to sound with the noise of Americans enjoying
themselves. Males.*

GUARD 2

Hey, listen, you can hear 'em boozing in their mess.

GUARD 3

The whole place, back there, 's like a miniature US!

GUARD 1

Bloody shopping mall, like downtown Milwaukee.

More conviviality from the walkie-talkie.

GUARD 1
(*to Guard 2*)

For fuck's sake turn off that fucking walkie-talkie!

GUARD 1

Cock!

GUARD 2

Nob!

GUARD 3

Dick!

GUARD 1

When you go back there you're in for a surprise.
The stuff they've got. You won't believe your eyes.
And you won't believe how it's all so bloody clean.

To Guard 3.

Hey did you notice their 'rubber goods' machine?

GUARD 3

Durex, like?

GUARD I

No, that's the point, US rubberwear's
called *Trojans*. They call 'em *Trojans*, theirs.
I wanted to get a packet, like, just to have a look.
Would it take my 50p's, would it fuck.
The machine takes only US dimes and quarters.
I tell you I wouldn't take my wife or girl in.
Them Yanks, yer know, lock up your wives and daughters.
And it's all fucking dollars, mate, forget your fucking
    sterling.
Everything they've got back there's entirely Yank,
Yankee shops, *Budweiser* (deadly brew!) Yankee bank.

GUARD 3

Trojans? Funny name for spunkbags. What's it mean?
Never noticed the Yanks' rubber goods machine.

GUARD I

There's another sells *Maintain* 'with male desensitizer'
And some Yankee joker's drawn a sort of chart
for measuring, he calls it a 'cock-sizer',
and do yer know where the graduations start
for US 'Standard'? Two foot bloody six!
I tell yer, bloody Yanks, they're obsessed with their pricks.
Then under-bloody-neath it some swaggering shit's
scrawled 'Sub-standard sizes for sub-standard Brits.'

GUARD 3

Yer, funny. I suppose they think that that's a joke.
If I knew who'd written it I'd bloody bash the bloke.

Trojans?

To Guard 2.

Come on, Mastermind, you ought to know
you're the one with Geoger and Eng. Lit. (O).

GUARD 2

Troy were a city, wan't it, years and years ago?
Destroyed by fire, gutted, rubble, dust, debris.

GUARD 1

Could they do that to cities in whatever it was BC?
Didn't have no Poseidon, Polaris, Cruise,
so what did those bloody Trojans use?

GUARD 2

Greeks, Greeks destroyed Troy. Chucked pitch-pine
firebrands, started a blaze. Fire does fine.

GUARD 1

Ay, fire does fine. But all we have to do's
press a button and release one of their Cruise.

GUARD 3

Our Cruise, ours, it's supposed to be half ours
even though there are only the two superpowers.

GUARD 1

The scientists since what's their names . . . the Trojans'
day
have come up with fire concoctions in a very big way.

GUARD 3

They've concentrated fire so it can be hurled
at any place we're fighting anywhere in t' world.
What'll be next? They've perfected fire
and that's what we're guarding at this fucking wire.

GUARD 2

We can press the button and fucking fuck the lot
but the Greeks did alright without the stuff we've got.

GUARD 1

Ay, lad, we've come a long, long way
from rubbing sticks together to the fires of today.

GUARD 3

'istory's a pile of shit. I got F in mine.
I bet the first thing they did when Troy got took,
the first thing them Greeks did was fucking fuck.

GUARD 2

Well, I know the first thing that I'd do
after ten years on the firing line . . .

ALL
(*singing*)

Shag the women and drink the wine
inky-pinky parlez-vous!

GUARD 1

Christ, but I could do with a screw.
I've been so long on this job my balls are turning blue.

GUARD 1

Cock!

GUARD 2

Nob!

GUARD 3

Dick!

GUARD 3

Yes, I think on that score the meeting is agreed!

GUARD 2

I'd like to be remembered for some heroic deed
enshrined in some historian of the future's words.

GUARD 3

Yer, how you guarded Greenham Common against a
bunch of birds.

GUARD 2

George Medal, Victoria Cross, DSO and bar . . .

GUARD I
Well guarding Greenham Common won't get you very far.
This isn't your World War I. You're hardly at the front
defending the Cruise missile against a camp of cunt.

GUARD 2
There's no glory in soldiering any more,
we're just nannies to these nukes in a modern sort of war.
I'd sooner have been a hero in them old Trojan Wars
than stand here guarding missiles against a bunch of
    whores.
I'd sooner have been wounded in World War I or II
(not lost a leg or owt like that, a little wound would do)
gassed at Ypres, shrapnelled at the Somme
than listen to these bastards shrieking Ban the Bomb!

GUARD 3
Don't know about gas attacks, but talk about pong
those bloody peace women don't half smell strong.

GUARD I
Yer, they don't have baths and they eat a lot of *Heinz*.
There's hot air in their gobs, and gas from their behinds.

GUARD 3
Two extremes innit that us lot are between
your hypershowered Yank and your Ms Unclean.

GUARD I
Cleanliness is next to godliness is what they say.
Those Yanks have at least ten showers a bloody day.
Know nowt about godliness, but I know them loos
get a lot cleaner the nearer they are to Cruise.
And you know the filthy toilets that we have to use.

GUARD 3
Could be worse, old son, you might well have to shit,
like those poor bloody women do, over an earth pit.

GUARD I

I'll tell you summat that that word Trojan means
and it's a bit more serious than your johnny machines.
And it's nowt to do with your ancient overkill
put into Cinerama by Cecil B. De Mille.
1948. With Berlin still the trouble
and international tension starting to redouble,
your US brought their bombs

Out to Women.

                              that no one's going to ban
and to meet the crisis drew up the masterplan
to nuke from bases, like this one here in the UK,
seventy Soviet cities with what was then your bomb.
Called *War Plan Trojan*!! and I dare say
that that's where they get their Trojan from.
To remind them when their thoughts might tend to stray
to a little screwing that they serve the USA.
And to let them know in the middle of a go
that they have a sacred duty to nuke old Uncle Joe.

Pause.

GUARD 3

So what were it about, this fucking Trojan War?

GUARD 2

Some bit of skirt, I think, some fucking foreign whore
and half of bloody Greece perished at the front.

GUARD I

Ay, where there's trouble there's allus cunt.

GUARD 3

And look at these cunts in their bloody benders.
Greenham fucking Common, what a place to send us.

GUARD I

If we have to stay awake, why should these cunts be
   kipping?

Let's wake 'em up. And when they look then we start
  unzipping.

GUARD 1

Cock!

GUARD 2

Nob!

GUARD 3

Dick!

*Then they begin chanting their abuse directed at the
benders where the Greenham Women are trying to
sleep.*

GUARDS

Are you out there, Phyllis, come and give us a fuck?
Are you out there, Cynthia, come and give us a suck?

Camp-followers are yer, after military cocks
sucking off a sentry in his sentry box?

How would you like a nice shot of warm come
right down your tonsils, up your cunt, your bum?
The semen of he-men's superior to that
your stubby little hubby squirts into your twat.

Oh I can feel their little fannies start to ooze
when I unzip my flyfront and flash 'em my Cruise!

Are you out there, Phyllis, come and give us a fuck
Are you out there, Cynthia, come and give us a suck.

*Behind the Guards' taunting, repetitive abuse is a
support 'choir' of American male voices coming from
the walkie-talkies.*

US VOICES

By Poseidon, those lousy Lesbian limey chicks
I think they're into dildoes not genu-INE dicks!

Listen, you goddam father-sucking whore
don't you know what God has given you it for?

We didn't trounce you limeys back in 1776
to get the goddam run-around from a bunch of dykey
 chicks.

*The combined abuse of Guards and US Voices rises to
a crescendo. There is a light inside a bender. From the
bender emerges the Greenham Woman/Lysistrata. The
abuse is stilled. She places a home-made improvised
cock on the wire in front of each of the Guards. The
Guards stand behind the large cocks, which might be
a cross between traditional Greek phalluses and model
Cruise missiles. The Guards stand behind the
projecting cocks trying to ignore the fact that they
look ridiculous.*

GREENHAM WOMAN/LYSISTRATA

A Bacchic debauch . . .

Indicating Guards.

a booze-up as they'd say

would cause a ten-mile tailback on the motorway.
A pop

GUARD 3

 piss-up

LYSISTRATA

for Pan, with Uncle Sam

donating Bruce Springsteen and buckshee Babycham –
if that were the occasion the charas'd congest
the car parks. Or a *Coca-Cola* Fest.
All-night rock and complimentary bars
and Greenham would be overrun with gaggles of guitars.
All night rave-ups with bags of booze
and every gate at Greenham would have mile-long queues.
But now where are they? Where have the women gone?

GUARD 1

To a Lesbian vibratorthon!

GUARD 2

A jaunt with gigolos. A great sex spree.

GUARD 3

A genital joy-ride. Fucks for free!

GUARD 1

And Cruise-shape dildoes from the MOD!

Enter Greenham Woman/Kalonike.

GREENHAM WOMAN/LYSISTRATA

Well, Kalonike, at least there's you.

GREENHAM WOMAN/KALONIKE

Now what's got into you? You look so down.
The *Cosmo* beauty column says you're not to frown,
you'll get crowsfeet and wrinkles . . .

LYSISTRATA

O so what?

You know women are a pretty rotten lot.
I'm pissed off with women if you want to know.

GUARDS
(*from behind wire*)

Here we go, here we go, here we go!

LYSISTRATA

Maybe I am gloomy. Maybe there's good cause
and maybe we are, like *they* say, just a bunch of whores.
Maybe that lot are right in their horrible abuse.
We're good for one thing only. Otherwise no use.

KALONIKE

Let's be glad we're good for that.

LYSISTRATA

                          I made it clear
it was important so why aren't they all here?

KALONIKE

It's hard for a woman just to leave it all behind.
What'll happen to the kids preys on her mind.
She leaves notes on the fridge where *he* can't fail to see
on how to warm fish fingers for the children's tea.
Notes all over, you know a woman frets
in case *he* feeds the kids with Pal meant for the pets.
Piles of catfood with a note on all the lids;
this is for the pussies, don't feed it to the kids.
Don't give Mary broccoli. It brings her out in spots.
Make sure Mark ties his shoelaces with proper knots.
Make sure that Samantha and Jonathan eat
their veggies up before they get a sweet.
David – dentist's! Thursday – Bonzo – Vet!
Notes with big red letters: DON'T FORGET,
Make sure Janet takes her pumps for gym.
Things really fall apart if they're left to him.
The list of DON'T FORGETS a woman sticks
on the wall's even longer than their

   To Guards.

                              pricks!
All the billion details of the daily life
of your average unpaid slave, the British wife.
The billion details of 'domestic bliss'.

LYSISTRATA

Trivia! Trivia! Compared to this!

KALONIKE

What is *this*, then?

LYSISTRATA

   A pretty big affair.

GUARD 3
(*from behind wire*)
We can provide that, you lot over there!

GUARD 2
Got just the ticket for you, haven't we, sarge?

GUARD 1
Comes in three sizes . . .

GUARD 3
large . . .

GUARD 2
large . . .

GUARD 1
and LARGE!

LYSISTRATA
Maybe it's still too early. Maybe.

KALONIKE
Too early, Lysistrata, you're telling me.
It's still only 411 BC.

LYSISTRATA
In that case the fate of Greece, all Greece,
which means both Attica and the Peloponnese
depends on women . . .

KALONIKE
O we're done for then!

LYSISTRATA
We're even more done for if we depend on men.
Every Spartan is going to die . . .

KALONIKE
Hurray, that means an Athenian victory.

LYSISTRATA

Everyone in Boeotia will be killed.

KALONIKE

But not the eels
they're absolutely scrumptious. Spare the eels.

GUARD 3
(*from behind the wire*)

Do you notice what everything they think of 's like?
Now it's bloody eels! I bet that one's a dyke.

GUARD 2

Hey I've got something better than a Boeotian eel.
Come on over here, love, and have a little feel.

GUARDS

One day we'll have a weapon and that day isn't far
to destroy selective targets in the USSR,
zap the Bolshie's buildings (by Poseidon and by Cruise!)
but leave a few nice items that a feller could use
like all the fucking vodka and the fucking caviar
and a Rusky cunt or two for soldier's perks,
nutbloodycrackers, a Bolshoi ballerina,
and nuke these bloody Greenham Greeks but spare
the fucking ouzo and a few jars of retsina
and a few of the young ones in see-through underwear.

LYSISTRATA
(*to Guards*)

Look, we're trying to pretend that this is ancient Greece.
I wish you'd give us just a little bit of peace.

GUARD 1

You'll get peace if we keep these weapons, pet.

LYSISTRATA

Those weapons haven't been invented yet.
We're still in the age of shields and swords.

GUARD I

Well they're not going to keep back your barbarian hordes.

LYSISTRATA

I wish you'd just shut up!

GUARD I

Right, Your Ladyship.
Listen, lads, lay off and they might do us a strip.

LYSISTRATA

Yes, your idea of theatre stops at striptease.
This happens to be a play by Aristophanes.
So try to be quiet and listen, PLEASE!

GUARDS

Here we go, here we go, here we go!

LYSISTRATA

We're NEVER going.

KALONIKE

(*seeing the Women approaching*)
They're all coming though.
The women from Anagyra. At least they've come.

GUARD 2

(*whispering to other Guards*)
Anagyra's probably ancient Greek for Brum.

GREENHAM WOMAN/MYRRHINE

Are we early?

Frosty pause.

Sorry, I'm late. OK?

LYSISTRATA

We need urgent action without delay
and you lot keep us waiting half the day.

GREENHAM WOMAN/MYRRHINE

I couldn't find my clothes. I had to creep
about in the dark. The children were asleep.
So here I am. What's the great idea?

LYSISTRATA

Wait till the Boeotians and the Spartans are here.
Then I'll tell you all my long-thought-out schemes.

GUARD 3
(*out of corner of mouth*)

Where's Boeotia?

GUARD 1

Bradford.

GUARD 3

Sparta?

GUARD 2

I dunno . . . East Cheam.

LYSISTRATA
(*turning on Guards*)

Look, if this were 1986
and we were into international politics
then the women coming here would have to be from
the superpower countries who possess the BOMB.

MYRRHINE

Look who's here now. It's Lampito.

GUARDS

Here we go, here we go, here we go!

LYSISTRATA

Welcome, Spartan sister.

Looks her over.

Mmm. Nice thighs!

LAMPITO
(*US accent*)
Yeah, it's the aerobics and the dancercise
we're into over there. Don't let your hands wander.
That ass comes from workouts with Jane Fonda.
She

Indicates equally big USSR woman.

uses anabolic steroids though.

USSR WOMAN
Capitalist hyena, that is not so.

LYSISTRATA
We're trying to stay in Greece, Ms Lampito.

LAMPITO
OK, then let me introduce our . . . Boeotian friend.

GUARD I
How do you do, you've got a very nice rear end.

LAMPITO
She's from Corinth.

LYSISTRATA
Welcome.

LAMPITO
Did you call
this meeting?

LYSISTRATA
Yes, I did.

LAMPITO
OK then tell all.

LYSISTRATA
Yes, but first let me ask you, aren't you all sore
seeing your children's fathers going off to war?

All of us here, in one way or another,
as lover, wife, daughter, sister, mother,
have got to the point where we've seen
too many of our men fed to the war machine.

KALONIKE

My old man's been gone five whole months in Thrace.

MYRRHINE

It's seven since I've seen a man about the place.

LAMPITO

Mine comes home on leave with weapons and pack
and he's in at the front door and out the back.

LYSISTRATA

No lovers either. And the Milesians betrayed
the alliance and stopped the dildo trade.
Economic sanctions cut off our vibrators
and other DIY helps for man-starved masturbators.
So if I told you, that after much, much thought
I've hit on a solution, can I count on your support?

CHORUS OF WOMEN
1

I'd do anything.

ALL
And so would I.

2
Anything. Anything. I'd quite literally die.

3
I'll get the village church to hold a bring-and-buy.

4
I'll do anything, O anything at all.

5
I'll put up a petition in the village hall.

6

I'll make cakes to sell at the peace campaign stall.

7

I'll do a sponsored swim round the isles of Greece.

8

I'd give my right arm to bring about peace.

9

I'd do absolutely anything to make war cease.

10

I'll go canvassing support on my evenings free.

11

I'll do anything at all. You can count on me.

12

Tell me to do anything and I'll agree.

LYSISTRATA

Good! That's wonderful. I always knew
that I could count on every one of you.
So now I can tell you. I have a dream
that war will end, and a foolproof scheme.
Are you committed, are you forward-looking?
It's quite a sacrifice. It may come as a shock.
Let's have a show of hands, those who say yes!

*All the hands of the Women go up with simultaneous
enthusiasm.*

WOMEN

We're with you all the way. But tell us. We can't guess.

LYSISTRATA

For the sake of peace we have to give up . . . fucking!
And totally abstain, but totally, from COCK!

GUARD I

Let's check the other gates. I can't bear
hearing women, even Greenham women, fucking swear.

*Exit Guards. All the raised hands come down.
The Women back away.*

LYSISTRATA

Myrrhine, where are you off to? You've gone quite white.

MYRRHINE

You know, I've decided it's OK if men fight.

WOMEN

1

It's only a little war, Athens and Sparta.

2

It's not as if it's global, Lysistrata.

3

It'll be over by Christmas anyway.

LYSISTRATA

There's no such bloody thing as Christmas Day.
Christ isn't born yet. It's BC four-eleven.

WOMAN 4

Not give up cock. I love it, me. It's heaven.
I'd rather walk through fire.

LYSISTRATA
(*to nearest Woman*)
What about you?

WOMAN 5

I think I'd rather walk through fire too.

LYSISTRATA

Bloody women! Maybe those back there

(*the Guards*)

are right

and all we do want is what they shriek at us all night.
Lampito, Lampito, sister. It depends on you.

LAMPITO
Well, life's pretty terrible if you don't screw.
But peace has to come before sex, so, yes, OK.

LYSISTRATA
You're the only real woman here today.

KALONIKE
But if we do start living like a bunch of nuns
how will that make men lay down their guns?

LYSISTRATA
Their swords, dear, swords. But what's a name?
In essence all male weapons are the same.

LAMPITO
Remember one of Greece's chart-topping ditties
called 'Menelaus and Helen's Titties' . . .

   Sings.

He'd wanted to give vent
to the rage that he'd long stored
but when he saw her bodice rent
he cast away his sword.

Before the longed-for bosoms bare
he dropped his sword and stood,
and then he said: 'Your life I spare'
as she always knew he would.

Thousands of men went to their death
to win him back his bride.
Her titties took away his breath
and his sword fell to his side.

She opened buttons 1-2-3
and her breasts were half on view.

With all there was still left to see
how could he run her through?

LYSISTRATA

All we need's our perfumes, our pubic tweezers,
the outfits of the professional cock-teasers.
We'll be like their pin-ups on the barrack walls,
their wankers' fantasies, and make their balls
ache and turn blue till they can stand no more
and on the point of bursting they'll put an end to war.

*Picking up the 'Glamourwear' catalogue flung over
the wire.*

Look at these undies our friends behind the wire
recommend for escalating sexual desire.

MYRRHINE

O, yes, I've seen their ads. I know them, Lysistrata,
plain cover catalogue with complimentary garter.

LYSISTRATA
and
CHORUS OF WOMEN
*(reading from the 'Glamourwear' catalogue in
the voice of the male morons who write the copy)*

1	Excita	2	Kitten	3	Camilla	4	Venus
5	Gypsy Rose	6	Siam	7	Tigress	8	Rosie
9	Lavinia	10	Natasha	11	Amazon	12	Wildcat
13	Madame	14	Maxine	15	LYSISTRATA!		

I

Loll about the lounge in a deluxe lingerie.
You'll have your geezer grovelling we guarantee.

ALL

ONE SIZE FITS ALL

2

Loll about your lounge in our deluxe lingerie
and his goggles will be glued on you and not page three.

ALL

ONE SIZE FITS ALL

3

Divinely delicious this explosive G-string. Wow!
Have the courage to wear this and he'll soon kow-tow.

ALL

ONE SIZE FITS ALL

4

Designer-style scanties exquisite art deco –
a dekko through the open parts. Go on have a go!

ALL

ONE SIZE FITS ALL

5

All men seek adventure. Go on give him some.
Open-nipple playsuits, colours: peach and plum!

ALL

ONE SIZE FITS ALL

6

Lounge about in this lace-fronted camisole –
more than a match for any feller's self-control.

ALL

ONE SIZE FITS ALL

7

Dress up in this one to serve his evening meal.
Tempting open crotch for extra man-appeal.

ALL

ONE SIZE FITS ALL

8

Open-crotch panties in gold lamé –
wear it when he comes home tonight and make his day.

ALL

ONE SIZE FITS ALL

9

In enticing black with polka dots this half-cup basque
will set you up a treat for your titillating task.

ALL

ONE SIZE FITS ALL

10

Partially open panties give a hint of you know what.
Just the way men like their dinners . . . served up hot.

ALL

ONE SIZE FITS ALL

11

Order number 40A, colours: mauve and peach.
Gets to those other parts mere undies never reach.

ALL

ONE SIZE FITS ALL

12

A leotard in leopard with strategic scoops –
just the thing, darling, for tripping with the troops.

ALL

ONE SIZE FITS ALL

13

Black and glittering and very very glam –
come on heavy with him as the leatherclad Madame.

ALL

ONE SIZE FITS ALL

14

Slinky catsuit clings to every feline curve.
You'll get the jungle din-dins that you deserve.

ALL

ONE SIZE FITS ALL

15

Suspenders and black stockings with straight black seams
guaranteed (years of research) to gratify his dreams.

ALL

ONE SIZE FITS ALL

16

With little gusset buttons these pink silk cami-nicks
will get your geezer going in a couple of ticks.

ALL

ONE SIZE FITS ALL

17

Suggestive little bows untied with ease
and a strategic gold tassel for an extra touch of tease.

ALL

ONE SIZE FITS ALL

18

Camisole in lamé and lurex mesh –
flash your flesh in this and he'll soon get fresh.

ALL

ONE SIZE FITS ALL

19

This little crotchless scanty's trimmed with fur.
Tease your tired Tarzan. Groovy! Grrrrr!

ALL

ONE SIZE FITS ALL

20

Special occasion sporran, O och aye –
wear it G-string fashion and wait for fur to fly.

ALL

ONE SIZE FITS ALL

21

And this little number with a touch of class
shows half of your pussy and the whole of your arse.

LYSISTRATA

So that takes care of the uniforms we'll wear.
Now gather round me. I want you all to swear
a solemn oath, never to fuck again
until war's been abolished by the men.
I swear all men, husband, lover or gigolo.

WOMEN

I swear all men, husband, lover or gigolo.

LYSISTRATA

If he comes near me with a hard-on will get a firm NO.

Pause.

If he comes near me with a hard-on, continue please.

KALONIKE

O all these approaching hard-ons make me weak at
the knees.

LYSISTRATA

I swear to live without it, entirely fucking-free.

WOMEN

I swear to live without it, entirely fucking-free.

LYSISTRATA
And slink about the lounge in the sheerest lingerie.

WOMEN
And slink about the lounge in the sheerest lingerie.

LYSISTRATA
Until his thing starts smoking he's so on fire.

WOMEN
Until his thing starts smoking he's so on fire.

LYSISTRATA
But not give in an inch to his passionate desire.

WOMEN
But not give in an inch to his passionate desire.

LYSISTRATA
And if he forces me against my will.

WOMEN
And if he forces me against my will.

LYSISTRATA
I won't fuck him back but just lie still.

WOMEN
I won't fuck him back but just lie still.

LYSISTRATA
I'll never ever wrap my thighs around his eyes.

WOMEN
I'll never ever wrap my thighs around his eyes.

LYSISTRATA
Or let him up the back however hard he tries.

WOMEN
Or let him up the back however hard he tries.

LYSISTRATA
and
CHORUS OF WOMEN

No blow-jobs, no hand-jobs, not even kisses
until he's going crazy for all he misses.

No slurping cunnilingus – cunnilingus, sister,
isn't that a bit of a tongue-twister –

No slurping cunnilingus, no soixante-neuf,
no togetherness of motion like the surfboard and the surf.

No soixante-neuf not even soixante-huit.
It's going in the freezer what he likes to eat.

No soixante-neuf, not even soixante-sept.
An unending hard-on's all he's going to get.

No soixante-neuf, not even soixante-six,
until he gives his promise to work for Peace.

No soixante-neuf, not even soixante-cinq
and strict surveillance so he doesn't wank!

No soixante-neuf, it's all soixante zero
until he stops behaving like a warlike hero.

No nothing, chum, closed legs and closed doors
until your mind is open to ending wars.

Your little prick's not going through its paces
until you've put an end to missile bases.

No generosity, no opening wide
until the world is free from impending genocide.

It's a headache (it's ballsache!) every night, my dear,
until you agree to a nuclear all clear.

From Athens to London, LA to Leningrad
if you've got a hard-on, mate, that's just too bad.

Take note Athenian Reagan, and Spartan Gorbachev
there's a female moratorium on having it off.

We're going to make sure that your balls turn blue
you'll suffer severe groinitis before we're through.
But when it's all over, you will only thank us
when we're making love together, and once more
you're in our beds, in a world with no war,
relieved of the strain of being warmongering wankers.

*Three Older Women now cut the wire, enter the base,
and occupy the sentry box, taking advantage of the
absence of the Guards.*

LAMPITO
What are those women doing in the base?

LYSISTRATA
Protesting against the spiralling arms race.
Our sisters are taking over the sentry box
and we'll lock the 'Acropolis' with cycle locks.
And while we're doing that, off you lot trot
on the Spartan equivalent of Aeroflot.
We'll get things going here and while you're gone
influencing the Spartan Pentagon,
we'll lock those gates, and *these*

(*cunts*)

                              and locked they stay
until we Greeks of Greenham get our way.

WOMEN
They'll send the law. No chance. Them and us.

LYSISTRATA
Let them send the forces and the fuzz.
No threats, abuse, or anything they use
will make us open up till they abolish Cruise.

They may force those gates open. *These*
are staying firmly shut till every man agrees
never to make war, and only then
will we open our locked gates and let in men.

227

*The Women outside the wire place bike locks on the
gates. One of the three Older Women who have
occupied the sentry box climbs on to the roof and
unfurls a peace banner, maybe that one which reads
REMEMBRANCE IS NOT ENOUGH. Guard 1 appears,
his walkie-talkie spluttering US obscenities. He rattles
the gates to no avail.*

GUARD 1

Now look what those bloody women have gone and done.
God! I sometimes wish they'd let me use my bloody gun.

*Guard 1 runs off. The Women sing. Then from deep
in the base come the sounds of the First World War,
the explosions, ricochets, shells, gas rattles, Maxim
guns. From the deep central entrance we see moving
towards us in slow motion the three who are now to
become three World War I Veterans. When they enter,
they are wearing the gas-masks of World War I, British
issue. As they move downstage the sounds of World
War I grow fainter. They approach, remove their
masks, and start marching with rifles. As they draw
near the gate they become old men, the kind of World
War I Veterans we still might see marching proudly,
if arthritically, past the Cenotaph on Remembrance
Sunday. When they stand behind the cocks on the
wire, the cocks detumesce and grow limp.*

WORLD WAR I VETERAN 1

Keep in step, old comrades, though now we're somewhat
  older
and these World War issue rifles are heavy on the shoulder.
First-class fighting men we were, young heroic fighters
slowed down a little now by rheumatics and arthritis.
Not so chipper maybe when it comes to up a hill,
joints being rusty, but I bet you, with a bit of drill,
we could present and slope and shoulder arms still.

THE COMMON CHORUS

WORLD WAR I VETERANS

1

Are we still up to giving these here Greenham wenches
a taste of what we gave the Boche in the Great War
    trenches?

2

Did our comrades suffer, did we trounce the Boche
to live to see these gals preaching pacifistic tosh?

US VOICE

And we didn't trounce you limeys back in 1776
to get the goddam runaround from a bunch of dykey
    chicks.

WORLD WAR I VETERANS

3

Did we volunteer for action, did we sign on, did we serve
to let women trespass on this masculine preserve?

4

Did we lose our youth, did we win against the Hun
to live to see the soldier made the butt of filthy fun?

5

We loved our dear old Blighty and the lasses we defended
but look now at these women here and how the
    country's ended.

6

We may look harmless now with our bad legs and arthritis
but once we stood erect and were proud to be good
    fighters.

7

We saw our comrades bloated and their bodies gnawed
    by rats.
You've no idea what war is, you pacifistic twats!

8

You go on about abolishing defence and guns
and you'll leave Britain open to tomorrow's warring Huns.

9

And after all our suffering and we got our demobs
we came back home to Blighty and found women in
    our jobs.

10

We came back home from the horrors of the trenches
and found women, wenches, manhandling our wrenches.

11

Pulling our levers, tightening our screws
and now, to cap it all, shrieking NO MORE CRUISE.

12

Were we gassed at Ypres, were we shrapnelled at the
    Somme
to have our daughters and granddaughters yelling
    Ban the Bomb!

13

Did the lads who shared our billets lay down their
    precious lives
to have this military Acropolis occupied by wives?

14

If we only had our Maxim I tell you for a starter
I'd mow down that amazon Lysi-fucking-strata.

15

(Language, Drances,* lots of ladies out in front.
Don't let me hear any bollocks, fuck or cunt.)

---

*A name in the original Aristophanes.

16

If I were a lad again I'd be proud to serve the Queen
and I'd turn these women yeller with a few whiffs of
    chlorine.

US VOICES

Listen, you old limeys to your Uncle Sam's advice –
get yourselves Cruise missiles with a cunt-seeking device.

Failing that a canister of chlorine gas
from the good old days, and failing that your ass.

The trouble with you guys is the goddam way
you turn all world history into Remembrance Day.

The World War I Veterans unpack a canister of gas.

WORLD WAR I VETERANS

Ay, gas, 22 April 1915
that was the date the Huns first used chlorine.
And only five days later, five fucking days
and us blundering and blind with eyeballs all ablaze
and comrades croaking from the Kraut's chlorine
27th of bloody April 1915,
women, bloody women have their pacifist pow-wows
over in the Hague with a bunch of fucking Fraus,
boatloads of the buggers, peacettes in petticoats . . .
I wish a Gerry sub had torpedoed all their boats.
Women, women, setting themselves up as being wiser
than us poor buggers at the front battling the Kaiser.
Could any idea be dafter,

2
dottier,

3
                    dopier
than peacettes in petticoats preaching their Utopia.

Cut to Greenham Women at Peace Conference.

WOMEN
If not now, in heaven's name when?
When the world has killed off all of you men?
Brothers, husbands. sons into the jaws of War –
whatever then could we want a world of peace for?

WORLD WAR I VETERANS
You had to hold your pow-wow in the bleeding zoo.

WOMEN
Yes, and behind the bars were the wild beasts, you!

Remembrance Day and Cenotaph; that's something
    there won't be
in any city on the globe after World War III.

Silence.

WORLD WAR I VETERANS
I was there so why shouldn't I remember?
The Germans used it April, we tried it in September.

Ay, Ypres and Loos, I got myself gassed twice
once by the Germans then by our own device.

You don't have to tell me. I was there.
These clouds of green vapour rolling through the air.

Before my eyes conked out, that green cloud that I saw
made me think we'd seen the end of ordinary war.

It tore your lungs to pieces. It clawed your eyes.

US VOICES
Yeah, yeah, but get on with it, you guys.

WORLD WAR I VETERANS
Eyes that couldn't see, but couldn't stop weeping,
days of deep stupor and nightmare-filled sleeping.

We all had our eyes bandaged because of the gas
like see-no-evil bloody monkeys made of brass.

We marched in a crocodile, the one behind
the other in a long line of the blind.

US VOICES
Yeah, I'm sure you've got a lot of heroic tales to tell
but get these women out of our (I mean *your*) citadel.

*As they fumble with their gas canister, the three Older
Women in the sentry box give them other things to
remember.*

CHORUS OF WOMEN
1
Why can't they remember, these would-be tough guys,
they once had hardly anything inside their flies?

2
The little willies we washed and dried
now stiff and unyielding and courting suicide.

3
Why don't you remember the powder on your bots
then being tucked up with your teddies in your cots?

ALL
If hist'ry retraced its steps along that bloody path
I could see you as my baby gurgling in your bath.

1
I see a blue romper suit with a white bunny tail
smeared with mud and blood and shit at Passchendaele.

2
I see my just-bathed baby riddled by a hail
of Maxim-gun bullets at Passchendaele.

3

I see the dimpled fingers learning Braille
because my boy is blinded at Passchendaele.

4

I see his naked body and his curly little head
burbling in his bath again but the water's red.

5

I see my baby in his bathtub with a blissful smile
but the bubbles all about him are blood and bile.

6

I see my baby with his little rubber duck
bobbing in a bathtub full of blood and muck.

7

I see my little baby with your milky breath
suddenly souring with the smell of death.

8

I see you my baby burping in your sleep
then coughing and choking with gas-filled lungs at Ypres.

9

Powdered in your nappy and the safety pin
suddenly a bayonet that gets rammed right in.

10

The nappy washed and rewashed, whiter than white,
full of grown man's shit as you run into the fight.

ALL

Why is my baby in bright red bathwater?
I didn't wash him for this World War slaughter.
We don't bathe our babies for this bloody slaughter.
Why are our babies lying in this red bathwater?

11

And after I've dried him and I'm putting on his vest
I see the shell-hole that's shattered his chest.

12

We clean the creases in his baby fat with a cotton bud
and find his later beer paunch oozing guts and blood.

13

Peeping through the bubbles his sweet little cock, it's
now the worm that winds in and out of his eye-sockets.

14

Is it only us remember these would-be tough guys
once had hardly anything inside their flies.

*The Women outside the wire have been responding to
this from the Women inside the wire by a keening that
began subdued and now rises as they converge on the
locked gates.*

WORLD WAR I VETERANS

Hey look out the enemy's going into action.

WOMEN

What you see here's only a millionth of a fraction.

WORLD WAR I VETERANS

Out with the gas can, remember Loos.

WOMEN

And remember it turned out no bloody use.

WORLD WAR I VETERANS

Remember the boys we were in 1915
and give those enemies of Britain a whiff of our chlorine.

Right get ready. I've got the Hun in range.

WOMEN

What you seem to have forgotten's that the wind will
change.
Like the new toys you've got stored in these bases
the stuff's going to get blown right back in your faces.

*The World War I Veterans release the green cloud
which envelops nobody but them. They choke in
ancient Greek:*

φυ φυ
ιου ιου
του καπνου

*Their eyes are blinded. The smoke clears. The three
Older Women come from the sentry box and tenderly
bandage the eyes of the World War I Veterans. They
put a bunch of poppies in their hands.*

WORLD WAR I VETERANS
We want to gas 'em and they give us bouquets!

WOMEN
To remind you of your mothers and your wedding days.

WORLD WAR I VETERAN 1
God knows it's true that I'd've gladly died
in battle to protect my mother and my lovely bride.

WORLD WAR I VETERAN 2
We were all of us ready to lay down our lives
to protect our little children and our helpless wives.

WORLD WAR I VETERAN 3
Even death wouldn't have been too much
of a sacrifice to make for my old Dutch.

*They are older geezers now, tearful and pathetic.
The punk girl who will later emerge naked as the
image of Peace goes through the hole in the wire
and tenderly guides them into forming a 'crocodile',
each with a right hand on the shoulder of the man
in front, a famous World War I picture. She leads
them slowly back into the depths of the base and
the rest of the Women keen for the dead in War.*

Enter the Inspector and two Policemen.

236

INSPECTOR

Female crime. Every month shows an increase
both here in Britain and in ancient bloody Greece.
Is this what they call 'keening' for the horror of the BOMB?
Sounds like a million moggies wailing for a tom.
Sounds more like the way them Easterns holler
for that other feller they should nuke, the Ayah-bleeding-
    tollah.
Doesn't sound British. If you get my meaning.
A bunch of Pakis now, they suit your keening.
It sounds more like our coloured brethren's tones.
Not my sort of music. I prefer Tom Jones.
I don't mind demonstrations. Everyone is free
to express him (or her) self in our democracy.
But certain things are sacred. The Queen. Her subjects
    who
lost their lives in either World War I or II.
They showed their banner REMEMBRANCE IS NOT
    ENOUGH
at the service (shown on telly) at the Cenotaph.
In my humble submission that goes too far
whatever your political opinions are.
Women protesting! We've seen it all before.
They were even at it in the First World War,
chanting slogans, chained to bloody railings,
All this jiggery-pokery, women's 'wailings'.
1915 they tried it on then
bleating for Peace and undermining men,
who had a dangerous job to do.
But there weren't so many anti- in World War II.
Women were supportive. Women toed the line
when it came to facing Hitler in '39.
Well, gentlemen, I think we've got ourselves to blame
if women start this Greenham Common game.
By Poseidon, if you let go the reins
then they're going to end up in Peace Campaigns.

Some of my PCs, though I'm not a bloke to chide,
display a certain laxness to the distaff side.
We do a lot of nights and while the cat's away
don't the little mice soon learn to bloody play.
Your intruder comes in a variety of guises
especially repair men with tools of all sizes.
Tupperware parties with the stress on *Tup*!
You never know what temptations might turn up.
I'm trained to spot the clues, and O I've seen her
casting dreamy glances at the vacuum cleaner.
Her and that salesman who egged her on to prove her
suction power stronger than his bloody Hoover.
We leave the gate wide open, wide,
and you wouldn't believe what walks inside.
Your postman whispering through the letterbox crack
'I've got a little something for you in my sack.'
Phoning the joiner, that's what they're all doing,
fitting the fixtures, a bit of the old screwing.
The plumber that comes round's not so bloody dumb
he doesn't know the pipes she wants him to plumb.
Carpet-fitter. Knock-knock! 'Come to lay . . .'
Little glances groinwards. Do I need to say?
There's two ways to deal with women: one's purdah
like our coloured friends, and the other's murder.
We let laxness in the home and when we're on the beat
they're giving someone else our little midnight treat.
We're out and about, enforcing British law
and they first learn whoredom and then denounce War.
If this is what happens when you treat her
like an equal, don't give her a millimetre
or she'll take six inches and it won't be yours.
Then they try to castrate us by stopping wars.
Domestic leniency, believe you me,
first it's sensuality, then it's CND.
First it's going out alone, with made-up faces,

then the next thing that you know surrounding missile
    bases.
One day it's taking classes, learning ancient bloody Greek
then it's aerobics and building a physique.
What's next you wonder, well one thing that's next
is our women getting missile systems hexed
with their witchcraft, wailing, all this, all this,
because in domestic matters men have been remiss.
You know we've given them far too free a hand
and the upshot of it is they'll destroy the land.
In my considered opinion they undermine the state
and as for Great Britain you can forget the Great.
It's my belief we're on the slipp'ry slope
because we've given women too much rope.
Now they've gone too far. They've cooked their goose.
Their necks are going to feel the tightening of the noose.
He's on our side. He's a bloke is Zeus.

Well, ladies, I think you should be knowing
that this is as far as Liberation's going.
Sorry to spoil your little fun, but from today
the only way you're going is Holloway.
I'm rather afraid that we're going to get tough.
The gentlemen of Britain have had e-bloody-nough!

   To Lysistrata.

You've locked these gates, madam. May we inquire why?

LYSISTRATA
Because the weapons in there bleed the country dry.

INSPECTOR
Locking the gates though. It doesn't make any sense.

LYSISTRATA
It's a protest against the money wasted on defence.

INSPECTOR

O so we're a paid up economist are we, miss? I see.
The FT index is all Greek to me.
Tell me, if you're an economist, miss,
about the money that gets wasted policing all this.
Have you ever thought about the cost to the nation
of policing your protest and your little demonstration?

LYSISTRATA

You won't need to do it once they withdraw
the missiles, and we've put an end to War.
The money stockpiled in that Acropolis . . .

INSPECTOR

Acro . . . Acro . . . is that some foreign lingo, miss?
English is all I ever need to speak.

LYSISTRATA

OK then, no more references to anything Greek!
The money represented by this wire fence
could be used on education if men had any sense.
The millions of pounds in your barbed wire barricade
could go on education here, or for Third World aid.
The billions committed to your missile base
could go towards helping the human race.
These destructive systems waste enormous wealth
better spent on housing, education, health.
The billions behind that guarded silo door
would feed more than 5,000 if we got rid of War.
Those millions in missiles and US personnel
could be spent on health care and making people well.
Those millions on missiles that you pour
along with human blood down the open drain of War.
Those millions, those billions stored in that concrete
could let the world's hungry learn to eat.
We protest against those billions that are poured
into payloads the nation can't afford.
Cash that's needed to house, feed, clothe, heal, teach.

INSPECTOR

Just open the bloody gate. Forget the Budget Speech.

LYSISTRATA

Inside blast-hardened bunkers housing Cruise
are millions the nation's being forced to misuse.
These palatial missile bunkers almost halve
the nation's resources and people starve.
Even if you never use your boyish toys
by taking from the needy deterrence destroys.
With Cruise missile money you could create jobs
for kids your kind will end up calling 'yobs'.
Their lives of unemployment don't make any sense
and the money needed is squandered on 'defence'.
And by jobs I mean some profession other
than killing the sons of a Spartan mother.

INSPECTOR

Now you've lost me. Where the hell is Sparta?

LYSISTRATA

Where your payloads are pointing. The Peloponnese.

INSPECTOR

Didn't catch the last bit.

LYSISTRATA

Forget it, it's in Greece.
And if you want to know, my name is Lysistrata.

INSPECTOR

Well – Miss, is it? – Lysistrata, or do we say Ms?

LYSISTRATA

When I've finished with your armies it'll be *Dis*Ms!

INSPECTOR

Your geography's confused, Ms. I do hope
your little ladies' commune's not into dope.

POLICEMAN

Shall we search them, Inspector? They look the type
that have their peace pow-wows with a hashish pipe.

OLDER WOMAN

I'll kick his knackers for him, the cocky little devil.

LYSISTRATA
(*restraining her*)

No, that would be descending to their male level.

To Inspector.

There's no confusion. *My* mind's clear
and there's no difference between there and here.
Since Hiroshima what we've done
paradoxically 's to make the whole Earth one.
We all look down the barrel of the same cocked gun.
One target, in one united fate
nuked together in some hyperstate.
So Greece is Greenham, Greenham Greece,
Poseidon is Poseidon, not just for this piece.
Not just all places, all human ages too
are dependent on the likes of us and you.
In the Third World War we'll destroy
not only modern cities but the memory of Troy,
stories that shaped the spirit of our race
are held in the balance in this missile base.
Remember, if you can, that with man goes the mind
that might have made sense of the hist'ry of mankind.
It's a simple thing to grasp: when we're all dead
there'll be no further pages to be read,
not even leaflets, and no peace plays like these
no post-holocaust Aristophanes.
So if occasionally some names are new
just think of the ground that's under you.
If we're destroyed then we
take with us Athens 411 BC.

The world till now up to the last minute
and every creature who was ever in it
go when we go, everything men did or thought
never to be remembered, absolutely nought.
No war memorials with names of dead on
because memory won't survive your Armageddon.
So Lysistrata! – (   )* – it's one name.
Since 1945 past and present are the same.
And it doesn't matter if it's 'real' or a play –
imagination and reality both go the same way.
So don't say it's just a bunch of ancient Greeks.
It's their tears that will be flowing down your cheeks.
So where we are, Greenham, ancient Greece,
doesn't matter. Their fates depend on Peace.
We've heard you men plan world-wide Apocalypse
and we went on serving dinner with sealed lips.
We went on sitting with our knitting in our laps
while you moved model missiles on your maps.
We heard the men's low murmur over their moussaka
and knew the world's future was growing a lot darker.
Serving the coffee we heard dark hints
of coming holocaust with after-dinner mints.
All this time supportive to the last
we nailed our colours to your macho mast.
I tried to discuss it with my husband, tried
to say he shouldn't vote for national suicide.
O, hello darling, did you vote Yea or Nay?
'Me, I'll always vote for Cruise to stay.
What's it got to do with women anyway?
Your province is knitting not national defence.'

INSPECTOR

O your husband, Mrs Strata, seems a man of sense!

---

* This parenthesis should be the name of the actress playing the role of
Lysistrata.

LYSISTRATA

A man of sense alright, if you can call
sense, wanting to destroy us all.
But male misgovernment grew more crass
and in the end we women couldn't let it pass.
Crasser and crasser, week by bloody week.
We could have told you if you'd let us speak.
You've set the world on a collision course
and still go on believing in masculine brute force.
We were driven finally out of sheer desperation
to devise a strategy to save the nation.
Perhaps it was the day we heard recruiters cry
that able-bodied men were in short supply.
And we decided that there was no point waiting
for men to end the war when it was escalating.
If men didn't want to staunch the flow of blood,
there was no choice about it, we women would.

(A big decision for an ancient Greek
not only not allowed to act, not allowed to speak.)

INSPECTOR

How can I stand here in the uniform of law
and listen to women, *women*, lecture me on War?
Us men sit and listen, us men submit
while *you* tell *us*, hell, no, shit!
Men give the advice and women take it.
Men enforce the law when women break it.
I'm a man. I say. You do. I wear the clothes
that give me authority and you wear those.

LYSISTRATA

Sexual identity, what a frightful bore
when the issue we're debating is the end of War.

To Women.

Take off his uniform. Who knows. Who knows.
Men are sometimes different without their clothes.

The Women undress the Inspector who is revealed to be wearing women's underwear under his uniform.

WOMEN
(reprising 'Glamourwear' song)
ONE SIZE FITS ALL!
Dressed like that, who knows, but you might find
you had a female side and change your mind
about war being a showcase for the male.
(If it were ancient Greece you'd wear a veil!)

LYSISTRATA
Though you're the stronger sex, play at the weaker
and be the listener while I'm the speaker.

LYSISTRATA
and
CHORUS OF WOMEN
We're going to dress up in that sort of groovy gear
until the men's cocks stick out right to here.

Eros. Eros. Bless your sexual co-workers.
Shoot your libidinous shafts from Piccadilly Circus.

When we've saved the country, we like you
will end up on a plinth as public statues too.

O Aphrodite, O Aphrodite,
bless me in my diaphanous nightie
and my scanties crucially see-through
and I'll end up a statue the same as you.

We'll use erotic means to stop the flow of blood
and end up a public plinth labelled MOTHERHOOD.

This is the time, you are witnessing the birth
of a new love of country meant to save the Earth.
MATRIOTISM, and no one has to die,
MATRIOTISM destroys patriarchy,
MATRIOTIC women save the Earth.

245

WOMAN 1

It'll be good to see an end of soldiers in town
pushing trolleys loaded with Newcastle Brown.

WOMAN 2

Like commandos on a mission you see them clear
the entire supermarket of its stocks of beer.

WOMAN 3

Their supermarket trolley loaded dangerously high
with the only sort of product they ever seem to buy . . .

WOMAN 4

Tins of Newcastle Brown, six-packs of Tartan
to give them lots of courage to fight against the Spartan.

WOMAN 5

Being buffers between the British and the US bases
affects their behaviour too in public places.

WOMAN 6

A bit belligerent and bloodshot from the booze
clomping into pubs and shops, and jumping queues.

WOMAN 7

And everyone too timid to ask them to desist
because *a*) they're aggressive and *b*) extremely pissed.

WOMAN 8

Whooping after women, with crude view halloo
full of the inky-pinky parlez-vous.

WOMAN 9

Frightening other shoppers, scaring the cashier
clanking with their purchases in military gear.

WOMAN 10

Their purchases are only ever one thing: BEER!

INSPECTOR

Ach, what do you know of war, you web-concocting
   spiders?

LYSISTRATA

Everything! We are the child-providers!
All war's victims started life inside us.
To improve your understanding let's reverse
roles even further. Here!

   Gives Inspector a 'baby' to hold.

                              Take this child to nurse.
Hold the baby close, see how it feels
then maybe reconsider women's peace appeals.
Hold the baby in a close embrace
and know why women hate your missile base.
No, let's not laugh at him. His female side
might help to hold us back from genocide.
Hold the baby closer, croon, try to be tender.
Break out of your imprisoning stiff gender.
Don't sing to the child that dark male lullaby:
Bombs-away-baby, you're going to die.

Mother the cannon-fodder for your War!

INSPECTOR
(*breaking down*)
Stop it. Stop it. That's too much. Please, no more!

LYSISTRATA

Then imagine waiting while the one you bore
the cannon-fodder of the future for
is away from home himself and at the War.
Worse off than those women who have known
a little love and now are left alone
's the girl, approaching womanhood, who waits
while war is wiping out all likely mates.

INSPECTOR

Men grow old, you know, not only you.

LYSISTRATA

Yes, but look what happens when you do.
Bald, decrepit, toothless a man still gets
into the knickers of nubile nymphettes.
But for a woman once she's over the hill . . .

INSPECTOR
(*rising to the occasion*)
Well, if a man can get a hard-on still . . .

GUARDS
(*from behind the wire*)
Here we go, here we go, here we go. Hooray.
Three cheers for an old man's hard-on's what we say.

LYSISTRATA
and
WOMEN

Your hard-on's the first sign of *rigor mortis*
an exit sign not one of excitation.
Death's Helltons and Death's Dusthouse Fortes
have their hot-lines open now for reservation.

Your obsessions with these cocks of yours,
their blood-bloated hardness, length and size,
has always led us blindly into wars,
because you can't bear *not* to seem tough guys.

It's time to die while you can still have flowers
and a memorial carved in stone with touching verses.
Time to be buried properly before the superpowers
make bulldozers and black plastic bags our hearses.

While they still make the cedar and oak coffin
I'd book one now while firms are still supplying
to carry you and your poor hard-on off in
before the superpowers start us panic-dying.

Die now while there's a time for tears and waking
with generous shots of whisky and cold ham.
The kind of funerals the Powers have in the making
is one mass grave for all of Birmingham.

So go and die while there's still time for weeping
beside the spot you chose for wife and self
while there's a time for grandsons to be keeping
their granddad's photo on the mantleshelf.

Here's some poppies from the people who still care
and baklava for the watchdogs at the dock.
Here's cash to give to Charon for your fare
to ferry you across Death's Holy Loch.

Go and die while there's still time for strewing
carnations on your coffin while folk cry.
A time to mourn before War's total ruin
blows flowers and the folk into the sky.

Go, die while you can keep your male illusion
your cock-bound fantasies of right and wrong
before corpses fuse in chaos and confusion.
Go, and we'll see you off with a sad song.

*The Women 'bury' the Inspector, and the cock is
buried in a separate coffin. The Inspector's coffin is
made from two discarded police riot shields so that
it is like Snow White's glass coffin. The Women bear
off the two 'coffins', the Inspector in the see-through
coffin and the cock in another.*

GUARDS
(*from behind the wire*)

1
There's more to this than meets the eye.

2
There's more to this than meets the eye.

3
There's more to this than meets the eye.
And we suspect a

1
Spartan

2
German

3
Russian SPY!

1
There's more to this than meets the eye.

2
There's more to this than meets the eye.

3
There's more to this than meets the eye.

ALL
These Greenham women have got to be
infiltrated by the KGB!
I don't believe what we've just seen.
They've been infiltrated, they must have been.

1
There's more to this than meets the eye.

2
There's more to this than meets the eye.

3
There's more to this than meets the eye.

ALL
The

1
Spartan

2
German

3
Russian infiltration

ALL
getting at the weaker sex to overthrow the nation.

1
There's more to this than meets the eye.

2
There's more to this than meets the eye.

3
There's more to this than meets the eye.

1
Russkies,

2
Jerries,

3
SPARTIES!

ALL
Subversive left-wing parties,
something subversive's been and got 'em.
Shock 'em to their senses, show 'em your bottom!

1
There's more to this than meets the eye.

2
There's more to this than meets the eye.

3
There's more to this than meets the eye.

ALL

To reassert the glory of the uniformed male
let's flash it at 'em and watch 'em quail.
Rise to the occasion, on the word of command
present your naked cock in your right hand.
Your country needs you, the Fatherland calls
for brave heroes who've still got all their balls.

The Women begin to re-enter.

When they look this way, flash it at 'em quick,
all they hang around here for's a bit of dick.
Flash it at 'em, fellers, and make the fuckers flinch.

WOMAN
(*not looking*)
If you took your hand away we could see the whole inch!

*The Women go into their benders. The light is failing.
There are shadows and torches inside the benders as
the Women begin settling down to sleep. There is a
sense of intimacy, solidarity, friendship, sisterhood.*

WOMAN 1

You know if we flashed back
the guards would die of a heart attack.
If one of us went out and stood in front
of one of them, and went and flashed her cunt,
the poor little lad would get such a shock
it would soon shame him to put away his cock.

WOMAN 2

Their foulness though, it makes me weep.

WOMAN 3

They'll go on all night and won't let us sleep.

WOMEN

Good night! Good night! You know it feels so good
and so secure, in spite of them, this sisterhood.

GUARDS

There's more to this than meets the eye.

They 'flash' as one of the Older Women pokes her head out of the bender.

OLDER WOMAN

Well, I hope there's more to that than meets the eye!

Darkness. The torches in the benders go out. The orange lights of the base fade down. Blackout.

ACT TWO

A later morning.

LYSISTRATA

I can't keep them here. They're all in need of it.
Prick-sick the lot of 'em. And ready to quit.
They seemed so dedicated but they desert
because their randy bodies are on Red Alert.
Women behaving like those lot say they do –
any little dodge to get themselves a screw.
Those foul-mouthed lots behind their barricade
are right: all women want is to get laid.
Every little dodge, every devious trick,
anything at all to get a dose of dick.
Every kind of lie, every sneaky stratagem
to get a stiff six inches into them.
Every fraud you've heard of, every ruse,
more concerned with cock than campaigning against
   Cruise.
They're all so randy, so screaming for a screw
it can't be long before the Peace Campaign is through.
I found one by the Orange Gate trying to hitch
a lift back to London, the treacherous bitch!
One by the roadside skirt half up her thigh
luring lorry-drivers into a lay-by.
There was even one about to sneak off to the bar
where the US personnel take R and R.
Women! Women! Traitors, they betray
our campaign sisterhood for one quick lay.

Woman 1 enters.

254

Here's one now, trying to slip away.
Morning! Off somewhere in a hurry, pray?

WOMAN I

Yes. Er yes, I'm sorry, have to I'm afraid.
I just thought of the milkman. He has to be paid.

LYSISTRATA

It's not important. You've got to stay.

WOMAN I

I'll give him what he wants and come back straightaway.

Enter Woman 2.

WOMAN 2

Shit! I've just remembered, the cat! The cat!

LYSISTRATA
(*to audience*)

Do you know how many times I've already heard that?
I know your pussy's dying for some Whiskas, dear,
but you and your pussy are staying right here.

Enter Woman 3.

WOMAN 3

I forgot to turn the gas off. Honestly.

LYSISTRATA

And we're trying to turn off World War III.

WOMAN 3

I only need a night to check. I don't want to quit.
I only want to go back for a bit.

Enter Woman 4 pretending to be in labour.

WOMAN 4

OOO the contractions! They've begun.
Phone for the ambulance. Don't stand there, run!

LYSISTRATA

Nine months' gestation in a single day!

WOMAN 4

OOOO the baby, the baby's on its way.

*Lysistrata knocks on the swollen belly of Woman 4
and there is a hollow metallic sound.*

LYSISTRATA

It's hard and hollow, and makes a funny noise.

WOMAN 4

Hard and hollow, just like all the little boys.

*Lysistrata reaches under Woman 4's clothing and pulls
out a helmet from World War I, as seen on the World
War I Veterans.*

LYSISTRATA

And what's this, this relic of World War I?

WOMAN 4

I was going to use it to bathe my little son.
You know the Greenham spirit: improvise.

LYSISTRATA

I know it's a pack of monstrous, shameful lies.

Enter Woman 5.

WOMAN 5

I don't want to seem alarmist but I've seen a snake.

Enter Woman 6.

WOMAN 6

Those bloody owls all night keeping me awake.
I haven't slept for weeks. Too-whit-too-bloody-whoo.

LYSISTRATA

What the hell's got into all of you?

You want your men. But imagine THEY
are equally desperate for a lay.
Just think of them restless and rigid in their beds
with only one thought always in their heads:
How long, O Lord, how long before the next screw?
So, please, persevere. Let's try to see it through.

Enter Kinesias Paeonides/Dick Dixon with a little boy.

KINESIAS

In comes I. Great God Almighty.

Brandishes cock.

Look how I'm afflicted by Aphro-bloody-dite.

LYSISTRATA

O goddess of all sexual desire
keep on adding fuel to the fire.

To Myrrhine.

Right, tease him. Serve him only the hors d'oeuvre.
But that's the only course you're allowed to serve.
A little kiss, maybe, but nothing more.
Just remember the solemn oath we all swore.

MYRRHINE

OK! OK!

LYSISTRATA

And I'll help to whet
his appetite while you put on your glamour set.

KINESIAS

OOOO I've got testicular tetanus, lock-cock.
Inches lust-winched to yards and hard as rock.

LYSISTRATA

Who goes there, friend or foe?

KINESIAS

Me!

LYSISTRATA

A man!

KINESIAS

Doesn't it show?

LYSISTRATA

Well if you're a man you'll have to go.

KINESIAS

I want to see Myrrhine before I do.

LYSISTRATA

You want to see Myrrhine and who are you?

KINESIAS

Her husband, Kinesias (Dick Dixon) is my name.

LYSISTRATA

Say no more. It's preceded you . . . your . . . fame.
Everything reminds her. Your wife's
obsessed with you. I saw her salivate
over a still-unopened crate
of a certain fruit consignment labelled *Fyffes*.
When we women chat, Myrrhine's little boast
is Kinesias (Dick Dixon) the man with the most.

KINESIAS

Call her!

LYSISTRATA

Do I get a tip, some quid pro quo?

KINESIAS

Waving his cock.

You can have the tip of this before you go.

LYSISTRATA

I'll bring her.

KINESIAS

Quick! I tell you chaps my life
has lost all meaning since I lost my wife.
The living room's a shambles. I sit on the settee
that used to hold us both and now holds only me,
so lonely that I've started talking to the TV.
Food that I used to love has lost its savour.
She was, I realise now, what gave it flavour.
Her love and care were the bouquet garni
that put my appetite for living into me.
Don't know where my clothes are. Can't get dressed.
I tell you I've never felt more depressed.
It's a dog's life doing your own cooking,
all the fucking housework, then no fucking.
All I can think of is this . . . this . . . growth.
The bed's not big enough to hold us both.
We sleep in separate beds. I'm not able
to have my breakfast sitting at the kitchen table.
It's getting out of hand. Jerking off won't work.
It's got too wide to get a grip on it to jerk.
It's very painful this phallic hypertension.
Had to have my trousers built with an extension.
The be-all and end-all of my being's THIS . . .
this . . . this . . . this . . . edifice.

MYRRHINE
(off, arriving)
He says he loves me but it's all an act!

KINESIAS
(indicating cock)
Isn't this clear demonstration of the fact.

MYRRHINE

No, I'm off.

KINESIAS
(desperate, pushing forward Little Boy)
No, please, Myrrhine,
look, the little lad, he's so much thinner.
It's for your little child that I appeal.

Gives Little Boy a poke.

LITTLE BOY
Mummy!

KINESIAS
It's weeks since he had a proper meal.
Or wash. Look at him. He's filthy. Look.

MYRRHINE
Can't his father bathe him, learn to cook?

KINESIAS
Come back, my darling, at least for your son.

MYRRHINE
(drawing nearer)
A mother's work is never done –
by men!

KINESIAS
God, she's so much more, much more
attractive than she ever was before.

MYRRHINE
(to Little Boy)
O let me give you a big kiss.
Your dad's a proper brute neglecting you like this.

KINESIAS
Listen, why do you pay any heed
to this bunch of dykes? Look at me. In need!
The whole house, everything's gone to pot.
You wouldn't believe the shambles.

MYRRHINE

        O so what!

KINESIAS

All the little knick-knacks that you had
the dogs have broken them.

MYRRHINE

        That's just too bad!

KINESIAS

I bet you miss our bed. God Al-bloody-mighty
you used to be pretty into Aphrodite.

MYRRHINE

I'm not coming back till you men negotiate
an end to the war.

KINESIAS

        When it's decided by the State
we'll do it.

MYRRHINE

        Well, you'll stay in that state till they do.
Till then, I'm not coming home to you.

KINESIAS

What about a quickie at least before I go?

MYRRHINE

I can't say I don't want to, but no! NO!

KINESIAS

Come on, I know you, always oversexed.

MYRRHINE

Here in front of the lad, whatever next?

KINESIAS

(to Little Boy)

Here, come here, darling.

Whispers.

Scram!
I want a word in private with your mam!

*Kinesias gives the Little Boy a toy wooden sword,
or pistol, to play with. One of the Women coaxes the
'weapon' off him and exchanges it for a dove on a
stick. He goes off, playing with it, at first bearing it
like a peace protester then suddenly making it into
a dive-bomber with appropriate noises.*

KINESIAS
Now come on, love, lie down, lie down.

MYRRHINE
Where?

KINESIAS
Any-bloody-where! Right here! I don't care!

MYRRHINE
But, Kinesias, Dick, I did swear a solemn oath.

KINESIAS
Bugger it. This thing's bigger than us both.

Kinesias moves towards her.

MYRRHINE
Wait! A groundsheet!

KINESIAS
The bare earth'll do!

MYRRHINE
O the ground's not good enough for you.
You big, strong, impulsive thing, so butch.

Myrrhine leaves for groundsheet.

KINESIAS

She was always one for that little extra touch
of comfort. Shows her love.

Myrrhine returns with groundsheet.

MYRRHINE
                    Up with your bum!

I'll just slip my clothes off, then I'll come.
Be with you in a jiffy. Damn, O damn!
Forgot the mattress.

KINESIAS
I'm terrific as I am.

MYRRHINE

I want you to be comfy!

KINESIAS
A kiss! Just one.

MYRRHINE

There!

Kiss.

KINESIAS
O wow! Go on then, run, run, run!

*Myrrhine leaves. Kinesias lies back on ground. Cock
rises. He sits up again. Enter Myrrhine with mattress.*

MYRRHINE
There we are, my love. Just like a proper bed.

*Kinesias lies back, up rises the cock. He sighs with
anticipation.*

MYRRHINE
Getting my clothes off!

Thinks.

> Something for your head!

KINESIAS

I don't want a pillow.

MYRRHINE
> I'd like one though.

Myrrhine leaves. Kinesias sits up and looks woefully at his cock.

KINESIAS

Poor cock, you're starving. The womb service is slow.

Enter Myrrhine once more with pillow.

MYRRHINE

I think that's everything.

Puts pillow under Kinesias.

> There you go!

I'll just slip off this bra.

> A blanket!

KINESIAS

> NOOOO!

I don't need the Bayeux Tapestry, a four-poster,
a Goblin Teasmade, a pop-up toaster,
a morning alarm call, a bedside book.
All I need, Myrrhine, is a FUCK!

Myrrhine leaves.

MYRRHINE

I'll be back in just a couple of ticks.

KINESIAS
(to cock)
Poor cunt-craving junkie, where's your fix?

Myrrhine returns with blanket.

MYRRHINE
Up! Up!

KINESIAS
Up! Up! Can't you bloody see –
I've been up since seven. *He's* been up since three!

MYRRHINE
You'd like some perfume?

KINESIAS
No more, PLEASE, no more!

MYRRHINE
You used to insist on it before.

Goes for perfume. Returns.

Hold your hand out. A little to please me.

KINESIAS
Pooh, *Chanel* bloody *No. 2* if you ask me.

MYRRHINE
O that's the one from Rhodes. That wasn't very clever.

Myrrhine makes to leave.

KINESIAS
No, it's the most perfect perfume ever.

*Sloshes it over himself, then gulps the rest down.
Myrrhine leaves.*

KINESIAS
God rot *Gucci*, *Nina Ricci* and *Chanel*.
Fuck all parfumiers. They can go to Hell.

Myrrhine returns.

MYRRHINE
This is so much better, smell.

KINESIAS
                              No more
little treats. I've got a better one in store.

MYRRHINE
OK, darling. I'll just slip off my shoes.

Kinesias lies back. The cock rises. He sighs.

But you will remember to campaign against Cruise
and work towards a Spartan Armistice?

KINESIAS
I'll seriously consider it.

Sighs.

                              Ah bliss!

Pause. Kinesias sits up. Myrrhine has gone.

Slowly the conviction dawns. O God she's gone
and left me with the hardest bloody on
I've ever had in the whole of my damned life.
At the crucial moment stood up by the wife.

*He sings a lullaby to his cock, which he nurses like
a baby.*

Cock-a-bye baby,
cock of my life,
it doesn't seem likely
that you'll lay the wife.

GUARD I
Cock-a-bye, cocky
but don't despair.
We know where you'll find
professional care!

GUARDS
Bollocks weren't created to suffer such a strain.
There's a limit to the agony a man's cock can sustain.

KINESIAS

O my knob is throbbing like a dynamo!

GUARD I

Ay, we had a gander and fancied a go.

GUARD 2

Weren't bad in her undies. Quite a show.

GUARD 3

You could tell she were a proper bastard though.

Enter the Herald, a dual twin of USA/USSR.

KINESIAS

Hello, hello, no, don't tell me. I know you two lads
you're the well-known ancient fertility ads.

HERALD

I am a herald, a preparatory ambassador
sent to initiate *détente* in the Cold War.

KINESIAS

Détente? If your concern is PAX
why the weapons peeping from your macs?
Or is it an affliction of the bollocks?

HERALD

The man's a lunatic, by Castor and by Pollux!

KINESIAS

But the evidence is there. Your balls do swell.

HERALD

My credentials. An emblem of authority.
A sort of staff of status in the Spartan nation.

KINESIAS

Getaway with you. You can't fool me.
We're all suffering from similar inflation.

Shows his cock.

Join the club. How are the Superpowers?
Proper cock-up is it, just like ours?

HERALD

Women! Women! Even my old missus,
with KEEP OUT signs on all their orifices.
Not so much as a distant whiff of cunt
until we've voted for disarmament.

KINESIAS

Now I see it. It's universal then
this female conspiracy against us men.
Contact your governments. Tell them this:
Urgent send envoys to sign an Armistice.
The problem's universal. All we need to do's
open up our flies for a frank exchange of views.

HERALD
(*leaving*)

No more SS20s. No more Cruise.

GUARD 1

Bloody marvellous how they get under your skin.
The one thing about women is you never win.

GUARD 2

With 'em, without 'em, they drive us round the bend.
But don't you think this hostility could come to an end?

GUARD 3

We'll be kind to women, if they'll be kind to men.
How about it, ladies, no hard feelings then?

*One of the Older Women goes up to the youngest of
the Guards, Guard 2.*

OLDER WOMAN

Well, if you ask me, you looked very silly
trying to impress us with your little willy.

What about your mother? What would she have thought
seeing her son doing something of that sort?

O poor lad, you've got something in your eye!

GUARD 2

Yer, I think it's a bleeding fly,
something like that, or a speck of dirt.

WOMAN
(*through wire*)

Here, let me see. O yes. It must hurt.
Look at me.

Pause.

Look up at the sky.
Look at me.

Pause.

There!

There's no need to cry.

GUARD 2
(*cross but crying*)

You've made it start watering, poking my eye!

WOMAN
(*dabs his eye through the wire*)

I'll kiss it better, love.

Kiss kiss.

There!

GUARD 2
(*backing off in acute embarrassment*)

Hey, you daft old bugger, don't you dare!

Enter the Ambassadors.

WOMAN

Here come the ambassadors from both blocs
bridging the gap between them with their cocks.

AMBASSADOR 1

We are following our pieces to make Peace.

AMBASSADOR 2

Enough rigidity. We want release.

LYSISTRATA

I'd better act. Or in a couple of ticks
they'll be tickling one another with their pricks,
or getting up one another's bum,
or blowing one another into Kingdom Come.

Gentlemen, without further hindrance, let or pause
PEACE emerges from the past of human wars.

*From the central entrance deep in the bases emerges
Peace, a naked Greenham Woman – the one we last
saw leading the blinded World War I Veterans back
into the depths of the base. Her body is smeared
with ash and blood as if commemorating 6 August,
Hiroshima Day, or the anniversary of Nagasaki. The
Women with pebbles and stones – out of which they
make a commemorative cairn – set up a rhythm to
bring Peace downstage. Three times Peace stops and
the rhythm stops. In the pauses we hear wolf-whistles
coming from as if deep in the heart of the bases. Peace
carries rolled up at this stage a banner of the Peace
Movement depicting the world in very bright-coloured
cloths over which is a disarmament symbol. When she
reaches the front of the stage she unfurls the banner.
The disarmament symbol on the world continues with
Peace's legs. Where the arms of the symbol divide is
exactly over the cunt of Peace.*

LYSISTRATA

Bring them together. Don't bully or cajole
like some pissed husband desperate for his hole.
Be gentle with them. They should be led
not like machos trundling women into bed.
If they won't join hands as friend to friend
then lead them by the part they do extend.

*The Ambassadors are led to the centre where Peace
stands. Their cocks form an inverted V, that parallels
the disarmament sign. They at once try to glance over
the banner to the naked Peace behind.*

LYSISTRATA

Before we finish off I'd like to say
that it's August 6th, Hiroshima Day,
which is why you see Peace smeared with ash and blood.
Yes, we'd all go back to 411 if we could.
It would have been good to turn back the clocks
and have a little romp with padded cocks.
The patriarchs of 1986
still battle for world power with their pricks.
Hiroshima, that world-transforming blast
makes it that much harder to reclaim a simpler past.
Besides if *Lysistrata* was put on then
every part would have been played by men.
So for the sake of theatre let's retrace
our steps. Forget this is a missile base
patrolled by these poor lads for the USA
and let's get back to our prenuclear play.
This is the Athenian Acropolis
where Athens and Sparta sign the Armistice.
So end the hostility between you two.
Why don't you make peace? What's stopping you?

AMBASSADOR 1

We'll make peace but these

*Points to areas on the world above the breasts of
Peace.*

are our spheres
of influence, and his country interferes.

AMBASSADOR 2

We'll make peace, *if* it's understood
that this territory

Points to area of the world above the cunt of Peace.

stays ours for good.

GUARD 1

Time for Peace feelers. I wouldn't mind.

GUARD 3

She had nice tits, and a gorgeous behind.

*Guard 2 is silent. The Women begin bringing thermos
flasks and sandwiches to offer the Guards through the
wire. The Older Woman gives food first to Guard 2.*

OLDER WOMAN

You look a bit peeky, guarding all night.
Here, aren't you hungry, have a bite.

From our secret stash of Harrods hampers
here's smoked salmon and vintage champers.

Food from Fortnum's we have stashed away
hidden in the bushes to celebrate today.

*All they have to offer is a thermos and sandwiches in
plastic bags.*

You know we get the odd crown-pattern wrapped food
parcel

a brace of pheasants or a grouse from Windsor bleeding
Castle.

The Women are unfurling all their bright banners.
Enter a Drunk Geordie Soldier returning for duty at
the base. He's very drunk and carrying what's left of a
six-pack of Newcastle Brown.

DRUNK GEORDIE SOLDIER
What's going on here, then? A bloody party,
a booze-up between your Athenian and your Sparty?

GUARD 1
You're not supposed to come in through the front.

DRUNK GEORDIE SOLDIER
Howay, let us in, man. Divvn't be such a cunt.
I've got to be doing your job tomorrow.
Do you blame us if I want to drown my sorrow?
Politicians of the world. My advice is this:
before you negotiate, go on the bloody piss.
They all look fucking wonderful. Even your wog
when you're looking at him through a haze of grog.
Know what I mean, pet? Here have a swig.
I'm not your average male chauvinist pig.
Howay, pet! I'll tell you something: booze
is the surest way there is to banish Cruise.
Know what, hinny, when you've had a few,
they all look lovely, even some of you.
Russkies, Yanks, Jocks, Japs, Chinks,
they're all one big family after a few drinks.
I'll tell you something else: the Brotherhood of Man,
the Brotherhood of Man's in this Brown Ale can.
Get everybody pissed. And just you watch.
World harmony's a matter of your beer and Scotch.
It works like that with birds. After fifteen pints or so
some old slag can look like Marilyn Monroe.
I've drunk with your Greeks, ancient and today's –

273

they all look lovable through an ouzo haze.
I'll bet them ancient Greeks swigged a lot of wine
then went bopping to bazoukis and singing *Auld Lang
    Syne*.
I'll tell you something. And you'll think I'm barmy
or just a bloody bastard 'cos I'm in the army,
but I've got a soft spot in my heart for CND.
(Now I wouldn't want anybody quoting me . . .)
Everybody, everybody has a right to say
that your Cruise should go back to the USA.
I bloody hate myself. I bloody hate
having to stand on guard at this bloody gate.
Give us a kiss, and I'll tell you something more.
I hate myself and I bloody hate War.
Honest, cross my heart, when I'm bloody pissed
I think even the Russkies have a right to exist.
Been pissed with Jerries, they're very nice chaps
not *Schweinhunds* when you've shwigged enough
    schnapps.
Now I'm going to have a few jars with the Yanks.
They're looking after us, they deserve our thanks.
Off to their Bob Hope Center, very nice place
tucked away at the heart of this missile base.
I'm telling you it's all so neatly planned
you'd think this desolation was Disney-bloody-land.
They're alright, Yanks, not bad for a laugh.
But I tell yer their beer is fucking naff.
Budweiser! Women's beer! I wouldn't give a glass
of that piss ('scuse my French) even to wor lass.
Tell you what, I'll toss you a few over the wire.
You can wash your faces in it, or douse your fire.
I'll bring you some six-packs from their PX store
and you can drink to disarmament and the end of War.

*Soldier lurches through gate towards the depths of
the base.*

LYSISTRATA

Now it's all over, we should celebrate
the glad reunion of mate with mate.
We hereby restore
sex, and abolish War.

Take your partners, hug and kiss,
the world's drawn back from the abyss.
Dance, celebrate creation
saved from man's annihilation.

GUARDS

War, it'll only survive in old soldiers' stories.
All our heroic deeds, our military glories.
If War's finished then we'll never get our gongs.
War'll go into museums where it, perhaps, belongs.
The Greeks resisting though outnumbered by the Persians.
Memories like that though help to form a nation.
Yes, the Greeks have their Marathon and our version's
standing alone against the Nazi until our Uncle Sam
came to help us out a bit and outstayed his invitation –
Marathon, the Somme, Dunkirk, Suez and Vietnam.
Gives me a funny feeling though that War's
gone the same way as the bloody dinosaurs.
Museums and old movies, miles of celluloid
of Coventry or Dresden, Hiroshima, Hanoi
have bombs dropped on 'em and systematically destroyed
and Peace will make them seem as far away as your
    old Troy.

Hey, but wait a minute, we'll be unemployed!

The only buttons anybody's gonna press
aren't the ones to nuke us into Nothingness
but Fast Forward Wind as *nostalgie de la boue*
brings us endless re-runs of World War I and II.

I betcha after a few years of world peace
all the old war films'll be on re-release.
You watch the figures on the home video charts
when the rush of War nostalgia actually starts.

We'll have to show the kiddies what they've missed
or else they won't believe that such things could exist.

History'll come to a dead end. I mean
wars, that's all history's ever been.

WOMEN

Well from now on it's taken a new turning
and there'll be a very different tale to be told.
From now on the only fires you'll see burning
are those in living rooms to keep away the cold.

Goddess of childbirth send increase,
send new babies from tonight's embrace.
Entrust the future to us here in Greece
standing in for all the human race.

Artemis, goddess, we beseech you, bless
everything that you create
brought back from the brink of Nothingness
and bless mate reconciled with mate.

Goddess, who wants the world to go on turning,
who wants the grass to grow, the trees to bud,
turn men's hearts away from bombs and burning,
turn men's hearts away from dust and blood.

Goddess walking the high mountain slopes
walking space and time from ancient Greece,
look down and bless our new fragile hopes
rooted in a future of eternal peace.

Goddess of sex, you from whom
comes the child, the tree, the flower,
bless the fruit of the glad womb
saved at the dark eleventh hour.

Britain's not a dancing nation
not like the ancient Greeks before us.
But the joy of reprieved creation
moves us as a common chorus.

Dance, dance, join hands and glide
in tune with the rhythms of the earth
released from the curse of genocide
pulsing with rebirth, rebirth.

> *As the Women dance, the Drunk Geordie Soldier
> emerges from the depths of the base erratically
> pushing a shopping trolley laden with Budweiser beer.
> He proceeds to lob the cans over the wire making
> grenade noises whistles and explosions. A Woman
> cuts a large hole in the wire so that they can be passed
> through. The Women start drinking them.*

WOMAN
(*to Guards*)

We've sung our song for the end of wars.
Come on, fellers, now it's your turn. You sing yours.

> *The Guards shuffle with embarrassment, then stand to
> attention and to the tune of 'Rule Britannia' sing:.*

GUARDS

Bless the women,
the women lead the way,
women, women, women, women lead the way.

Thank you ladies,
Lysistrata was a scream
but a

1

    stupid

2

      stupid!

3
stupid!

ALL
DREAM.

Well, that's enough of ancient Greece.
We've got to live in our own age.
Tell those who won't join in your peace . . .

*They raise three walkie-talkies out of which comes a
repetitive US Voice.*

US VOICE
We'll nuke 'em back to the Stone Age.
We'll nuke 'em back to the Stone Age.
We'll nuke 'em back to the Stone Age.

*At this point enter a real Police Inspector with police
and bailiffs who proceed to destroy the Women's
benders.*

INSPECTOR
Right, I'm nicking the lot of you for breaching the peace!

Blackout.

End of Part One.

Part Two

*Again we see the wire and gate of USAF, Greenham
Common. Now it is winter. In the background near
where we imagine the silos are are two watchtowers with
a search beam each. In one is Guard 1 (Poseidon) and in
the other Guard 2 (Athena). There is one old Greenham
Woman (Hekabe) on the ground in front of the wire.*

GUARD I (POSEIDON)
From salt, up from deep salt water, up –
POSEIDON, Poseidon, me. Down there below
in Europe's bitter waters the NEREIDS . . .

GUARD 2
The what?

GUARD I (POSEIDON)
NEREIDS:

*Begins to count them off in a military roll-call. As
he punches out the names in staccato bursts, female
voices pick out the names of the Nereids and make
something flowing and female out of them. The two
ways of delivery heighten musically the divisions
created by the wire. The female voices make us aware
of the Greenham Women in their benders, intoning
the names of the Nereids as ancient female 'allies'
under the dominion of Poseidon. It is as if they are
dreaming themselves as Nereids while they still sleep,
though the barking roll-call of Poseidon is, like the
obscene taunts and chants of Part One, designed to
wake them in the early hours.*

Actea
Amphinome
Apseudes
Autonoe

Agave
Amphitrite
Arethusa

Amathea
Amphitroe
Asia

Beroe

Callanassa
Ceto
Cranto
Cymatolege
Cymothoe

Calypso
Cleo
Crenis
Cymo

Callianira
Clymene
Cydippe
Cymodoce

Dejanira
Dexamene
Doto

Deopea
Dione
Drymo

Dero
Doris
Dynamene

Eione
Eucrate
Eumolpe
Eurydice

Ephira
Eudora
Eunice
Evagora

Erato
Eulimene
Eupompe
Evarne

Galataea
Glauconome

Galem

Glauce

Halia
Hippothoe

Halimede

Hipponoe

Iera

Ione

Isea

Janira

Laomedia
Ligea
Lysianassa

Leucothoe
Limmoria

Liagora
Lycorias

Melia
Mera

Melita

Menippe

Nassa
Nesea

Nemertes
Neso

Neomeris

Opis	Orythra	
Panope	Pasithea	Pherusa
Phyllodoce	Pione	Plesaura
Polynoe	Pontoporia	Pronce
Protomedusa	Protomelia	Psamathe
Sao	Spio	
Thalia	Thoe	Themisto
Thetis		
Xantho		

GUARD 2

Yeah! Say that again . . .

Guard 1 (Poseidon) begins again but only goes as far as opening his mouth.

Milk, honey, olive oil, and goats they get
there in their grottoes from those whose way
had to go over water, as a plea for peace
over the waves as their boats crossed the ocean.

Begins again.

From salt, up from deep salt water, up –
POSEIDON, Poseidon, me . . .

GUARD 2

Tell 'em who Poseidon is. You've done the Nereids.

GUARD 1

I don't need to. They all read their news
They all know POSEIDON's an underwater CRUISE.

Resumes.

From salt, up from deep salt water, up –
POSEIDON, Poseidon, me. Down there below
in Europe's bitter waters the NEREIDS

Doesn't allow Guard 2 in again.

deploy their beauty in a circle dance.

Ever since PHOEBUS and me laid our stone circle
round Troy with tackle that mortal masons use
I've had a soft spot in my heart for PHRYGIA.

GUARD 2

Phrygia! That's a frigging fine name for this freezing dump!

GUARD 1 (POSEIDON)

It's smouldering now. Sacked and gutted by the Greeks.

Crammed with commandos the wooden womb,
an inspired invention of some backroom boffin,
a quiet scientific man, a boffin from Phocis,
made rubble and debris of this burg that I built.
The Wooden Horse they're going to call it in stories.
They were welcoming death when they whooped for
    the Horse.
The green places of gods are charcoal and ash.
The gods of green places forced out of their groves,
the sacred stones still gummy, still tacky with gore,
the sacred stones stained with the carnage of men
not cockerels' or goats' throats slit for a god.
And Priam, high prince of Pergamum, Troy,
the leader of Ilium, lies cold on the altar
he dedicated himself to ZEUS, the DEFENCE GOD.

The Greeks drag the spoil, the gold loot, the booty,
the armour and weapons of those they have slaughtered
in clanking cartloads down to their galleys.
The jewels from women's warm bodies,
necklaces, anklets, breast-cushioned brooches,
beautiful jars to store oil in or cook with
heaped onto wagons to be shipped off HOME.

All they need now is the wind in their sails

and they'll go back home to their women and children,
these Greeks who have seen the seed in the ground
flourish as cornstalks ten times since they brought
war to this shoreline, ten harvests ago.

HERA and ATHENA . . .

> GUARD 2
> Hera and Athena, who are they?

GUARD 1
One's Zeus's missus. And Athena you play!

GUARD 2
I'm not playing a lass, Troy or no Troy.

GUARD 1
You'll play who you're told to and like it, my boy!

> GUARD 1 (POSEIDON)
> (*resuming*)

Hera and Athena in alliance against me
got me defeated, so I'm now gutting Troy
and the altars where people once worshipped POSEIDON.

Deities are nothing to a desolate city.
The crushed don't find much to thank their gods for.
There aren't any prayers when a culture collapses.

There's a clamour along the banks of Scamander
as the women of Troy are allotted their masters
for their beauty, their breasts, their child-bearing bodies,
or their backs to bear burdens, chosen for bondage,
and labelled for various regions of Greece –
Arcadia, Thessaly, Athens, Cos, Corfu,
The Peloponnese. Boeotia, the islands,
for the fishermen, farmers, the olive-growers.
the keepers of bees in rock-hillside blue boxes,
for the brothels of cities, the beds of tormentors.

All those still not assigned to their masters,

these chicks here, cooped up down below me
waiting to hear what their conquerors want.
Among them

Shines torch on bender.

somewhere, Helen of Sparta,
a captive with captives. Now Helen of TROY.

*Torch beam searches for Hekabe among the benders,
then finds her asleep on the ground before the wire.*

And that figure there, she's had the most suffering,
that's HEKABE huddled in the chill of her sorrow
though half of her pain she hasn't heard yet:
her daughter Polyxena, ritually slaughtered
at the tomb of Achilles, for his bed after life.
Her husband, King Priam, hacked down and unburied,
her children all slaughtered, except for CASSANDRA,
a virgin, Apollo sends visions, a virgin.
She's AGAMEMNON's. He won't consider her sacred
when he kisses his concubine . . .

*The Guard 1, sex-taunter of Greenham Women,
surfaces from the god he is playing. He shouts in his
own voice towards the benders.*

. . . cracks open her cunt!

Back into the US accent of Poseidon.

This was a fabulous city before. So long!
So long, Ilium! ATHENA brought your tall towers down.
But for her, maybe, you wouldn't be rubble.

Guard 2 becomes Athena.

GUARD 2 (ATHENA)
Can we bid our old hatred goodbye?
Can Athena now speak to Poseidon the strong?
We're kin, Poseidon, kin, you and I.

GUARD 1 (POSEIDON)
Yes, speak, Athena, we both belong
in the bonds that bind the gods of the sky.

GUARD 2 (ATHENA)
I'm glad of your grace. I have something to say
which touches our interests, lord of the sea.

GUARD 1 (POSEIDON)
Some message from Zeus has come your way.
You've brought a message from the gods down to me?

GUARD 2 (ATHENA)
No, I want your power to give help to Troy.

GUARD 1 (POSEIDON)
No more hate left then for what you helped to destroy?

GUARD 2 (ATHENA)
Say first if you'll give me the help that I seek.

GUARD 1 (POSEIDON)
Yes, but who are you helping, Trojan or Greek?

GUARD 2 (ATHENA)
My old foes will be happy when I make the Greeks pay.

GUARD 1 (POSEIDON)
Your allegiances waver every-which-way.

GUARD 2 (ATHENA)
Pay for that insult made of my shrine.

GUARD 2 (ATHENA)
And the Greeks somehow chose not to punish the act.

GUARD 1 (POSEIDON)
But without your assistance Troy wouldn't have been
sacked.

GUARD 2 (ATHENA)
Now though I want them to suffer in turn.
Give them a bad time. Do it for me.

GUARD 1 (POSEIDON)

Before they set sail, or later at sea?

GUARD 2 (ATHENA)

When they think that they're half way home from Troy!
Zeus will pour down torrential rain, unending hail,
billows of black breath out of the heavens.
He's offered to give me his missiles of thunder
to smash the Greek ships and gut them with fire.

And you, Poseidon, make the ocean heave
with shouting surge and whirlwinds of spray.
Make the Greek coast choke with the corpses,
white bloated cadavers sun on Greek beaches.
That should teach them to keep my shrines sacred
and respect all the other gods besides me.

GUARD 1 (POSEIDON)

Done! And that's all you need as my consent.
I make the whole ocean strain until bursting –
Mykonos, Delos, Scyros, and Lemnos,
corpses lumber their beaches, clog the boat anchors,
come up with fish-shoals as ghastlier catches.

Go to Olympus, and there take in keeping
those missiles of thunder Zeus promised you.
Then bide your time till the Greeks weigh anchor.

Fools! Fools! Who devastate cities,
leave holy places levelled, and graves
violated, molesting the rest of the dead.
They reap what they sow: Desolation.

*Guards 1 and 2 are made broody by Poseidon's final
words and lapse into silence as dawn reveals the
waking Hekabe.*

GREENHAM WOMAN (HEKABE)

Up! Head up, old girl! Up off the ground! Up!
Straighten up, if you can. Head up. Back straight.

Troy's no longer Troy! So we . . . I'm no queen!

Courage! 'Fate bloweth where it listeth.'
Don't ram your ship of life slap into the rollers.
Ride the waves . . . not much choice, have I, really?

Such a lot of crying to do. A lot of keening.
Country gone. Children gone. Husband, King Priam, gone.
Our life-sail once swollen with favour and fortune
collapsed to a kerchief of shrivelled extinction,
a snotrag of nothingness that once-bellying sail.

Is it best to clam up, or let it all spill,
really let go and keen all our afflictions,
not the least of which is to sleep on hard ground –
not exactly a *Slumberland* this ground piled with stones!
Not pleasant for old bones like mine used to better!
My head's splitting! Temples pounding! Sides *aching*!
I have to keep shifting from this foot to that
to get any ease, swaying like those ships there waiting,
the Greek fleet rolling to the sway of my grief.
I get comfort from rocking myself to and fro,
tears flowing. Wretchedness has music too.
Misery sings, but I doubt it goes dancing.

> *Hekabe moves closer to the waiting ships in the
> auditorium, fascinated by them, peering at them,
> swaying at their motion at anchor. Then she starts
> singing. If ever we hear the sound of the ocean it is
> the swish of traffic passing Greenham, or the hum
> of a generator, its throb and rhythm.*

Ships, ships, ships on fast oars
from the Greece where we'll soon be faring,
speedily, speedily came to these shores
with battle brass roaring and blaring.

Battle bugles baying for blood
and bawling for Helen returning.

She left Menelaus, crossed the flood.
Her heat was the cause of Troy's burning.

So I squat on my hunkers and rock to the sway
of the terrible ships that will take us away.
Those terrible monsters, they mesmerise me.
They will take all us women over the sea.
And I squat on my hunkers and rock to and fro
to the ships that dropped anchor ten years ago.

I once sat on a throne, straight-backed and gold-crowned,
now the ship of my life, she's been run aground.

Because of loathsome Helen's lust
the city behind me is blazing.
My man and my sons they banquet on dust,
the sons I spent my life raising.

So I squat on my hunkers and rock to the sway
of the terrible ships that will take us away.
These terrible monsters, they mesmerise me.
They will take all us women over the sea.
And I squat on my hunkers and rock to and fro
to the ships that arrived here ten years ago.

I once sat on a throne, straight-backed and gold-crowned
now the ship of my life, she's been run aground.

Helen put thousands into the grave
and the Troy that's behind me might never have been
and I am beached up by fate as a slave
who was launched on her life as a queen.

I once sat on a throne, straight-backed and gold-crowned
now the ship of my life, she's been run aground.

Outside the camp of occupation forces
I sit a prisoner, soon exile and slave.
I've pulled half of my hair out from resentment and protest.

Widows, bereaved mothers, fatherless daughters,
virgins honeymooning on Greek forces' gang-bangs,
Troy's smoking. Join me in keening for Troy.
Come, come, little fledgelings, under my wing.
I'll lead you in keening as once before
we honoured the gods with our singing.
I beat out the time with King Priam's sceptre.

Shouts.

We sang, and the gods used to listen . . .

*From the various benders emerge the Chorus of
Greenham/Trojan Women. The Chorus will eventually
each have the modern name of a Greenham woman.*

CHORUS
Hekabe! Why are you shouting? Why the commotion?
Has there been news? Have things been decided?
You frightened us, shouting, as we lay in our benders,
brooding inside about losing our freedom . . .

HEKABE
You can see the Greek rowers already on board.

CHORUS
Are they getting things ready to take us away
far away from all we once could call home?

HEKABE
I don't know what's happening. But fear the worst.

CHORUS
Hey, come on out, the rest of you, out of your benders.
Our slavery's sealed. They're setting sail soon.
Better get ready to start being slaves . . .

HEKABE
Not Cassandra. Best leave her inside,
my poor crazed little baby. She shouldn't come out.

Though she's a priestess those men will abuse her.
She should be kept from the pawers and gropers.
I couldn't bear that on top of what's happened.
Troy! Troy! Troy! You're all finished.
The dead have left you, the living are leaving.

CHORUS
(emerging from benders)
We're scared. We're frightened. Tell us the news.
They're going to kill us. We're being taken to Greece.
If that's what those sailors preparing there means.

They look at the ships in the auditorium. The traffic
swishes by. The generator hums.

HEKABE
I've been out all night. Too scared to sleep.

CHORUS
Has he been yet, the man with the news?

HEKABE
Any moment now, we'll know our new masters.

CHORUS
Will it be Argos? Phthia? One of the islands?
Wherever they take you, it's a long way from Troy.

HEKABE
And whose slave will I be? Whereabouts?
An old woman like me, a useless dependent!
What work will they find for old bones like me,
opening and shutting the door, a nanny to children?
Me, who held the highest honours in Troy.

[Maybe reprise snatch of swaysong.

I sat on a throne straight-backed and gold-crowned . . .]

CHORUS
I
It's a long way to fall, no wonder you weep!

2

No more weaving, at least not on those wires.

3

The last time I gaze on the graves of my forebears.

4

The last time!

5

The last time!

6

The last time!

7

Instead, drudgery.

8

Or dragged off to bed.

9

God rot the night some Greek gets me down!

10

Drawing water maybe.

11

The springs of Pirene.

12

I only pray that it's Athens they ship us to.
They say there's justice, and the city's blessed.

1

Not Sparta!

2

NOT Sparta.

3

Sparta spawned HELEN.

4

To bow and scrape before the sacker of Troy.
Menelaus, imagine being a slave to that monster.

1 2

If it's not Athens, Thessaly would do,
nestling in the foothills of Olympus.
It's fruitful and wealthy, so I've heard say.
And SICILY

CHORUS

It might not be bad by the Ionian Sea . . .

Here's one of them coming, the herald, with news!
Whatever it is he seems in a great hurry.
Our slavery in Greece is about to begin.

Enter Guard 1 (Talthybius) with Guards 2 and 3.

TALTHYBIUS

Hekabe, I think you should know me by now.
I've been to and fro between Troy and the Greeks
for the whole of the duration. Talthybius! With news!

HEKABE

It's happening, all that I feared in my mind.

TALTHYBIUS

Yes, it's happening. You've all been 'assigned'.

HEKABE

Thebes? Thessaly? Where? Tell us our lot.

TALTHYBIUS

One man for you each. Together, you're not.

HEKABE *and* CHORUS

Tell us the worst then. Who goes to who?

TALTHYBIUS

One at a time. One at a time. That's all I can do.

HEKABE

Who gets Cassandra I'd first like to know.

TALTHYBIUS

Agamemnon. King Agamemnon. That's where she's to go.

HEKABE

Slave to his Spartan wife! What a terrible plight.

TALTHYBIUS

No, to keep the king happy in bed at night.

HEKABE

Apollo, he promised she'd always stay chaste.

TALTHYBIUS

I think it's that sanctity tickles his taste.

HEKABE

O the trappings of priestess, they aren't worth a thing.

TALTHYBIUS

It's rather an honour to be fucked by the king.

Silence.

HEKABE

The other, my youngest, where did she go?

TALTHYBIUS

It's about Polyxena you're wanting to know?

HEKABE

Whose bed is she flung in? She's gone to whom?

TALTHYBIUS

She's gone to do duties at Achilles' tomb.

HEKABE

My girl guard a grave? O please
what kind of strange Greek customs are these?

TALTHYBIUS

Consider her happy. Your daughter's fine.

HEKABE

Does she still see the light, this daughter of mine?
At least I can celebrate she still sees the light.

TALTHYBIUS

Everything's . . . been seen to. She's fine. She's alright.

HEKABE

Andromache? What of her? What?

TALTHYBIUS

Son of Achilles. She fell to his lot.

HEKABE

And who gets me, with one foot in the grave?

TALTHYBIUS

You go to Odysseus. You're Odysseus' slave.

HEKABE

A slave to that dirty, despicable liar,
that despiser of justice, that defiler of right.
His tongue made white black, black white.
Sisters, sisters, weep for me. Of you all
I'm brought the lowest with further to fall.

CHORUS

That's you taken care of. What about me?
Which Greek brute's taking me over the sea?

TALTHYBIUS (GUARD I)
(to Guards 2 and 3)

Quick, bring Cassandra out of her bender.
She's got to be given to King Agamemnon.
She's the commander's. She's got to go first.
Then the rest have to go to whoever's got them.

Sees light in the bender.

What the hell's that? That light there inside?
God, don't say they're starting burning their benders,
setting fire to themselves to frustrate our intentions
of lugging them over to Greece into bondage.
For those born in freedom, bondage is beastly.

Thwacks on the plastic of the bender.

Come on! Come on! Death could well be the best
but if I don't deliver you I'll get the chop . . .

Guards 2 and 3 begin to drag on a foot. Cassandra's.

HEKABE
No! No! Nothing's on fire. It's only Cassandra,
my daughter. Don't harm her. She's special.

*Enter Cassandra from the bender. Punk hair, half
shaved, half some brilliant green dye. Leather jacket
with many studs, including hooks from which later
the woollen web can be strung. Lots of peace badges
over jacket. Safety pins in ears. Peace signs painted
on cheeks. Wrapped also in a bright peace banner.
She has been silent a long time since her rape by Ajax.
When she speaks she sings or chants the part of
Lohengrin we associate with the Wedding March,
'Here Comes the Bride'. Starts, speaks, goes back to
tune, as though the whole occasion were her 'wedding'
to Agamemnon. She brandishes a torch or a 'bouquet'.*

CASSANDRA
Light up all sides!
The God of Brides!

At the king's side
the Argos bride!

O I'm in luck –
a royal fuck!

Here comes the bride
of genocide.

Here comes the bride
of regicide.

What a fine thing
to be poked by a king!

I'm slave to you.
I'm yours to screw.

My legs are spread
on the king's bed.

My legs are wide
Sir Genocide.

How blessed I am
in this royal ram.

A royal bed
to lay my head.

A killer king
waving his thing.

Your tears are shed
over the dead,
but I'm so happy at what is to be.

You all mourn Troy
but I will know joy
though I go to Hades he'll go there with me.

I'm being laid
by Sir Rough Trade . . .

I wave the light
for my wedding night.

You mourn the dead
I dance to bed
and my deflowering will be my delight.

Circle round me
the bride-to-be.

> *Cassandra is inducing Hekabe and the Chorus to*
> *dance with her . . .*

Dance after me
Please 1-2-3.

Sing! Sing! Sing! Sing!
for the bride of the king.

> *Hekabe is almost carried away and involved in a*
> *dance like they used to do 'when Daddy was alive'.*
> *A humouring of the 'crazy' Cassandra. Cassandra*
> *dances away to the wire and the Greenham gate.*

CASSANDRA

Bouquet and veil
veil and bouquet.
Blood marks the trail
to my wedding day.

> *Cassandra goes up to the wire and examines the*
> *woven CND letters we saw plaited froms rags into*
> *the wire at the beginning of Part One. She adds to the*
> *letters lower-case 'assa' between the C and N, and -ra*
> *after the D, making her name C assa N Dra. As she*
> *weaves she sings.*

CASSANDRA

Cock, Nob and Dick
hard as a stick
into Cassandra and over with quick.

Dick, Nob and Cock
hard as a rock
into Cassandra then limp as a sock.

Cock, Dick and Nob
a blow by blow job
into Cassandra who won't weep or sob.

Then she tries to get through the wire into the base.

CHORUS

Hekabe, Cassandra's crazy again.
Stop her before they abuse her, these men.
They'll start getting brutal if they have to give chase.
Watch her, she'll claw her way into the base.

*Cassandra has lit candles beneath her name. Guards
2 and 3 pull her back from the small hole in the wire,
and stomp out the candles with an unnecessarily
violent stomp. Cassandra is returned to her mother.
There is a burst of American voices from the
walkie-talkies on the hips of the Guards.*

HEKABE

The torch the god holds up for wedding days
throws here the shadow of a blacker blaze.
Cassie love, I had such high hopes for you.
A ceremony, not Greek swords and spears
goading you to some brute's bed to be *screwed*.
Give me your torch. Marriage! It's a mockery.
A blasphemous travesty of what bridals should be.
Sisters, rescue the candles Cassandra lit.
Let's keen and drown out her mad wedding song.

*The Women begin to 'keen' under and over the 'Here
Comes the Bride' of Cassandra. They begin the
Greenham ritual of the 'web'. Cassandra holds the
centre of a length of bright-red wool which the
Women weave into a symbol. When they are finished*

the black leather spider-web with green hair at its
centre, Cassandra speaks:

CASSANDRA

Mother, make a garland for my head.
Be glad I'm being sent to that king's bed.

If I seem slow
then make me go.

If APOLLO's any good at prophecy
there'll be less hell in HELEN than in me.
Through our royal wedding that great chief
will fall from his greatness and come to grief.

HELEN was hell.
I am as well.

That brutal king
to death I'll bring.

His palace wall
like Troy will fall.

As murder came
and Daddy died,
he'll get the same
through his sweet bride.

Here comes the bride
of homicide . . .

End of 'web'.

No more of that! I can't and won't tell all –
how the bloody axeblade's going to fall
on my neck, but not on mine alone,
right through flesh and marrow bone.
From Agamemnon's forcing me to bed
a son will hack his mother dead.
Yes, I know you think I'm crazy, high.
I am, but these are truths you can't deny.

Troy's death is peace
compared to Greece
celebrating victory and asking itself why.

Because of one hot woman and her lust
at least ten thousand Greek men bit the dust.
To win back Helen who all men despise
the king killed what was precious in his eyes
and surrendered to his brother to beat Troy
the life of his daughter, his pride and joy.
And what were these cruel sacrifices for?
These past ten long years of murderous war!
For Helen who was no better than a whore.

Helen was hot
for the whole lot,
and went as willing as anyone could.

And Helen whored
of her own accord
and out of her whoring flowed endless blood.

We know HELEN.
She was willing.

She couldn't wait
to meet her fate.

> *Guard 3 is inclined to sing along to this anti-Helen,
> anti-woman part, and Cassandra turns on the Guards
> and silences them with a very clear-eyed speech about
> what happens back home when the troops are away
> on a ten-year campaign.*

CASSANDRA

And they came in their thousands to this shore
and laid their lives down far away. What for?
Defence against aggressors? Beating back attack?

Getting some harsh oppressor off their back?
No! And when the poor sods come to lose their lives
they don't get laid to rest by loving wives.
Back home in Greece their abandoned children grow
but what they look like their dads no longer know.
His body gets cremated. A few white dusty ounces
left in a place the newscaster mispronounces.
Back home the widows die, the wives grow sour.
Old men have no sons in their last hour.
They weep for loneliness. At their last gasp
they miss a son's firm reassuring grasp.
Dying alone and frightened and no heir
to weed their graves, light candles, *care*.
How thankful they must be, back home in Greece,
it took you ten whole years to make this peace.

The men left with your wives, too old, too young,
except to use the finger, or the tongue.
What happened here was bad. What will you find
has happened to the loved ones left behind?
That little girl left crooning in her cot
is ten years later sucking you-know-what,
not a pacifier, some foul old geezer's prick.
What you'll find back home will make you sick.
When you set sail for Troy, what was she? Four?
That's ten years for your daughter to turn whore.
Those toddlers waving flags in tiny fists
selling themselves to senile masochists.
Adolescents with no paternal checks
cruising the midnight streets for drugs and sex.
That little boy, sweet in his sailor suit,
now works the bathhouse as a prostitute.
His little brother waving the Greek flag
as you sailed out is serviced by a fag.
You don't need seers to tell you in ten years

a place can fall to pimps and profiteers.
The old men left in charge just grew too old
and everything was chaos, uncontrolled.
Your suffering here. It won't take long to bore
the folks back home with stories of 'your war'.
Your families less familiar than your foes.
Which is why you want us with you, I suppose.

Half your comrades urns of ash with names
left in the marketplace and no one claims.
Bits of leather jerkin, a beloved spear,
but nobody left to clutch them with a tear.
You want celebration, sick and tired of war,
and diffident strangers greet you at your door.

While cannon-fodder's fed into the maw
of that ever-ravenous monster, War,
what's happening back home while you're abroad
your fathers dead, your wives and daughters whored?
The thriving city-states you left behind,
drained of resources, rapidly declined . . .

Your wives, yes, yes, they loved you. But ten years
is too long to resist some lecher's leers.
Never knowing when the Trojan War might end
what woman wouldn't want a present friend
rather than a man, no matter how good-looking,
who wanted her to live ten years without fucking?
Or, as the Trojan War led many to discover,
another woman made a better lover.
She shudders when she hears the armour rattle
on the doorstep, hubbie home from battle,
home with his macho wants, his male demands,
his callous, wandering, war-coarsened hands.

The walkie-talkie on the hip of Guard 3 splutters in
a US accent to the tune of 'Here Comes the Bride':

US WALKIE-TALKIE

We know the likes
of you lot are dykes
and into dildoes not genu-INE dicks.

*Cassandra presses on, without registering the
intrusion.*

CASSANDRA

At least the men of Troy died in defence
of what they loved. That makes a bit more sense.
Dead they were carried homeward where
their flesh got washed and dressed with loving care.
Wife, mother, sister saw they had the best
and their home soil's where they were laid to rest.
Between the battle skirmish and the fray
they went home to sleep with wives, to play
with their children, and know some joy
denied the Greek invaders outside Troy.

Sir Genocide
takes me for bride.

I'm dragged to bed.
The king's soon dead.

Here comes the bride
of homicide.

TALTHYBIUS

If Apollo hadn't driven you crazy, my girl,
you'd suffer for what you said just now.

My commanders are just about to set sail.
The last thing they need is that sort of talk.

To audience.

I can't fathom it myself, those higher up
have no more nous than those who mean nothing.

I mean here's Agamemnon, in charge of the Allies,
the whole Panhellenic pact, the son of a king,
falling for this, smitten by this maniac.
Me, I'm just a poor soldier, but I tell you, me
I wouldn't touch her with a fixed bayonet.
I could no more fuck her than fly.

Turns to Cassandra.

Right, look, I know you're not quite right in the head
so all that aggro against Argos, that hooraying for Troy,
we'll pretend never happened. I didn't quite catch it.
The wind on this beach being so blustery, OK?
But best come on now, love, into his ship.

To audience.

Can you imagine our *king* screwing that?

*Cassandra's reaction to him is to 'talk posh' as both a
member of the Trojan royal house and the concubine
of the herald's king.*

CASSANDRA

My good man! Hark at the minion! This messenger boy!
People with your job are really despised
universally, government lackeys,

Drops into US accent.

'licking ass'.

I'm a witch. I close my eyes and see the future.
That Odysseus my mother is supposed to be slave for
has a bad time coming, if he only knew it.
He'll look back on the war and regret that it's over.
My death's a picnic compared to his pains.

Ten years of war
then ten years more
before Odysseus gets back, then alone.

The woes of Troy
he helped to destroy
won't be the half of the woes of his own.

I go to my groom
stretched in death's gloom
their highest commander brought down so low.

My corpse and his
the precipice
and there washed in torrents of thunderous flow.

Him and me feasts
for the wild beasts.

What's a commander when dogs in the street
work over his body like so much raw meat?

She lets fall the wrapped-round peace banner.

Ta-ra these trappings of prophet I wore.

*The Guards cut the strands of wool that make the
web round Cassandra. Long trails of red wool hang
from her leather jerkin.*

Right, where's the ship? Take me on board.
Spread the sails wide to catch the first wind.

You've heard of the Furies 1-2-3.
Two are in hell and the third one is me.

*Thinking of the dead she goes to the ground, addresses
her dead father and brother, then goes limp in the
'passive resistance' way.*

Dead brother, dead dad, get ready to greet
the ghost of Cassandra you're going to meet.
Wait there in Hades. When I come down
I'll be wearing in glory a victory crown,
the crown of victor, for I'll destroy
the house of Atreus, destroyers of Troy.

*She goes limp. Guards 2 and 3 drag her off with the
red wool strands trailing behind her like blood, and
the prophecy's fulfilment of her bloody death in the
future. Hekabe picks up the remaining strands of red
wool, and hugs them to her. She sinks to the ground
in the place where Cassandra addressed the dead.*

CHORUS

Don't let the old woman lie there on the ground.
Lift her up. Can't you see she needs help?

HEKABE

I want nobody's help. Just leave me be.
Let me lie here on the ground where I seem to belong.
Everything I've borne, am bearing, will bear,
forces my feeble frame towards the earth.
Gods! Gods haven't been much good to us.
But their names spring to our lips when we're oppressed.
Misery squeezes the old prayers from our mouths.
Despair makes us pray without thinking.

And troubles make us turn to the past,
a past that was happy. Which sharpens our pain.
When prayer doesn't work a song can console
though old blessings only rub salt in our wounds.

HEKABE

I was of royal blood, and wife to a king
and I bore him sons. O many fine sons.
You wouldn't find their like in the whole of Phrygia.
I don't think that any Trojan or Greek
could ever have been as proud as I was of them,
so proud . . .

       And I had to watch them being hacked down.
I cut so many locks of hair for their graves
I'm almost bald now. And his father, his father . . .
These eyes saw him butchered in a spot supposed sacred.

My daughter, whom I'd reared for good matches,
ripped from my protection. My daughters brought up
for fine husbands now serving invaders.
I'll never see them. They'll never see me.
To crown, to *crown* it all, the fate left to me.
To go to Greece in my old age, a slave
to do work I'm eminently suited to –
concierge with a bunch of big keys,
the mother of Hector, cowering, curtseying,
baking cakes for them, kipping in the kitchen,
one who slept in a bed for a queen.
Tattered old rags over tatters of flesh.

All this, all this because of one . . . fuck!

Cassandra, my special one, with gifts from the gods,
this isn't how I saw your virginity taken.
Polyxena, Polyxena, what's happened to you?

Not one son, not one daughter left to console.
I once had so many . . .
So why should I stand up? Who can I lean on now?

Here's your slave. She lived so well once in Troy,
drag her off to sleep on rocks and in mud
and cry herself to the sleep of death.
The only time a person's truly happy . . .
Nobody's happy this side of death. Nobody.

> *Silence. They are all gathered round their fire brewing
> a kettle.*

CHORUS

1

Let's keen for Troy.

2

There's that new song.

3

There've been hundreds of songs about our city.

4

But none about its destruction before.

5

Our songs weren't so gloomy before the war.

6

No, not so tearful before the war started.

7

Now we may sing, but we're so broken-hearted.

8

Let's sing it, though our hearts aren't at all strong.

The keening for Troy:

A four-wheel truck
brought the Wooden Horse,
the vehicle of doom
right through our gates.

The doom-convoy
was wheeled into Troy.

Its insides were primed with destructive force
and when the monster shook
metal death rattled inside its womb –
death and slavery the Trojan fates.

And we couldn't wait to let the monster in . . .

A wagon on wheels brought the horse of wood
into these gates, and there it stood
and all our houses soon ran with blood.

Outside it glittered
with a silvery sheen.
And metal arms clattered
in the death machine.

And we couldn't wait
to drag it through the gate.
And we couldn't wait
to embrace our fate.

And the Trojan people shouted with joy:
Our troubles are over. The gods have saved Troy.

Our troubles are over, come out and see.
Drag the thing into the sanctuary.
It seems that the gods have heard our plea.

They sang and they cheered, the people hurrayed.
They believed now the Greeks would never invade
and brought in this thing, and they were betrayed.

JUST AS WE ALL SAID HURRAY
TO THE WOODEN HORSE FROM THE USA.

The young and the old they all sang along.
They welcomed the monster. It made them feel strong.

This cunning contraption made of mountain pine
they hauled like a launched ship into the shrine
of Pallas Athena; then the blood flowed like wine.

With rope and tackle the thing was towed
into the goddess's concrete abode
ignorant of the monster's true payload.

And the tracks it made were where blood flowed
and along the gutters of every Troy road.

> *During this 'song' the gates of Greenham Common
> are being opened by the Guards as if admitting the
> Cruise convoy. There is 'Cruise music'. The walkie-
> talkies of the Guards crackle with language and
> instructions and counting, a counter-music to that
> of the Women.*

CHORUS

Night fell and everywhere that you turned
the blackout was lifted and the torches burned.
Singing and music once more filled our ears
and people doing dances not done for ten years.

The nights for ten years had been intense and black
with all torches doused for fear of attack.
Now everybody left their torches alight
and left them burning brightly all through the night.

And I was singing along with the rest; the joy
of war being over had intoxicated Troy.
We were singing and singing and singing when
the whole city rang with the cries of strange men,

men with blackened faces. All celebration froze.
Singing was choking, music death-throes.
The thing we'd welcomed had been jam-packed
with Achaian SAS with their faces blacked.

Before anyone had a chance to sound
the drums and the bells we use for alarms
there were men with blackened faces all around,
blood already dripping from their brandished arms.

The dying, the screaming, the terrifying din
then we knew what monster we'd let in.
Out of hiding more bloody than before
to all our street parties came invited War.

Into the party the uninvited one
taking off a husband, father, son.
While everyone's enjoying the respite from grief
in walks War, the sly life-thief.

Scared kiddies wake up and scream in their cots.
Troy's soon full of lost fatherless tots
who hug their teddies and suck their thumbs
and howl for a mother who never comes.

Jubilant bandsmen done to instant death,
their horns still vibrating with blown breath.
Fluteplayers slumped with suddenly slit throats
and the air still filled with glad flute notes.

And children who'd been gratefully chanting gods' names
are running on the roads with their flesh in flames . . .

And with our husbands dead
and headless, in the very same bed
and lying still warm beside,
the killers drop their swords and thrust
into our bodies with another lust
and leave Greek seed inside.

And these are the brutes whose brats we'll bear
when we're shipped overseas to be slaves over there.

*The gates of Greenham Common camp are now fully
open. Guards 1, 2 and 3 are pushing children's prams
heaped with weapons. They are the weapons from
all wars and include Greek helmets, World War I
helmets, a Maxim gun, grenades – an 'anthology' of
weapons, the primitive to the sophisticated, at least
up to World War I. It is as if the silos are an arsenal
of weapons from the earliest times to Cruise, from the
Trojan War to the Third World War! As the prams
leave the gates and turn we see a boy (Astyanax)
dressed in a bright anorak and brightly coloured
scarf, a contrast to the soberer anoraks of the Women.
As he draws level with the gate, one of the Greenham
Women becomes Andromache.*

CHORUS

Hekabe, look, here's Andromache, look!
She's got your grandson, Astyanax, with her.

Where are they taking you with all those weapons?
I suppose they'll hang on their walls back home?

GREENHAM WOMAN (ANDROMACHE)
(*the ensuing speeches overlapping*)
Our new masters are dragging me away.

HEKABE

Ah!

ANDROMACHE

Cry for me –

HEKABE

Ah!

ANDROMACHE

. . . for my suffering . . .

HEKABE

God!

ANDROMACHE

. . . my misfortune . . .

HEKABE

My kids! My kids!

ANDROMACHE

Not any more.

HEKABE

It's gone. All this. All we had. Troy.

ANDROMACHE

Ah!

HEKABE

Troy's smoke. A cloud in the air.

ANDROMACHE
(*speaking to the ground where 'the dead' are*)
Hector, Hector, come back to me!

HEKABE

It's my son you're calling. He's dead. He's dead.

ANDROMACHE

Look after me again.

HEKABE

Drag me down to death with you.

ANDROMACHE

Such a desire to die!

HEKABE

Such suffering, that's why!

ANDROMACHE

The city . . .

HEKABE

One thing on another.

ANDROMACHE
(*suddenly vehement*)

It was Paris who brought the gods down on us.
Your son and his lusts made Troy fall.
His bodily functions put paid to us all.
Paris, your son, and his damned roving eye.
Troy's ash, and your son Paris is the reason why.
He is the reason that the vultures fly
swooping down on the corpses out of the sky.

HEKABE

Troy, emptied of life. It makes me cry.
Will there ever again be such pain as ours?
If the dead can see us, they'll be glad they're dead.

CHORUS

Tears, tears. They're good when you're broken-hearted.
Sad songs can help when the spirit's defeated.

ANDROMACHE

You're a hero's mother. My man, he killed scores
with this weapon. Now look at me.

HEKABE

The gods lift some people up to the top
of the tower of life. Some they let drop.

ANDROMACHE

Well, here's me with your grandson, spoils of war,
trophies, prizes. The high brought low, people made things.

HEKABE

Fate's terrible! Cassandra just now . . .
those men dragged my own child from my arms.

ANDROMACHE

God! Another male rapist gets the poor girl!
As if Ajax hadn't already abused her enough.

There's worse to follow . . .

HEKABE

                There always is.
One hell's always at another's heels.
Terrors tread on each other's shadows.

ANDROMACHE

They killed Polyxena. At Achilles' grave.
Butchered in cold blood as a gift for a corpse.

HEKABE

Ah! So that was the messenger's riddle!

ANDROMACHE

They let me stop. I covered her with something.
I squeezed out a few words over her body.
They waited a while till I'd said a few words.

HEKABE

How could they kill her in such a brutal way?

314

ANDROMACHE
She's lucky she's dead. She's happier than me
still with some life left to drag out.

HEKABE
Child, life and death are poles apart.
Death's nothing. In life there's always a chance.

The bleakness of Andromache makes Hekabe take
Astyanax to her, as if to prevent the hope he
represents being blasted by his mother's despair.

ANDROMACHE
Mother, that brainchild's better aborted!

I'll tell you what I think. It's more consoling.
Being dead 's like never having been
and death seems better than a life of pain.
The dead feel nothing. Nothing hurts the dead.
Once you've known happiness and had it stolen
you never stop hankering to have it back,
always haunted by what you're now missing.
It's as if Polyxena never existed.
Now she feels nothing of what she suffered.

Me though, I aimed my hopes high
and the more I had, the more there was to lose.
All the virtues wives are meant to have
I cultivated, for your son, Hector's sake.
I never went out, never created suspicions
by being seen in places where women get
a reputation, whether fitting or not!
I entertained no loose talk in my house.
I'd learned the difference between right and wrong.
I never picked quarrels with Hector. I stayed calm.
I knew when to insist, though, and when to agree.

I suppose these Greeks got wind of how I was.
My 'name' preceded me, dug me a pit.

From the moment they caught me, Achilles's son
marked me down for his. A slave to those butchers!

If I stamp out the image of my man
and prise my heart open to let a new one in
don't I betray the dead? But the alternative's
to cherish the dead and be showered with loathing.
But don't they always say: one night in bed 's
all it takes to break a woman in.

GUARD 2
(*from behind wire*)
Yer, one fuck's enough to mek her like 'er new jockey!

ANDROMACHE
I can't stand a woman who flits
from first to second man without a qualm.
Even a cart-horse parted from its mare
and teamed with some other hauls its load sullenly
languageless beasts without our higher nature.

Hector, sweetest love, you were all I needed,
noble, intelligent, wealthy, and all man.
You got me a virgin from my father's house.
You were the first. The first man in my bed.
And now you're dead, and I'm to be shipped
over to Greece to be slave to a killer.

> *Hekabe is staring out into the auditorium with
> Astyanax – to sea, where the ships are at anchor. She
> covers his ears so he doesn't hear his mother's black
> despair. She rocks his head to and fro, humming the
> 'swaysong' from before.*

ANDROMACHE
So don't you think Polyxena's better off?
You're weeping for her. My suffering's worse.

And that hope you say there always is in life.

I've lost it all. I've no more illusions.
It would be nice to believe in some sort of future.

CHORUS
It's the same with us. We all have those feelings.

*There is a sense of blocked hope, futility. It seems
that it is up to Hekabe, who in some ways has
suffered most, once more to find the flicker of hope,
somewhere. She takes Astyanax nearer the ships to
look at them as if they were something exciting for
the boy. Through looking at the ships with him she
finds a metaphor that gives her a view of the spark
of hope in the blackness.*

HEKABE
(to Astyanax, looking out at the ships)
I've never been on a ship before either!
But I know them from pictures and stories –

If there's a storm at sea . . .

*Hekabe sees Astyanax is frightened, so reassures
him.*

. . . not a real bad one!
Do you know what those brave sailors do?
They do all they can to keep the ship going.
One takes the helm. Look, there, that thing's the helm.
One wrestles with the sails. One mans the pumps.

*Astyanax goes forward, fascinated by now, to look
more closely at the ships so that Hekabe can say the
rest to Andromache, the grown-up stuff.*

But when the sea's too swollen, the storm too frightful,
they give in to fate, and go with the swell.
Me, I'm mute in the face of misfortune.
The billows of misery are way over my head.

317

Forget his daddy. Tears for the past can't help you now.
Do what your new master wants you to do.
You know very well how to win his regard.

Astyanax runs back to his granny.

Then perhaps one day this grandson of mine
might do something extraordinary, for Troy.
Or his children, or his children's children.
They might find their way back over the sea,
rebuild the city, and restore our Troy.
So try to endure. For the sake of this boy.

*Hekabe is looking at the Troy the descendants of
Astyanax build when she sees Guard 1 (Talthybius)
enter.*

Look, their messenger's back. Now what?

Enter Talthybius and Guards 2 and 3.

GUARD 1 (TALTHYBIUS)
(*to Andromache*)
Your husband, Hector, was the best of your bunch.
But all that's over. Please don't hate me now.
I didn't volunteer to bring you these decisions
the Greeks have just taken with the joint command.
I didn't want to be the one . . .

ANDROMACHE
Be the one, what?
Finish the bad news you were going to break.

TALTHYBIUS
The decision's that your son's going to be . . .

ANDROMACHE
Not with the same master, him and me?

TALTHYBIUS
He won't be any Greek master's to own.

ANDROMACHE
Not leave him behind in Troy on his own?

TALTHYBIUS
It's bad news I'm afraid, not easy to break.

ANDROMACHE
Bad news isn't easy either to take.

TALTHYBIUS
They're going to kill him, since you force me to speak.

ANDROMACHE
That's worse than me being raped by that Greek.

TALTHYBIUS
There was a debate. And Odysseus won.

ANDROMACHE
What worse can happen now? My son! My son!

TALTHYBIUS
It's on account of him being the son of one so great.

ANDROMACHE
And I hope all his own children meet the same fate.
What will they do with him? My boy! My boy!

TALTHYBIUS
He has to be hurled from the top tower of Troy.

Andromache seizes Astyanax.

TALTHYBIUS
Now then, my love, don't make it difficult.
We'll take him in the end. Be sensible.
All you can do 's behave with some dignity.
You'll have to comply. You're all on your own.
Your husband's not going to rise up from his grave.
It's one woman against the whole might of Greece.
Come on, my dear. Don't put up a struggle.

Face the facts. Look, if you annoy the troops
it will only turn out all the worse for you.
And the boy won't get buried. They won't allow
any mourning. No tears shed over his tomb.
Face the facts. Look, give in to to us quietly
and your boy might not have to be left unburied.
Be reasonable, and the Greeks might be too.

ANDROMACHE

O my darling. O my darling, my little treasure.
They're going to kill you. I'll be left all alone.
Your father's noble qualities which meant
deliverance to some meant death to you.
Your daddy's bravery's bad luck for you.
I thought I was bearing a son to rule Asia
not a babe to be butchered like this by the Greeks.
Are those tears, little one? You understand, don't you?
Your little fists cling so tightly to my clothes,
a bird without wings seeks the shelter of mine.
Your daddy's ghost won't come out of the ground
bearing his weapons in defence of his son
and none of his comrades, no, no men from Troy.
Hurled head first down from that sickening height,
unpitied, your breath bashed out of your body.
It smells so sweet, your breath, my little baby!
These breasts nourished you and all for nothing.
It takes so much trouble to bring up a child.

Give your mother a kiss, and let's say goodbye.
Put your arms round my neck, and give me a kiss.

You think yourselves so civilised, you Greeks,
and look at the atrocities, you savages.
What's my boy done that you should take his life?
Helen! Who said you were Zeus' daughter?
Your fathers were legion: Evil, Hate, Murder, Death

and every loathsome thing bred on this earth.
Zeus' daughter! A plague on all mankind.
Damn you! Those eyes of yours. Look what they did.
This devastated place was once so beautiful.

To Guards.

Take him, take him. Hurl him to his death
if that's what you want. Then you could eat him!
What's one child more when all of us are doomed?

Begins singing to the tune of 'Here Comes the Bride'.

My child to doom.
Me to my groom
waiting to breed his Greek brats from me!

With my son dead
I go to the bed
to bear more Greeks for their military.

One hot embrace
kills a whole race.

TALTHYBIUS
(to Astyanax)

Come on, kid. Let your mam go. Time's up.
We've to go up that tower to the top of Troy.
And there you've got to die. Those are my orders.

To Guards.

Take him!

Guards take Astyanax.

To carry out orders like these
you need a heart a lot colder than mine.
You need to have no conscience and no pity.

Exit Guard 1 (Talthybius) with Andromache.

HEKABE

Now they've taken my grandson from me and his mother.
What can I do? All I've got for you is tears,
The only action we've got left is mourning.
The city. Now you. What's left to lose?
You take us all with you when you fall.
All of us plunge to oblivion with you.

*During the next 'song' the Women are thinking of the
progress of Astyanax up the tower, which could be the
watchtower we see behind the wire.*

CHORUS

The boys of Troy have always been
the most beautiful boys you've ever seen
and when Zeus caught a glimpse of Ganymede
washing himself by Simois stream
he lifted him off to satisfy HIM
and fill his golden winebowl up to the brim.

And his hand doesn't shake
and he doesn't spill a drop
and the god's heart doesn't break
when Troy gets the chop.

And his hand doesn't shake
as he pours out God's booze
and his heart doesn't break
when he sees Troy lose.

A city won't get saved by good connections
if those connections are what are called gods,
most of which anyway are crude male projections
obsessed with flashing their divine erections
and if they held free Olympian elections
they wouldn't get voted back in, the sods!

Up on Olympus where the time stands still
he sees what we suffer and he doesn't spill
a drop of the wine that he pours for his lord

who looks at Troy's ashes then back at him
and the golden wine-bowl he's filled to the brim
and he stares not at us but at the boy who poured.

And Zeus gazes at Troy's ashes, then back at him
the boy who filled his winebowl up to the brim.
You'd think that Priam's brother Ganymede
could have used his Trojan charms to intercede
and as he poured the wine for the Lord of the Sky
begged him to save Troy from its misery.

But his hand doesn't shake
as he pours out God's booze
and his heart doesn't break
when he sees Troy lose.

And his hand doesn't shake
and he doesn't spill a drop
and the god's heart doesn't break
when Troy gets the chop.

And Tithonus he's made it to the bed of Dawn
and he looks on human suffering and stifles a yawn
and they go for a drive the length of a day
and cities being gutted are just sights on the way
back to the heavens, where what happens down here
doesn't squeeze from Tithonous the tiniest tear.

And the Trojan boy
will lovingly caress
the breasts of Dawn
as Nothingness

as Nothingness
engulfs the Troy
where he was born.

Horrible how the creatures of the Earth
taken off into the air

look down on their place of birth
once they've got up there.

And the brother of Priam
pours wine for his lord,
not once does he weep
not a drop does he spill.

And the grandson of Priam
of his own accord
from Troy's walls will leap
of his own free will.

What good does it do to have a god-in-law
when he lets you get defeated by the gods in war?
What good is it having in-laws in the sky?
when they glance down from their heaven and let you die.

> *The Women have been watching the progress of
> Astyanax up the tower and on the last line we are to
> imagine him falling and landing with a dreadful
> crunch on the ground. The 'die' also marks the
> beaming entrance of Guard 3 (Menelaus).*

GUARD 3 (MENELAUS)
(*looking up, like the Women*)

That bright sun up there's just how I feel inside!
Today at last I get my hands on HELEN, my wife.
I'm MENELAUS, a man who's been much wronged.
I know you all think I came to Troy for the woman
but you're wrong. It was the man I was after.
The treacherous guest who made off with my wife.
He had it coming to him. And it came. It came.
Him and his country, they've paid the full price.
Now I've come to see to the woman, her.
I can't bring myself to say her name. My wife.
She's amongst this lot somewhere, like one of them.
The soldiers who fought this campaign to retrieve her

have assigned her to me to finish her off,
or if I want, take her back with me to Argos.
That's what I'll do, postpone the execution,
take her to Greece for those back at home
to take vengeance on her for all of their fallen.

To Guards.

Go into the benders and bring the bitch out.
Haul her out by the hair. Those lovely locks –
lousy with corpses, crawling with carnage!

HEKABE

Whatever it is that keeps the world going,
whatever you are, you're beyond human knowing,
whether you're god, or Nature, or man's mind,
I appeal to you. You creep up on mortals
and somehow create some semblance of justice.

MENELAUS

What's that? That's a rum sort of prayer.

HEKABE

Kill your wife, and earn my gratitude.
Don't look at her though. She'll cage your heart.
She makes eyes slaves, brings cities down,
burns houses to the ground. She has such power.
I know. You know. All who've suffered know.

Helen is brought out from a bender.

HELEN

Menelaus, are you trying to frighten me?
Getting your men to be so rough with me.
I understand that you must loathe me now.
Just tell me this. What's your decision?
Yours and the Greeks', do I live or die?

MENELAUS

There was unanimous agreement: death!

HELEN

Am I allowed to state my case, and show
that if I die, my death would be unjust?

Pause.

MENELAUS
(*not looking at Helen*)
I came to kill you, not to hear your case.

HEKABE
(*relishes the hope of 'justice' she has now discovered*)
Hear her! She shouldn't die unheard.

Provided I can state the prosecution.
Things happened inside Troy you're unaware of.
When you've heard the whole then it'll seem
all the juster that she's put to death.

MENELAUS
It seems a waste of time. We don't have much.
If you want to play at courtrooms go ahead.

It's you I do it for, though, not for her.

HELEN
I realise that no matter what I say
you hate me so much that you won't reply.
I'll have to imagine what your charges are
and answer each with some grudge of my own.

Pause. Turning on Hekabe.

She's the cause of all this horror, her!
She's guilty of this city's downfall, and of mine.
The mother of PARIS. Priam 's also guilty.
He ignored the omens of the firebrand dreams
and let the new-born Paris live. Then what?
Paris had to judge between goddesses, that's what.
At loggerheads, Athena, Hera, Aphrodite.

Athena said, Choose me and conquer Greece.
Hera would make him the King of all Asia.
And what did Aphrodite offer? She offered me.
She told him what the beauties of my body were
and that they could be all his, if she were the winner.
She won. He got me. It was a good thing for Greece.
It wasn't overrun by armies from Asia.
Greece wasn't occupied by barbarian hordes.
Greece isn't now an occupied country.
Good for Greece, maybe. But not good for me.
Sold for my beauty, reviled, and deserving
honours and glory for what I went through.

Yes, I know what you're thinking. Why?
Why did I creep so furtively away?
The son, that disaster that woman gave birth to,
came to Greece with a goddess beside him.
You bade him welcome then pissed off to Crete.
The question I ask since you won't ask it
is, was I in my right mind when I fled,
when I left my country to go with a stranger?
Blame the goddess, not me. The only god
the king of gods can't handle 's love.
Zeus rules Olympus and kow-tows to love.
Blame Aphrodite. Aphrodite, not me.

The other point you'll make against me 's this:
once Paris was dead and buried and the gods
stopped caring which man used my bed,
I could have left Troy and gone home with the Greeks.
I tried! I tried! These guards will vouch for me,
these men on the watchtowers, these patrols,
time and again found me trying to break out,
letting myself down on a rope I'd concocted.
The Trojans had no more use for me, but one,
Deiphobus, took me by force and kept me in Troy.
I was forced, Menelaus, forced. What right

have you to condemn me as you do?
I lived in bitterness, abused and raped.

If you want to play at gods, then go ahead.
Only an idiot would take a god's role.

CHORUS
(to Hekabe)
Come to their defence, your son, your country.
Don't let her smooth-talk lead him astray.
Eloquence and evil. A frightening combination.

HEKABE
I think first I ought to stand up for the gods
this woman's slandered with her shameless lies.
Would the high-goddess Hera be so crass and stupid
as to bargain with Argos to bribe a barbarian?
And Athena let Athens fall into Asian control?
A childish fiction, that contest on Ida.
Why would Hera want to be Miss Olympus?
To get herself a better husband than Zeus?
Was Athena suddenly hot for a husband
when she *begged* her father to let her stay virgin?
You make the gods fools to cover your guilt up.
No one in their right mind's going to believe you.
You say that – excuse me for laughing –
you say Aphrodite was my son's companion
when he first came to the house of Menelaus.
She could have brought you to Troy without budging,
brought you and your little town, and not even left Heaven.
My boy was certainly the handsomest of men.
You fancied him, that's your Aphrodite!
Aphrodite's only the lusts of the flesh,
aphrosyne/stupidity, it's got the same root.
You saw my son in all his fine Trojan gear
glittering with gold, and went berserk.

Argos couldn't hold you, that small-town place.
Once out of Sparta, and installed in Troy,
paved, as you thought, with gold, you could break out
into the luxury you'd always craved
when the means of Menelaus cramped your style.

What else? Oh yes! My son took you by force.
Did anyone in Sparta hear you yell out
for help? There was plenty of help about.
You came to Troy with Greeks in hot pursuit.
They were locked in combat. And if the Greeks
won a skirmish you'd praise Menelaus
only to make my son jealous of his 'rival'.
When we won though, Menelaus didn't rate a mention.
Always ready to embrace the winning side.

And all this talk of trying to slip away!
This claim you were kept here against your will.
When did you ever try to hang yourself
or stab yourself? Better women might
who couldn't bear being parted from their men.
Time after time I begged you to make off.
My son, I said, can find himself another woman.
I'll help you escape back to the Greek ships.
Did that meet your approval? No. You adored the palace
where you were kow-towed to, grovelled to.
And look at you, the way that you're dressed here.
You can't feel any guilt to dress like that
before the man you've been unfaithful to.
No sackcloth and ashes, no shaved head for you!

Senses Menelaus becoming impatient.

Menelaus, no. I'm almost finished now.
All I want to say is 'To thine own self be true.'
Kill her. You owe it to your country and yourself.
Kill her. Start a precedent. Adultery means death.

329

GUARDS
(from behind the Greenham wire)
Gallivanting gets you the gallows
cheating gets you the chop
Drop 'em where you shouldn't
and it's the long, long drop.

You tell 'em, granny
they should keep their fanny
only for the man who provides their bread.
Tell 'em no whoring or they're dead.

CHORUS OF WOMEN
Silence those Greeks who'll call you a wetleg.
Show what you're made of and kill your wife.
You came through a whole war now to be scared?
Show us what you're made of, Menelaus.
Show us what you're made of and kill your wife.
You were brave before the Trojans, why not her?
He's a hero in battle and a coward with his wife.

MENELAUS
Yes, I know she left me of her own free will.
Aphrodite's a fancy name for fornication.
Come on, they're waiting to stone you, the men.
For what you made me suffer is it slow enough, stoning?
You'll be taught what it means to dishonour me.
Stoning will teach you to shame Menelaus.

HELEN
It *was* the gods, not me. Forgive me, please.

HEKABE
(seeing Menelaus weaken)
The thousands who fell here. Remember them.

MENELAUS
(gazing at Helen)
Shut up, you old fool. I'm not impressed by her.

To Guards.

Take her aboard. Lock her up till we sail.

HEKABE
She should sail in a separate ship from you.

MENELAUS
(leaving, calling back as Greenham Gates open)
Has she gained weight while she's been here in Troy?

HEKABE
They say: once in love, always in love.

MENELAUS
Not when what is loved becomes something else . . .

But maybe you're right. In separate ships!
When I get her to Argos, there she'll die
a death full of shame, for a life full of shame.

*Menelaus is now behind the wire, and the gates of the
Greenham base have closed. He is therefore free to
say what follows with the male venom of 'behind the
wire', now as Guard 3 again.*

GUARD 3 (MENELAUS)
She'll be an example to all you damned women!
Keep your foul bodies to yourself. Chastity –
you don't seem able to learn that lesson.
Put her to death and maybe the example
will put fear into the hearts of all you whores.
All you whores need teaching a lesson!

*This reversal to the abuse we had at the beginning
of Part One makes the next Chorus more Greenham
than Troy. The two fires, the fires of the Women's
camp and the fires in the siloes and Troy.*

CHORUS OF WOMEN

So Zeus, you've abandoned us all.
So Zeus, you've let Troy fall.

So Zeus, you've abandoned the lot.
So Zeus, you've let Troy rot . . .

The altar flames that made a bond
between us on Earth and you beyond
have all lost their fragrance and now smell
of rubble and debris and the stench of hell.

Flames can nourish, can transform,
flames bake bread, and keep us warm
but the flames like those of Troy
do nothing, nothing, but destroy . . .

FLAME comes in two different sorts
but it's the same source that they're from,
one gives life, and one aborts,
one bakes bread, one's a bomb.

One makes you gather round its glow
the other makes you flee,
one says YES to life, one NO
and I know which one's for me.

The fire in the candle keeps
the threatening night at bay,
a glow of warmth where a child sleeps
until it's dissolved in day.

The other fire makes only nights
it chokes children into coal.
It extinguishes all other lights
and the sunlight in the soul.

The nightlight flames, the wedding brands,
the flame of oven and kiln creates.
The same element in other hands,
chokes, burns, asphyxiates.

The fire with this use or that use
how come they're both one flame?
What's the point of calling Zeus?
No one answers to that name.

There's our fire and their fire.
The infernal or the feeding fire.
Eternal midnight, or new dawn
on our side of the wire.

On this side of the Greenham wire
the peace candles are all ours.
The other side the terrible fire
is ten zillion candlepowers.

One is the fire that warms a room
that a family sits beside,
the other fire's the fire of doom,
the fire of genocide.

Does he care, does he care,
the great one way up there?
Is he moved when he takes a look
at Troy in ashes? (Is he fuck!)

Does he care when he sees, is he concerned
does the smoke sting his eyes
does he smell the smell
as houses and people and cattle are burned
and Troy turns to cinders? (Does he hell!)

What did they mean to that great one up above
our candles, our keening, our dancing in a ring,
our emblems of peace, our prayers for love?
What did they mean? (Didn't mean a thing!)

Somewhere my darling without a grave
wanders round Troy a troubled ghost.
THEY wouldn't let us bury our dead

and I have to wander on the swell and the wave
till we're brought to the conquerors' coast
and the vast walls of Argos glowering overhead,
built by giants, full of foreboding and dread.

Our girls who see their city in flames
are bound for places with strange-sounding names
and cry: Mother, why isn't our ship the same as yours?
Mother, they're taking us to faraway shores!

Our sweet little girls as foreigners' whores.

And while we watch the fading horizon
and Troy's getting farrer and farrer,
Helen's putting her come-hither eyes on
and calmly applying mascara.

We see our disappearing shore
we remember our men and start keening,
and the one who killed them, the Spartan whore
is no doubt in her cabin preening.

Helen who left a putrefying smell
of corpses and rubble and debris
came through it all and stinks of *Chanel*
and while we are slaves, she'll go free.

The one whose lust shed all that blood
must have a heart of stone
if all she thinks she needs to smell good
is her deodorant cologne.

So for the fire between her thighs
and for the fire that left Troy ash
I hope there's a fireball that fries
her and her ship in one flash.

She thinks that she can cover her shame
with a perfume atomiser,
so I hope that the sky flashes out its flame
and I hope the skyball fries her.

Horror follows in horror's tracks.
Look, they've killed Astyanax.

> *Enter Guard 1 (Talthybius) with the dead Astyanax.*
> *He carries also the 'shield of Hector', a modern see-*
> *through police riot shield, from the 'arsenal' of real*
> *weapons in the silos.*

TALTHYBIUS

There's just one ship left to take off the rest
of Neoptolemus's loot.
The commander himself's just put out to sea.
He's had bad news of trouble back home
so he's left and taken Andromache with him.
I couldn't help crying myself when she wept
and she said farewell to this place and goodbye
to the grave of her husband, Hector.
She begged me one last favour, to bury the kid,
your Hector's lad, who's been thrown off the walls.
She also begged that this shield could be left.
It's Hector's. She didn't want that on her bedroom wall
when her new master took her off to his bed.

She wanted it using for the kid's coffin . . .
since there isn't one of stone or of cedar.
She asked for his body to be given to you
to be covered and garlanded, the best you can do
under the circumstances. She would have done it
if her new master hadn't hurried her off.

So when you've done to the boy whatever you do
we'll throw some earth over him and set sail ourselves.
There isn't much time for anything fussy.
The wind we've been waiting for 's finally here.

I've saved you one job. I stopped at the river
and took the lad's body and washed off the blood.
While you do what you do I'll dig him a grave.
That way we'll save time, then set sail for *home*.

*Exits, then returns with the cardboard dove on a
stick, now stained with the blood of Astyanax. Then
Talthybius exits quickly. From this moment on there
should be a sense of hurry, bustle and urgency from
the Guards on their side of the wire, walkie-talkies
occasionally blurting, and a sense of slow solemnity
from the Women on their side of the wire as they
prepare the body of Astyanax for burial on the
see-through plastic shield.*

HEKABE

Put my son's shield here on the ground.
Its familiar shape breaks my heart open.

You Greeks have sharp weapons and blunt wits.

You must have feared this little boy a lot
to go to the lengths of devising this death
that crowns all the carnage accomplished before.
Were you scared that the boy would rebuild Troy?
The whole city's gutted and you're scared of a kid!
When his hero father and a thousand like him
couldn't do anything to stop Troy falling.
That's a shameful sort of fear that I despise.

To Astyanax.

My little darling, what a way to die!
If you'd died defending Troy, or even known
youth and marriage and a king's command
you might have known some happiness. If
happiness exists in such things as that.
You only had your nose pressed to the glass
where life's later joys were on display.
My little darling, what a way to die!
Those little curls your mother used to trim
so carefully and kiss, the rough stone walls
scuffed off. The skull glints through like a grin.
Death, his smile we can't wipe off our faces.

Your little hands, so like your daddy's were!
Limp and lifeless. Sweet little lips
that once made a promise to me, stiff and cold.
You bounded on my bed one day, and said:

'Granny, if you ever die, I'll cut
my biggest curl for you, and bring my friends
to where you're buried and say *bye-bye*!'
Now the granny puts the boy into the grave,
landless and childless, *I* bury *you*.
All that loving care, those kisses and caresses,
those sleepless nights it takes to raise a child.
For what?

        Your epitaph. What should it be?

'A little child is herein laid
killed by the Greeks, who were afraid.'

   Making sure the Guards hear her.

The Greeks will read it and blush for shame!

   Picks up the 'shield of Hector'.

You'd have had your daddy's shield when you grew up.
It can be your coffin now. You won't grow any bigger.

   Puts her arm in the strap.

His grip's imprinted on the handles still.
Ah, his shield. The crook of Hector's arm.
The rim's all rusted with his running sweat.
He held it to his chest. His sweat streamed down
in the heat of combat from his beard and brow.

Let's find something in the stuff we've got left
to wrap this pitiful little body in.
We don't have a lot to make much of a show.
Sweet little love, everything I have is yours.
Ah, only fools feel fortune lasts for ever.

Whatever controls our fates is like a madman
lurching about, half drunk, half a dancer.
We may be happy a while. It doesn't last long.

*The Women decorate the body of Astyanax and the
shield with such emblems and things as they can find
on their side of the wire.*

CHORUS
They've all got some precious relic left from Troy
they've managed to cling to, to honour his death.

Each Woman puts something on the 'bier'.

HEKABE
Your granny gives you what's left of your city
destroyed by damned Helen, who also killed you.

These aren't the prizes I thought you'd win at the games.

CHORUS
Your words go through me. Hector's heir.
Look at the poor mite lying there.

HEKABE
(*to the tune of 'Here Comes the Bride'*)
You should have been
wed to a queen
and dressed in rich robes not in poor rags like these.

This shield of yours
finished with wars
takes you on your journey to those down below.

CHORUS
Let Earth receive
him while we grieve
and keen for the corpse that we carry away.

HEKABE
Your granny can't kiss you better any more.
Your daddy will hug you when you get below.

The Women take the shield with Astyanax lying on it and hoist it aloft with solemn ceremony, 'keening'. The Guards are waiting impatiently on the other side of the wire. The keening may use the tune 'Here Comes the Bride'. This is the lowest point for the Chorus and once more the responsibility of unearthing even the smallest spark of hope is with Hekabe. The Women begin moving slowly towards the gate.

HEKABE
(who can no longer bear watching the 'funeral')
Wait! Listen!

The Women with the body of Astyanax pause.

HEKABE
It seems to me that all this time the gods
have wanted nothing but our pain; Troy's fall.
Troy they seemed to hate more than anywhere.
They were futile, all our sacrifices.

BUT if they hadn't brought us down so low,
face down in the dust, we'd disappear for ever.
Whereas now we are stories everyone will tell.

Now, go and take his little body to its grave
with these shreds of respect we've given him.
I don't think the dead care how they are buried.
It's us, the living, who cherish such vanities.

The Women bear the decorated riot shield as far as the gate in the wire and lay it down slowly at the open gate. The Guards drag the shield through the gate, close the gate on the Women, then pick up or drag the shield to wherever the hole is for it to be buried in. The hurry and lack of ceremony in their action is in marked contrast to the ceremony of the Women. They stand back from the gate and look up at the watchtower from which Astyanax was thrown.

339

CHORUS

1

His mother had such high hopes in him.

2

Now they're all dashed.

3

Born with everything. A high birth.

4

A high place to be flung down to the earth.

As the Women look up at the watchtower they see something else.

CHORUS

What's happening there?
Those flaming torches in the air.

GUARD 1 (TALTHYBIUS)

Your orders are to set fire to Troy.
What you're guarding's for use not decoration.
Your orders are to level Troy. Then leave.

To Women.

Your orders are when you get the signal leave
for the ships that are taking you to Greece.

To Hekabe.

You too, I'm afraid, old girl. Go with these guards.
Odysseus won you. And you're his slave now.

HEKABE

So this is it! I knew it had to come.
We're leaving home and seeing Troy on fire.
Up, let's take one last look at Troy, what's left of her.
The pride of Asia won't even have a name.

They're burning you and taking me away.
Gods, why call on them? I did before
and not one deigned to listen to my prayers.

*Starts to run forward through the half-open gate to
the base.*

Into the fire and die with all I love.

She is easily caught by the Guards.

TALTHYBIUS
Poor soul! You're almost off your rocker now.
Grab hold of her. Don't treat her with kid gloves.
Get her to Odysseus. She's his. His prize.

HEKABE
Those gods I thought were ours. Do they see?

CHORUS
They see alright but still the city blazes.

That once great city Troy's no longer Troy.

It's one big fireball now, the city. Look!

Troy's flying into nowhere on a cloud.

*We begin to see the headlights of the Cruise convoy
approaching the orange lights of the base as night
comes on.*

HEKABE
(*on the ground where the dead are*)
Children, listen, I'm not far from you now.

CHORUS
(*beginning to talk to their dead and all on the ground*)
If we can't call on the gods let's call on the dead.

HEKABE

Those are who I'm calling. I'm near death.
Listen. Listen. Tell them how we suffer.
They are taking us like cattle to market.

CHORUS

Pain. Slavery. Far, far away from home.

HEKABE

Priam! Priam! No one could bury you.
You're unaware of all I'm suffering.

CHORUS

Hacked. Murdered.
First blood. Then fire.
Soon you'll fall and won't even have a name.

HEKABE

That great cloud covers everything.
Smoke covers the ruins where I lived.

CHORUS

Not even a name. Troy's vanished for ever.

HEKABE

Did you hear it?

CHORUS

Yes, it's Troy falling.
Falling with such a great thud to the ground.
The earth shakes and trembles beneath us.

*The Guards, helped by police and bailiffs removing
the benders, begin to drag off the Women, who go
limp. Hekabe is alone with the headlights of the
convoy behind her. When the Guards return for her,
she rises to her feet, slowly, painfully, but unassisted.*

342

HEKABE

Come on, old girl, up. Totter towards the ships,
and life as a slave. But slavery's still *life*.

*Exit Hekabe. The headlights of the convoy move
forward unimpeded towards the audience. There is the
'Cruise music', the babble of US-accent walkie-talkies,
then:*

Blackout.

End of Part Two.